YOUROPEANS!

This is EUROPE

(ACCORDING TO ITS DOCTORS, HAIRDRESSERS, POLICE OFFICERS, SEX WORKERS AND OTHER EXPERTS)

BY MARK SCHALEKAMP

ISBN book 978-90-816566-0-3
ISBN e-book 978-90-816566-5-8
NUR 740

All rights reserved
No part of this publication may be reproduced and/or made public by means of printing, photocopying, microfilm or by any other means and/or using any other medium, without the prior written permission of the publisher.

Published by Juliette Publishing B.V., September 2016
Originally published as *Dit is Europa*, March 2016
by Maven Publishing B.V.
English translation Kris Kohlstrand
Cover design Lennart Wolfert
Layout Sander Pinkse Boekproductie
Author photo Rink Hof

This book is based on the Youropeans-project:
www.youropeans.eu
Mark Schalekamp can be contacted via e-mail:
mark@youropeans.eu

CONTENTS

INTRODUCTION
7

1. Project Youropeans: 278 cities, 8 categories and 232 interviews
13

2. And that is why the EU doesn't work
23

3. The police in Madrid have 650,000 followers
29

4. Doctors are paid under the table in Eastern Europe
45

5. Become an entrepreneur in Estonia or Ireland, but not in Southern Europe
59

6. The wisdom of Europe's hairdressers
75

7. Nobody knows a sex worker
85

8. Artists are always hard up, except in the Soviet Union
99

9. Famous Swedes are listed in the telephone book
113

10. Immigrants, refugees, asylum seekers, expats: the newcomers
123

11. You'll always be a foreigner (even if you can sing the national anthem while standing on your head)
143

12. How about the new neighbours?
153

13. The North-South divide: Zorba is not lazy, he just enjoys life
175

14. East-West: the Russians are coming
187

15. The EU is a cathedral. But how big should it be?
203

16. Even the former chairman cannot say what a European is
219

17. The values trap
241

18. The urban legends of Brussels
259

19. It's the communication, stupid!
277

Epilogue: Mark does a few city trips
285

Tips for city trips
293

Notes and thanks
309

INTRODUCTION

'Do you play golf?' Gedas asked.

'Only rarely, and very badly,' I replied.

He said it was a shame, since the centre of Europe was located next to a beautiful golf course.

'The centre of Europe?'

Yes, it was only about a 30-minute bus ride from the city, and he thought I should see it.

So the following day found me strolling through a small recreational park built in 2004 when Lithuania became a member of the European Union (EU). A column with yellow stars at the top, located at the edge of a compass laid out the on the ground, marked the spot. I reached it by walking up a path flanked by 28 flag masts; the Dutch flag dangled limply somewhere in the middle. Birds sang, a rabbit hopped off into the grass, and from behind a clump of trees came the intermittent sound of a golf club hitting a ball. According to the national tourist board, the geographic centre of Europe is an official tourist attraction, although the wooden information kiosk/souvenir shop was closed.

I missed the first bus back to Vilnius: I should have signalled

Introduction

more clearly that I wanted a ride, explained the driver of the next bus an hour later.

In Hungary, in Tállya, there is also a monument claiming to mark the geographical centre of Europe. And if you include Iceland, the Azores, and the European islands, the geographical centre is located in the Estonian town Mõnnuste. They are planning to erect a tourist centre there. Belorussian scientists have calculated that the geographical centre is located somewhere within their borders. The geographical centre may also be located in Slovakia, Ukraine or Poland.

The geographical centre of EU has also been calculated, and in 1987 it was somewhere in the middle of France. Since 2013 it has moved to northwest Bayern. The shift is easily explained: the size of the EU changes with the admission of every new member. This is where the 28 flagpoles should be located, not in Vilnius. And there should be 44 of them, which is the number of countries on the European continent. Or 51 if you include Azerbaijan, Georgia, Kazakhstan, Russia and Turkey, only part of which lie in Europe, and Armenia and Cyprus, which are geographically Asian, but culturally and historically European. It is neither the first nor the last example of a tendency to confuse Europe with the European Union.

Approximately 600 million people can call themselves Europeans; as of the end of 2014, the EU united 507 million of them. Including the 232 *Youropeans* that I interviewed between June 2013 and February 2015, eight in every EU capital: a doctor, a hairdresser, an entrepreneur, an artist, an immigrant, a sex worker, a local celebrity and a police agent. I was looking for striking differences and surprising similarities between them, with a view to creating a website and this book.

Why? For several reasons, the first being that it is necessary. Those 507 million people are all members of the same club: members of a union which has become increasingly important in recent years, and which plays an ever greater role in their daily life, whether they like it or not. Once you're in the club, you can work wherever you like, travel freely, and if you're a student, study for a time at a foreign university. The result is that members are visiting each other's countries much more frequently. I have seen this in my own city, Amsterdam, in recent years: more and more tourists, in all shapes and sizes. Tourists from China and the US, immigrants from Africa, as well as French expats, temporary labourers from Poland and Slovakia, Bulgarian sex workers, Spanish students, pickpockets and au-pairs from Romania, city trippers from Austria and Estonia. They live on my street, if only for a weekend, sit next to me in the underground, and stand in front of me in the queue for the supermarket. New neighbours.

On 1 January 2014 nearly 2 million people of non-Western origin and 1.6 million Western immigrants lived in the Netherlands. Most of them live in the cities, where they also make up a relatively large share of the population: since 2011 first and second-generation immigrants have accounted for over half of Amsterdam's population. These figures only include people who are registered, i.e. students and trainees; temporary employees, sex workers and pickpockets are not included. Nor are tourists.

I soon got to know most of my new neighbours, but I did not like all of them. The man at number 16 who pricked a hole in the football my friends from school and I accidentally kicked into his garden (every half hour). Or my downstairs neighbour in Amsterdam who had apparently left months before, leaving behind a marihuana plantation. But we usually got along. I feel more at home in a place where I know my neighbours and the neighbourhood, where I can find a restaurant where the waitress recognises me, and where I can go running along a fixed route. If I know my neighbours, I am willing to be tolerant, and if they occasionally party until the early hours, instead of getting angry, I'm glad to see they're enjoying themselves. You see what I mean.

You can measure social cohesion on the basis of how well people know their neighbours. Not an attractive term, but it is how the willingness of the members of society to cooperate with one another is usually described. Ten years ago, it was one of the focal points of my own company, Robin Good, which conceptualised and organised projects and events designed to help companies make their social involvement more tangible, and move from words to deeds. Sometimes by getting the neighbourhood involved, often by bringing people together who would not otherwise have much contact with one another. Examples include *Amsterdammers Ontmoeten Elkaar*, a project in which handicapped and non-handicapped joined forces to help other residents of Amsterdam. Or the organisation of the Amsterdam World Cup, an annual big two-day football tournament, but also an event where Amsterdammers with international roots have a chance to meet one another.

The Dutch have a saying: unknown is unloved. But the opposite is also true: getting to know people can foster understanding and greater social cohesion, which in turn makes people happier. There is nothing 'airy fairy' about this; business thrives when people know trust each other. I wanted to try to put into practice as a journalist what I had been doing for years as an entrepreneur: getting better acquainted with my neighbours. I hoped that writing about it would also help others to get to know their neighbours, and strengthen the ties within the European club. Or least make a modest contribution towards strengthening those increasingly important ties.

That was my initial excuse for starting the Youropeans. And I was casting around for a new project – I had arrived at the decision to write a novel, and before that to start a business, in the same way. This has become something of a speciality for me:[1] the same recipe, the same ingredients. The project always has to be creative, positive, have some commercial potential, and be socially relevant. The new element in this mix was travel. I had done so only reluctantly in recent years, having developed a fear of travel, and I wanted to confront that fear. And confront it I did, even though there were moments – alone in a hotel room in Sofia, or lost in Budapest – when it wasn't always easy.

1

PROJECT YOUROPEANS: 28 CITIES, 8 CATEGORIES AND 232 INTERVIEWEES

What do Europeans think of their work? Their country? Europe? The Eurobarometer – the European Commission's opinion poll – has been putting this question to 1,000 European in every member state since 1973. These interviews are conducted in person, but also online, and they produce interesting data, which also has scientific value: because N = 1000 × 28.

The result of my interviews was N = 8 × 28, because I interviewed 8 people in 28 countries, in the timespan of just one year. Completely useless as scientific data, but my results were different: a wealth of opinions, experiences and anecdotes from real people, who had their own story to tell about Europe: *the people's Europe*.

The eight professions were chosen at random. I tried to cover society as a whole: from high to low, from left to right.

- The **doctor**. Doctors have a university education, and social standing; they are usually part of the country's elite. Most of the doctors I spoke to worked in a hospital although I also met general practitioners, a psychiatrist and a dentist.

- The **entrepreneur**. Good people by definition, but I confess to being prejudiced. For me, as a former entrepreneur, I see them as optimistic, commercial and hard working. I spoke to a wide range of them, young and old, rich and struggling, and so their place in society also varied. In general, however, they tended towards the right of centre. My only criterion was that the entrepreneur in question should have at least eight employees. A one-person company without personnel is not an entrepreneur.
- The **artist**. Generally left of centre. This category included painters, musicians (two hard rock guitar players), actors. Of all my interviews, these were often the most entertaining, but they were also long because 1) artists are apparently very loquacious, and 2) they have a lot of time. And I had to produce a transcript from every two-hour long recording.
- The **policeman**. Of police woman (men outnumber women 18 to 10). Preferably a street cop instead of a spokesperson. They are key figures in society, the representatives of Authority. Not my favourite category to start with, but in the end I liked them more than I thought I would.
- The **hairdresser**. I had no affinity with them, not because I disliked them, but because it's been ten years since I last visited one: once a week I use clippers to shave off the sparse hairs on my skull. Beforehand I would have placed them near the bottom of the social ladder, but the hairdressers surprised me. Many of them were well-informed about world events, had an interesting take on those events, and were also entrepreneurial, managing their own chair or business.
- The **sex worker**. I started out calling them prostitutes, which did not go over well in the business, and also had an unfavourable effect on their willingness to cooperate. Sections of my novel *The Parvenu* were set in the Red Light District of Amsterdam, which I lived close to at the time, and I have met enough sex workers over the years to be amazed by the caricatures of their profession: dumb, common women who practise a profession that is so disgusting that they must be doing it

against their will. Involving them was a kind of project within a project, which I hoped would counter the prevailing view. I also hoped that talking to 28 workers about their job would give the knowledge I needed to draw some conclusions about sexual morality in Europe. Nor did I have any objection to including such a mediagenic category. 27 women and 1 man (shemale Melissa), from escorts to strippers.

- The **immigrant**. The outsider can provide a refreshing view of his or her new country, and in the case of immigrants from other parts of the world, also an interesting perspective on Europe. I gradually realised that the differences between different immigrants were too big to include them in one category, and I began to divide them into expats and immigrants. More about that later.
- The **local celebrity**. The joker category. It ranged from politicians such as Herman van Rompuy and Felix Rottenberg, (a Dutch former politician and now a political commentator) and athletes such as the Slovenian Olympic ski champion Tina Maze to the London-based stand-up comedian Omid Djalili. The only criterion was that they had to be familiar with their city. It was a good excuse to interview playmate Cathy in Vienna, but celebrities are by definition mediagenic, and I hoped that their inclusion would attract more media coverage and increase the project's impact. That was after all the purpose of the whole undertaking.

I interviewed a total of 232 Youropeans: 127 men and 105 women.* The average age was 39.6. The youngest were hairdressers Joni and Angelique (in Helsinki and Berlin) and sex worker Nicola (in Bratislava): 21. The oldest was the priest Anton, who is a *local celeb* in Bratislava: 85 (after our interview he drove me back to the city centre in the pouring rain. Without glasses and without incident.)

---

* 232 and not 224 Youropeans, because in some cities I interviewed more than one entrepreneur or local celebrity.

Project Youropeans: 28 cities, 8 categories and 232 interviewees

Each interview lasted approximately fifty minutes, and there was no set list of questions (although the police in particular expected that, and some agents, like the uncooperative Irishman Dennis, wanted to work through the questions I had emailed him in advance as quickly as possible. In that short space of time I tried find out how the interviewees felt about work, various social issues and their country, whether they felt like Europeans and how they viewed the EU. Their responses were of course varied: in the Baltic States, they talked about the long arm of Russia, in Athens about the economic crisis.

I wanted to use the interviews in two ways. The first was to produce an edited version, shortened to roughly 1,000 words in English (sometimes translated if the conversation had been held in German, Dutch, Spanish or French) that could be posted on the website www.youropeans with a photograph of the interviewee.* There they would be grouped city-by-city in a way that was eye-catching and attractive enough to encourage visitors of this site to get to know their fellow Europeans: the main goal of my project.

The second involved using the interviews as raw material for this book, in which I want to connect the dots and highlight noticeable differences and similarities. Ideally, the book would be a good read and would be available in all of the European Union's 23 languages. So that we can all become one big happy family.

HOW DO YOU FIND A YOUROPEAN?

I started my *tour d'Europe* in Lisbon in June of 2013. You have to start somewhere, so why not in the city that was at the top of my personal list of the most pleasant, beautiful capital cities (and it still is). Moreover, it was a city where I knew people, which would make it easier to find interviewees. One of my acquaintances, Marta, put me in touch with her own hairdresser Mauro, and

---

* The photographs are also displayed in this book, in the middle pages. A selection was exhibited in Brussels, Amsterdam and in various villages in Northern Italy.

on 3 June 2013, in the Rua Serpa Pinto in Lisbon, he became the very first Youropean.

'I only recently became a hairdresser; I studied mathematics and worked in IT for a long time,' Mauro said. It was quite a change, his friends agreed, was he gay now? He wasn't he said, speaking in Portuguese with Marta translating, because Mauro didn't think his English was good enough. I heard that a lot but usually their English was pretty good – better than my Portuguese/Romanian/Lithuanian in any case. The three of us were sitting on trendy, i.e. uncomfortable, chairs next to a client who was waiting her turn. Mauro's colleagues continued cutting and colouring, but I could see in the mirror that they were keeping an eagle eye on us: people come to hairdressers for a haircut, not an interview. Especially not an interview about Europe. I asked him what he thought of Europe, but a swelling chorus of hairdryers made him difficult to understand, even for Marta. After twenty minutes or so Mauro was ready to get back to work; he posed impatiently for a few photos.

Mauro was followed by 231 Youropeans. I found them in different ways, sometimes by accident, like the entrepreneur Karoli, whom I met on the bus from Riga to Vilnius. We were sitting in the two comfortable leather seats that formed the last row of the business class section. There is no train connection between the Latvian and the Lithuanian capitals, but this coach was just as good, and it only cost 20 euros, including a bottle of water, an apple and WIFI. At least you can make good use of your time this way, but before we both got to work (earphones in, bashing away at our laptops) I had a brief conversation with my neighbour. As the bus slowly manoeuvred its way out of Riga, I found out that Karoli was from Estonia, and although she was only 31, she was a serial entrepreneur who started her first company when she was sixteen, and had twice been named Europe's Young Entrepreneur of the Year. I don't think I could have found a better candidate for the entrepreneur category of Youropeans in Estonia, and I interviewed her in Tallinn a few months later.

Or take the Viennese Youropeans Coco, Cathy and Martin, respectively an artist, a local celeb and a doctor, whom I met thanks to Mario, the owner of a modelling agency, and Vienna's first drag queen. With real breasts, at least a C-cup, which he showed me on a Facebook photo. Thankfully he did not unbutton his shirt to show me the real thing. According to him, it is a medical miracle, which occurs in 1 out of a 100,000 men, but pills may have given nature a helping hand. I met him through other people, and was invited to visit his office, which was staffed by him, a charming assistant, and his right-hand man Marcus, who was as fashionable as he was eccentric: he was tall and thin with a Dali-like moustache.

'Are you sure you're not gay?' Mario asked as he fired up another Marlboro. *Circus Mario*. 'Right, so who do you plan to interview? Her? Pleeease… she looks terrible. I'll give you her,' he said pointing to a gorgeous model whose portfolio was displayed on the wall behind him. She was the Playmate Cathy, a local celebrity, but Marco also put me in touch with Coco and the doctor Martin. As a bonus he got me a place in a casting call for an Austrian beer brand that same afternoon, not far from his office. 'It's right up your street,' he said, looking me over from top to bottom like I was steer in a cattle market. The casting call went well, but I will not be the new face of Schloß Eggenberg Hopfenkönig.

Usually, however, the process was not as effortless, and finding Youropeans was hard work. There were three ways of doing so: 1) simply walking into their place of work, 2) connections, or 3) through official channels, such as with police agents. I usually found hairdressers along the first street I encountered, and after a few refusals, the fourth or fifth agreed to an interview right away, or said they would be happy to talk to me the next day. No, hairdressers were not a problem. Just look around and see how many salons there are in your own city.

Artists were also relatively easy to find, in the same way that I found doctors, expats/immigrants and entrepreneurs: though connections. Facebook was also helpful. Placing a notice that I was on my way to Vilnius/Prague/Luxembourg and looking for interviewees always resulted in a few good responses and some local contacts. Embassies — especially the smaller ones — were sometimes helpful; those in London, Paris and Rome made it abundantly clear that they had other things on their mind. But the Dutch embassies in Valetta, Riga, Prague and Madrid did what they could, as did the EU representative in Bratislava and Tallinn. The local journalists I contacted so that they could interview me for their newspaper of TV station also provided assistance: every now and then a local celebrity popped up in their well-filled rolodexes.

And it was a good thing too, because local celebrities are often difficult to approach. And who qualifies as a celebrity? I had already specified *local*, not wanting to reach too high and force myself to score the one real celebrity in Vilnius. London, on the other hand, is full of celebrities, but a local London celeb is usually so famous that they can't spare 30 minutes for anything less than *Rolling Stone, Vogue* or *The New York Times*. I tried. I was told that the children of David Beckham, Elle Macpherson and Claudia Schiffer all attended school right around the corner from where I was staying in upmarket Bayswater. I hung around near the school for two mornings and saw a lot of Porsche Cayennes, and yummy mummies with children in school uniforms, but it was apparently not David, Elle or Claudia's turn to do the school run. This category did provide an excuse to approach a few of my own personal heroes, but Goran Ivanišević was not in Zagreb when I was there, Agnetha Fältskog refused politely and Johann Cruyff, Amsterdam's most famous citizen could not be persuaded (I was, however, not unhappy with Felix Rottenberg and Pierre Bokma).

Hard work, as I said, but sometimes I got lucky and someone took over for me, as in Bucharest: a Romanian living in the Netherlands heard about Youropeans and appreciated the fact that I was helping to dispel prejudices about her country. She took care of literally everything, from interviews to address instructions. In Cyprus I stayed with a friend from college, who is now the director of a telecom company and packs considerable weight on the island. When his charming secretary put in a call to someone, they answered, and an interview was easily arranged.

I had to locate the sex workers myself, as no one admits to having one on their list of contacts. As Eva, a sex worker in Amsterdam, said: 'None of my friends knows one.' Their work anonymously. When I explained the project and listed the categories, they frequently joked 'Oh, so I'm the prostitute'. Prostitution exists everywhere, but it isn't always legal. Often it is the sex worker who is punishable, although in some countries, like Sweden, it is client. I could usually find online sites offering sex work, varying from escort services to independent operators, but that was only the start; as soon as I telephoned and mentioned that I was a journalist, most of them hung up. I conducted a number of interviews under false pretences, showing up as a client and not revealing my real intentions until a little later, when I had gained their trust.

And finally, the police. It is not easy to get an appointment; you have to work at it. Submit an official request, for example, which was a lot more complicated in some in some countries than in others. The Netherlands was a piece of cake: the communications officer understood the project, and arranged an interview within a day. She happened to have read my novel, which helped my case.

Unfortunately, no one in Bulgaria, Slovakia or Lithuania had read it. In most of the Eastern European countries the procedure was as follows: after searching an outdated website written in a language I do not speak (and in Bulgaria in an alphabet I cannot read) I would find a telephone number. Often no one answered the phone, but sometimes I got a receptionist who spoke no English/French/German and therefore hung up after a few minutes of further confusion. Further inquiries sometimes produced an email address, but no one ever replied to my emails.

On at least ten occasions, I was unable to finalize my appointment with the police until the next-to-last day of my visit, and had to travel directly from the police station to the airport. It was the bureaucracy, explained one of my interviewees. Every decision requires the approval of a supervisor, who in turn needs to consult his or her boss, and so on and so forth.

My Youropean was often a good agent who spoke openly about the profession — perhaps my interviewees had been carefully chosen with that purpose in mind. They usually spoke a language I understood, and if I was unlucky, used an interpreter, who was often a communications officer who made sure that the officer was not too open. That happened in Bratislava, Prague and Bucharest.

Most of them enjoyed being interviewed, with the exception of the Irishman Dennis. He clearly viewed it as a chore, and he explored every possible escape route. His first excuse was that he didn't want the conversation to be recorded. The second was that he did not want to be photographed. But his superior officer had agreed, and so after his initial refusal, and a ten-minute phone call with a boss, he returned to the interrogation room (!), looking like a criminal who had just been forced to surrender to a SWAT team. 'Ok,' he said, 'you've got 15 minutes.' And with a stopwatch in his hand he made sure that the interview did not last a second longer.

In time, things went more smoothly, and my requests were granted more easily: the police could consult the growing number of interviews on my website and conclude that my intentions were honourable (although Dennis may not have been all that happy when he saw his interview online a few weeks later). At least I wasn't arrested.

NOTE FROM THE AUTHOR, AUGUST 2016

The interviews in *This is Europe* were conducted between June 2013 and January 2015, and I finished writing the book in November of that same year. At the time, Europe was not yet the target of frequent terrorist attacks, and the prospect of a Brexit still seemed fairly unlikely. Times have certainly changed, but the subject of my book has not: Europe is Europe.

2

AND THAT IS WHY THE EU DOESN'T WORK

Dutch journalist Rob Wijnberg once said[2] that the word Europe in the title of a newspaper article is like the forecast of a rainy day for the owner of a beach club — it's a miracle that you are reading this book at all. Very little is written about Europe and the EU, although that has changed since the influx of refugees ceased to be an Italian (or Maltese) problem, and became a European issue, sometime around the spring of 2015. Even then, most of what we read is about other European countries and how they are responding to the problem, not about the EU.*

Claes de Vreese, professor of political communication at the University of Amsterdam, has been studying the way European elections are reported in 27 countries since 1999. According to him, in the early years the Netherlands provided the least coverage of all 27 countries, although that figure has crept up to about the average. I noticed this during the Youropeans project, which got

---

* When this book is published, in March 2016, the Netherlands will be halfway through its year as EU chair, which will probably result in a (temporary) Dutch peak in interest in the EU.

little publicity at home in the Netherlands before the publication of the book, while my visit made the front page of national newspapers in Hungary and Romania, and Slovenia, Estonia, Latvia, Lithuania and Croatia all devoted solid articles to the project. As a result of the lack of coverage, the Dutch have little interest in the EU, although there are editors-in-chief who argue that the opposite is true, i.e. they do not provide much coverage because readers and viewers are not interested. (I have noticed they tend to assign themselves a passive role, whilst I am more inclined to think it is the newspaper, and not the reader, who decides what is news.)

Another consequence of this hit-and-miss reporting is that people in the Netherlands have very little knowledge of European affairs. When the political activists from the Dutch *Geen Peil* movement called for an advisory referendum in March 2016 on the EU association agreement with Ukraine, they did so with the help of posters featuring outrageous quotes from equally outrageously Europhile politicians. Jean-Claude Juncker, chairman of the European Commission was quoted as saying 'Most Europeans don't understand the decisions being made anyway.' Dutch politician Alexander Pechtold opined that 'Europe is too complex to stuff into a referendum.' Unfortunately, both statements are true.

The complexity, but above all the level of knowledge, has consequences for the way in which the media cover European issues, which they tend to avoid until, for example, impending European elections force them to examine the issues. 'If an issue isn't really on the agenda, you can't suddenly have a serious debate about it,' De Vreese said.[3] 'Because there is little or no continuity in Dutch reporting on Europe, the media cannot assume even a basic level of knowledge on the part of general public.' And so the media prefers simple frames, such as in the last elections when it all boiled down to 'do we want more or less Europe?'.

De Vreese concluded that in countries where former prime ministers and other government ministers stand for European offices, there is more coverage. A familiar face helps. So does a good conflict: countries where there is a lot of conflict about Europe provide more coverage. Herman van Rompuy, former chairman of the European Council, was acutely aware of the difficulty of addressing all Europeans at once. 'He believed that national government leaders should actually be on the frontline, explaining European policies, because together, they are those policies,' said his former assistant Luuk van Middelaar, who is now a political columnist. But national leaders do not do this, and it is highly questionable whether they would have allowed Van Rompuy to go over their heads and speak to all of Europe.

Moreover, what podium could he have used to do that? The newspapers are less likely to write that 'Juncker believes' or 'Tusk thinks' than they are to report that 'Merkel wants' and 'Cameron demands'. There are no truly European media. In my hotel rooms I sometimes zapped to Euronews, which devotes a portion of its programming to the EU, from which it receives an annual subsidy of 15 million euros. There is no European newspaper.* Back in the nineties, the media magnate Robert Maxwell took a stab at rectifying this with *The European, Europe's first national newspaper*, but it went under in 1998. There are a few good European news blogs and sites, but their readership is limited. The only successful European station is Eurosport.

HERMAN, YOUROPEAN #196, LOCAL CELEB IN BRUSSELS

No, he does not have Obama's swagger, or Putin's raw charisma, I think as I follow Herman van Rompuy up the stairs to his room in the offices of his party in the EU, the *Europese Volkspartij* (EVP) His former party, because two months earlier, on 1 December 2014, his period as chairman of the European Council ended. He now has more time on his hands: my 10.30 appointment is his first of the day. A man of slight build wearing a long, sensible grey

---

* *Neweurope* is a weekly publication, and in April 2015 the US-based *Politico* started publishing a weekly European edition, but their target readers are primarily Brussels insiders.

coat, but carrying an elegant calfskin briefcase. He unlocks the door, switches on the light and we sit down, he on a couch next to a lowered European flag.

'Go ahead,' he says, and I take my first misstep: 'The EU was originally an economic union.' Van Rompuy interrupts me, his eyes piercing behind small, round lenses. 'That's so typically Dutch, and it is incorrect. The underlying idea was no more war, the peace ideal. And the economy was an instrument, not an objective. I see that in debates in the Netherlands, but certainly also in Great Britain, the economic motive is always at the forefront: "what's in it for us?" People are for or against Europe only insofar as calculating citizens believe that it directly benefits them. The founding fathers of the European Union sought an end to centuries of war, and wanted to find the most pragmatic way of doing so.' I have a feeling that Van Rompuy has told this story at least ten thousand times, but the tireless teacher in him is willing to tell it again. 'So they did it via coal and steel, the basis of the weapon industry. By transferring national control to a supranational body. That was the EGCS, later the EEC, which eliminated internal customs controls and introduced a common export tariff. When that had been completed, there was a move towards creating even closer ties within the common market, and finally towards the introduction of a common currency. That was a giant step towards integration, and a major hand over of sovereignty on the part of the nation states. But during that time, the economy was always a tool.'

'You are still young, of course, but you saw the birth of the EU. How did you experience that?'

'I was brought up in the European mindset. At the Jesuit College here in Brussels. Where I was a student from '59 to '65, the teachers were enthusiastic about the European ideology. Every year there was a kind of mini-Erasmus project, and a group of ten or so interested students took a fourteen-day trip through Europe with other boys – yes, at the time it was only boys, unfortunately – from Nijmegen, Berlin, Genoa and Evreux. It made Europeans of us. No longer focussed only on our own little group. It has sometimes been said that this was the noblest period in European history, and that it was it felt like to us. In the first rush of idealism there was even talk of the demise of the nation state. I have managed to hold on to that drive, even during my five years in the European Council.'

He takes his time, and does not mince his words. When I leave I give him a copy of my first novel, The Parvenu. His nickname is 'Haiku Herman' and so I sign the book:

So very diverse
Yet so very much alike
The Youropeans

My first haiku, composed on the underground just before the interview.

'Ah, that's how you spell Youropeans. Interesting.'

No, Herman van Rompuy does not have a lot of swagger. But I do not find it hard to imagine that he had what it takes to be the chairman Europe needed: intellectual, committed and accessible. A bridge builder. A decent man. And how many of those do you see in politics these days?

3

THE POLICE IN MADRID HAVE 650,00 FOLLOWERS

30 The police have, to put it mildly, a problem with professional deformation. 'During holidays I take pictures of my foreign colleagues. I pay special attention to their techniques, uniforms, and badges,' said Christian from Bratislava. He is not the only police officer who enjoys a busman's holiday: many of them simply walk into a foreign police station, introduce themselves, and are given a tour. Would bakers do the same? Some of them, like Igor from Slovenia, even stay with their foreign colleagues. He wanted go to London, and the IPA, the International Police Association, put him in touch with a retired Scotland Yard officer who had a spare room for him. 'It was wonderful,' said Igor, a jolly man in his forties. 'We shared a cup of tea every day, and discussed police matters.' Sometimes they contact one another online, for example via Policelink, a US-based community where the police upload films, mostly from their dash cams. 'It's fascinating to see how Americans deal with situations,' John said. He was a gentle giant working in the canine unit in Copenhagen. 'You know, we may do things differently, but we are all cut from the same cloth.' And it gets worse. Halfway through my tour I discovered that police officers also trade badges,

like little boys do with football cards. 'I ask foreign colleagues for them when I'm travelling, but I always carry a few in my pocket when I'm working here in Tallinn, so that I also have something to trade,' Lea said. The most coveted badge – the equivalent of that one impossible-to-find football card – is that of the British police. Bobbies are not allowed to give away their badge, which is the property of Her Majesty the Queen.

It says a lot about the officers' level of involvement: many of them also have a brother, uncle of father in the police force as well. Most of them have wanted to join up since they were young, and they remain with the police their whole working life, although many retire at a relatively young age. Serge in Luxembourg was so anxious to wear a uniform that he joined the army six days after his seventeenth birthday, the youngest ever according to a newspaper article. Four years later he became a gendarme, and now, at the age of 45, he is a presenter on Luxembourg Police TV. And looking forward to retiring in a few years – at 50.

'What will you do?'

'Play golf all day.' And he already has a handicap of five.

Stefano from Rome, a 50-year-old *carabinieri*, only played with soldiers when he was a child, and Igor caught the bug from reading *Sherlock Holmes* as a boy. ('But are you a detective now?' 'No, I'm with the border police'). When she was 4 years old, Verona, the chief of one of Amsterdam's neighbourhood police stations, watched the police pump the water out of a village pond in order to retrieve a pistol, and knew exactly what she wanted: more excitement and sensation. But she also wanted to be able to help, because she knows how to handle herself, whether in a shoot-out or giving CPR. She is small, just 1m65, but fierce: 'Whereas others walk away from tension, I step forward,' she said.

It was a fraught decision for Kestutis, Lithuania's highest-ranking police officer. 'In 1991, when we finally gained our independence, everyone did what they could to help the country recover. We were very patriotic. I had just finished law school, and my way of helping was to join the police force.'

It was a less obvious choice for some of the others. László, for example, was rebellious, and angry with everyone, especially after he was refused admission to the university. He had wanted to become a teacher. Now, thirty years later, he leads the Hungarian police force's information programme for schools, and so it all worked out in the end.

Paulo was a professional football player in Portugal, earning a decent salary, when he got injured. And so he ended up in the police force. 'Because it is a stable job, with the chance of a promotion.' Theognossia from Cyprus said more or less the same. She wanted to be an actress but ended up doing a commercial marketing course before finally deciding to join the police force. 'At least I'm sure of having a job and reasonable working hours. Nothing else is certain in this country.'

To serve and protect, the motto of almost every police force, is a deep-rooted belief, and they all take it very seriously, regardless of their role or rank: border police, head of the transport department, Frontex, Interpol, traffic police, chief inspector, team leader, sergeant, lieutenant, canine unit or commissioner. And most of them were incredibly dismissive of rank, arguing that the number of stars and bars on their jacket was not important. Except for Martins from Riga, who although only 25 already had four gold stripes on his coat. According to him, 'A soldier who doesn't want to become a general isn't worth his salt.'

The police. Most of my interviewees couldn't wait to join up, but I had always been wary of them, especially after I launched my own career of petty crime around the age of fourteen, stealing Marlboros from the supermarket, Heineken flags from the snack bar and advertising posters from bus shelters. The cops caught me every now and then, and made me report to the station; as a student I also spent a few hours in the cell. Around the same time I developed a strong aversion to authority, something which plagues me even today, in the extremely post-puberty stage of my life. To be honest, I found it thrilling to being entering the lion's den of my own accord rather than being sent there by my parents following a call from the police, casually strolling past rooms where weapons were kept and seeing gun holsters draped over chairs. Rooms where people were having lunch: I saw a can of Seven-Up on a desk, family photographs, and glass display cases (every police station has a display case full of prizes related to the national sport: football cups in Southern Europe, ice hockey cups in the north). They had hobbies, some of the police women were very attractive, and some policemen were witty. Just like real people.

LONG, CREEPY CORRIDORS IN BRATISLAVA, OPEN CURTAINS IN AMSTERDAM

The most remarkable interview I had was with Christian, in Bratislava. I was surprised to find that we would not be alone: we met in the office of one of his superiors, where I was seated next to him on a narrow couch. Leonora, an interpreter, sat on one side of the room, next to an information officer, while the police chief — an imposing woman in her fifties — was seated directly across from me on an equally imposing chair.

When I walked into the station ten minutes before I had noticed two statues on either side of the big front door. A man with a machine gun and a uniformed woman on the left, and three workers wielding radar equipment on the right side. I asked Christian if he could tell me anything about them. The interpreter rattled away, the press officer scribbled along with her, and Madame Police Chief watched. 'No,' he said. End of it. His thin hands lay in his lap, his fingers fidgeted with his hat. Out on the street he was respected, but here, at the head officer, the pistol on his belt might just as well have been a cap gun.

'Have the police changed since 1991, when the country was still communist?' I asked. He didn't really need an interpreter to answer my question, but he waited a long time before he said: 'I don't know, I didn't work here then.'

'And why are there only pictures of commissioners from after 1991 in the corridor downstairs?'

'The Slovakian police have only existed since 1991,' the press office said, speaking out of turn. That is the official line, but the police were the same; the same men, perhaps in a different uniform. The old spirit still haunted the sober building with its long, dark corridors. This is where Bratislavans were interrogated and mistreated in the 1960s. Among them the priest Anton, now 85 years old, the local celebrity for Youropeans, who was interred in a prison camp for ten years because he was a 'dangerous' priest (he was later also excommunicated by the Catholic Church for the same reason – Rome and Moscow had something in common after all.)

The interview was over. The officer was sent outside to play, the interpreter went home, the press officer looked pinched, and the boss presented me with a goody bag containing an alcohol test, a pen, a keychain, a notepad and rain poncho bearing the logo of the Bratislavan police. It was nice of them, and certainly a radical departure from the past.

Communist statues and creepy corridors in Slovakia: the buildings housing the police told their own story about a country. In Estonia, Finland, Luxembourg and Sweden they were new and shiny. In Amsterdam East, the police occupied a former school building right in the heart of the district. The neighbours, just four metres away across a tiny garden could see into the police station, partly because no one in the Netherlands closes their curtains, not even the police. The Dutch police apparently feel they have little to hide, and they even use volunteers to help out with their filing. (Volunteer? For the police?! My 15-year old self would have found this completely bonkers.)

The Berlin station near the Tempelhof airport is unmistakably German: a massive steel and leaded glass building with a small entrance that makes you feel even more insignificant. When I arrived my papers were carefully examined before I was allowed to wait just a fraction too long for Mrs Jabukowksi. The trek to the interview room was long, up one stair and down another, past closed doors while Frau Jabukowski, who was in her early thirties, maintained an icy silence next to me.

POVERTY AND CORRUPTION GO HAND IN HAND, ALSO IN EUROPE

The prosperity of a nation is reflected in its police stations. Romania, and certainly Bulgaria, are poor. They are subject to special rules, and their admission to the EU was strictly supervised. There the police stations are run-down and the pavements are cracked and full of potholes. In Bucharest I was directed to a branch office in a distant suburb, a long taxi ride away from the beautiful, touristic city centre. Every few hundred metres the streets got dirtier, the apartments blocks greyer, and some streets were unpaved. The taxi pulled into the station's parking lot, which was dotted with broken down police cars, some of them propped up on crates, and a doghouse. There were police officers sleeping in at least two of the cars, it being just after lunchtime.

I interviewed the policewoman in a room that was also her boss's office. The cardboard packaging from a plasma television set stood in the corner next to a stack of moving boxes, and the computer on the table was fast acquiring value as an antique. During the crisis all government salaries had been slashed by 25 percent, said Mariana, who was charming, and wearing her best uniform. 'We think it is unfair because we guarantee public order and safety.' That didn't seem to me to be the most relevant argument against salary cuts, but I kept my mouth shut. And because I was in danger of missing my next appointment on the other side of the city, one of her colleagues offered to give me a lift in a car that was still functioning. For thirty minutes we raced through the city's infamous rush hour traffic, siren wailing (exciting but embarrassing).

Sofia, Bulgaria, is as least as poor. The waiting room of the main police station stinks of urine, the receptionist is missing at least six teeth, and the glass windows of his booth are pitted. The poverty explains the corruption of the Bulgarian police, Anton said. He is responsible for security at major events such a football matches, and so his room is decorated with scarves from Real Madrid, Liverpool and AS Roma. 'When people are poor, they are open to gifts from the public. For example, to the idea that you can avoid a traffic fine by slipping a police officer a little something if you get caught speeding. In countries where the salaries are good, in your country for example, they won't risk their career, but here the temptation is bigger.'

Low pay is a problem in Croatia as well. 'He is paid more than I am,' Ana said, pointing to a waiter at the sidewalk café in Bogovićeva Street where we are sitting. In Zagreb, everything, even an interview with a police officer, takes place at sidewalk cafes. In the nineties, the concept of an office garden was introduced in the Netherlands, but today we work at home (possibly in the garden), in cafes (making one cup of coffee last all day; not very profitable for the owner), or in offices that do not look like offices. Zagreb, however, has office streets, where people sit from 9 to 6, holding meetings, entertaining clients, or calling their suppliers, and even after that many of them stay on to meet up with friends. Their social life is conducted outside, and it is not at all unusual to have never been to the house of someone you have known for ten years.

'I earn 500 euro a month,' said Ana, who was even more charming than Mariana. 'I'm guessing the waiter earns 900, plus tips. But we have no money. Not even enough to buy patrol cars. Not enough munition to use for training. And worst of all are our uniforms, pfff!'

'Old?'

'No, ugly. Really unacceptable.'

'Grounds for resignation,' I said.

She agreed.

In Ireland, the crisis has put pressure on salaries. 'But what are you going to do about it?' Dennis asked.

'Go on strike?'

'Not allowed.'

POLICE COOPERATION

The police in Europe work together, most notably via Europol, which was founded in 1999 and has its headquarters in The Hague. Crime has gone international. Kestutis, the burly police officer from Vilnius, is a member of the management team. Europol has no executive authority; it focuses primarily on sharing information between countries. This, according to Kestutis, is not enough, and its powers should be expanded. 'Europol's current mandate is too limited. But that is a political decision, part of the bigger political debate about where national legislation ends and European law begins. 28 countries with 28 different viewpoints make it almost impossible to reach consensus.' There is cooperation on a smaller scale between Estonia, Finland, Latvia and Poland. This is common practice in many places in Europe: The Danes work closely with their Swedish and Norwegian colleagues, but of course we know all about that from the television series The Bridge (*Broen* in Danish and *Bron* in Swedish). 'We train together and we coordinate our working methods,' John said. The Greek riot police share their extensive experience with foreign colleagues, and Romanians offer their Western European counterparts assistance in dealing with pickpockets. Sometimes cooperation is unavoidable, especially for small countries: the Luxembourg police are trained in Belgium, because it would be too expensive to maintain training facilities for so few people.

THE UNIFORM IS SACROSANCT

A few years ago a popular song in the Netherlands described it as a country where children call their father by his first name, and uniforms are not sacrosanct. If a girl nicks a police officer's hat during some mass event like King's Day, she does not risk going to prison. You can say *fuck you* to a Dutch police officer (though my country's Supreme Court has recently ruled that the police cannot be referred to as 'antfuckers', which is what the Dutch call nitpickers). That is not the case in many other European countries. Frau Jabukowski from Germany has no first name, and police officers in almost all countries are addressed in the polite form of their language, except for Denmark and Sweden (and in Ireland and England, of course, since English does not have a polite form, or depending on your point of view, no impolite form). The Danish police use the informal form of address because the polite form creates distance, Danish police officer John said. In his view, the distance has become too small, and there is now very little respect for authority. 'Thirty years ago the presence of a police officer could stop a fight. That is no longer true. I sometimes think that the fun doesn't begin until the police arrive.'

And in Belgium? 'It's not what you say, but how you say it,' according to the Flemish officer Nancy. 'But I don't like it when people in the streets immediately use the informal 'jij'. She is also unhappy with certain changes in society, including the fact that police interventions go straight onto YouTube. They pick and choose what they show, and sometimes that is police violence, but not what happened beforehand.

The situation in Southern Europe is very different. Portugal, for example. Paulo volunteered to drive me to my next appointment, an interview with a local celebrity (Salvador Mendes de Almeida) he wanted to meet. Paulo was a friendly ex-footballer in his thirties, but once I got into his police car I understood what I had also heard from others earlier that week: the police are no laughing matter. 'The law has given us the authority to do what we do, and that is to protect people. We deserve their respect,' he had said during our interview. Traffic was heavy in Lisbon, and the car in front of us ran a yellow light. 'Red light,' Paulo said and he immediately turned on his siren and flashing light. The miscreant pulled over instantly and the policeman took down the license plate number. 'He'll get a warning, not a fine,' he said by way of explanation, possibly because he had seen the surprised look on my face. Yes, the Portuguese obey the police, and they are respectful: *sim senhor* is the only acceptable way to address an officer.

The police also have a great deal of status in Madrid. One of my standard questions was: where do they police stand if the king or president has the highest social ranking, and a criminal the lowest? Most politely placed themselves 'somewhere in the middle'. Not Victor. 'Directly under the king,' he said with steely conviction. He meant it. 'Because we are here to help people.' The exception to the Southern European machismo was of course a woman. Her male colleagues take a different view, but the Cypriotic beat cop Theognossia – tiny and adorable – said: 'I think it is important to get along with the troublemakers in the neighbourhood. They need to see me as a person instead of a police officer. They all know me, in any case.'

'Do they make jokes about your name?' (I know I would)

'No, they like it.'

THESE DAYS YOU'RE NOT EVEN ALLOWED TO HIT SOMEONE!

Modern police forces are familiar with their own image; they keep regular tabs on it. And they think it is important to have a good image. It used to be different: we were *bad cops* but now we are all *good*. Really. At least according to Ana from Zagreb. 'Before '91, before independence, people were afraid of the police. But it's not like that now. Things really have changed. You used to be able to give a detainee a whack, but now if they complain at all, or say 'they're kicking me', I'm in big trouble.'

Stefano from Italy said: 'We are feared, but less than in the past. These days young boys tell me to *vaffanculo*, right to my face.' The police officer's response depends on where that boy is: in the north or in the south. 'In Southern Italy, organised crime is part of daily life, and that makes our work easier, because the rules are more bendable. In Bari I could throw a criminal a few punches, but not in Milan. There you have to stick to the rules when you approach a criminal.'

The Greek and the Hungarian police had the biggest image problem. 'Things were going well,' said László, who is an information officer at schools in Budapest, 'until the demonstrations in

2006. They turned into riots in which around a hundred police officers and thirty protestors were wounded. One agent was shot in the eye. But the press portrayed the police response as aggressive; they gave a totally distorted view. Even judges turned against us. Within a few months everyone hated the police.'

He couldn't say whether things were better now or not. But the evening before I (participating journalist!) had walked along in big protest march against a proposal to tax internet use: 150 forint, roughly 50 euro cents per downloaded gigabyte.

'That would make an ejaculation really expensive,' my first friend on the march joked, 'one of those films is easily a few GBs .'

The crowd, some ten thousand strong, surged forward across Andrássy Avenue, the Champs-Élysées of Budapest, moving in the direction of the head office of Fidesz, which rules the country with a two thirds majority secured by entering into coalition with the openly anti-Semitic, homophobe party Jobbik. Every now and then someone shouted a slogan (presumably something like 'down with them') that was picked up by others until it rolled through the crowd.

The police, who were lined up in formation along the street, were in full riot gear: helmets, battle fatigues, shields resting at their feet. They line up in this same formation for the local gay pride event, to protect Hungarian homosexuals, but apparently the odd homophobe is able to breach the line. The police looked fairly benign at this point but that all changed when the protestors reached the head office and threw a computer through a window. Then they made good use of their batons, and I adopted a slightly less participatory approach to my work.

In Athens, also in 2008, the police shot and killed a 15-year old school boy, which led to a wave of protests that lasted for weeks. The Greek Spiro, surprisingly small and slight of build for a riot policeman, was in the thick of it. 'It got worse and worse. At one point, the Molotov cocktails were filled with phosphorous, which is almost impossible to extinguish.' He stood up and demonstrated how he tried to beat the flames from his clothes. 'People called us murderers. Some doctors refused to treat our wounds. Before that, half of the population respected us, but afterwards only 30%.' They had to change, and they did. An example? 'Before we responded immediately if we were attacked, now we wait, and we wait. It was difficult, I have to admit.'

'70% have a favourable view of us,' Lithuanian police chief Kestutis said. If it is true, it is a remarkable improvement, since the police were extremely unpopular in most of the former communist countries (the Baltic States were actually part of the Soviet Union). And the KGB, the secret service, was even more unpopular. Older residents still shudder when they walk past their former headquarters in Vilnius, Riga and Tallinn. They are now museums, and it is possible to visit the interrogation rooms, cells and execution rooms. It didn't require much fantasy on my part to imagine how gruesome Soviet tactics were: the walls of the KGB museum in Riga are still flecked with blood.

'The government used to be strong,' Anton in Sofia said. 'One agent for every one thousand people was enough. During Soviet times, people knew their rights, but also their obligations.' That's one way of looking at it.

POLICE TV

It is easier to score in the popularity polls in some countries than it is in others. Finland is a case in point. Joanna explained the trouble caused by a small group of radicals. The police maintain contacts with the troublemakers, the leaders of gangs of football hooligans, for example. The same is true of Malta, where the police know all of the bad guys. Luxembourg, which is only slightly bigger does have a problem with criminals, most of whom come from other countries. Long live Schengen! 'They think that everyone here is a millionaire. But they aren't,' Serge added, just to be on the safe side. There is a high incidence and breaking and entry, but few murders. Only six last year, all of which were solved.

Image is important, and it can be improved. The police can

change their behavior, but that isn't enough. It's all about communication, and in today's world that means using social media. The police too. The police in Madrid already have 650,000 followers. 'Only the FBI has more,' Victor said. He is the press officer, and immensely proud of this achievement. 'But we don't follow anyone else,' which is odd thing for the police to say. But later, when one of Victor's colleagues went online I could hear the old-fashioned sound of a computer seeking a modem: *crackle, crackle, peep, ring*. The Madrid police twitters, but at what speed?

The Viennese police have 10,000 likes on Facebook. 'Number 10,000 was a fifteen-year-old girl last week,' Patrick said. I am a bit wary of such statistics. The one millionth customer in a shop is never a shabby old man, but always a fresh-faced person who fits the desired customer profile to a tee. 'She got a tour and ride on the police boat.'

It is all very pro-active — another communication buzz word — and the police communicate themselves in order to 'prevent inaccurate stories', according to Patrick, who works in the city that had just narrowly missed being named the world's most liveable, partly because of its safety record. In Austria, if you're unhappy about how you've been treated by the police, you can ask for their telephone number, which make it easier to lodge a complaint. 'It's a big deal here. No one has ever asked for my number.'

Luxembourg takes it one step further. Serge is going to be the anchorman on Police TV, at least until he retires and starts golfing all day. But the police In Cyprus are also active. They send the whole neighbourhood a text message when there has been a break-in somewhere, and they ask for tips. They do the same in Madrid, where it works very well. They have already arrested fifty drug dealers following tips via social media. 'It is, Victor said,' the future of police work.

'Civilians as informers? Don't I know that formula from somewhere, for example from the DDR (former East-Germany)?' Victor does not approve of the comparison. I shouldn't be communicating that kind of nonsense.

MY FAVOURITES

3 Spiro, Athens. Now a cook for the police, formerly with the riot squad. He worked mostly on Sundays, at football stadiums. Half of top teams come from Athens, so there was a derby, and riots, every weekend.
'Were you ever afraid?'
'You bet I was. It is very stressful for eleven officers to face off against two thousand people. I had to run for my life.'

2 Joanna, Helsinki. After fifteen minutes the sweat was still pouring off her face. She had bicycled to work, normally a distance of 25 kilometres, but she had taken a detour because of the fine weather, and ended up cycling 40 kilometres in full uniform, including a bullet-proof vest.

1 Ana, Zagreb. She uses astrology in her work. 'When I stop someone, I sometimes need a few minutes to judge a person's character. I recently encountered a Turkish boy, and something didn't feel right. He turned out to be a Libra, which is not good: they are talkers, manipulators, charmers. My supervisors don't approve but I know that the FBI once researched the link between crime and astrology signs.' I don't tell her that I'm a Scorpion, because they're no good, I once read.

4

DOCTORS ARE PAID UNDER THE TABLE IN EASTERN EUROPE

46   In Riga I ended up paying a visit to the hospital. The hotel doctor sent me there after I developed a strange allergic reaction on my arm one afternoon. I was expecting an A&E department in a sterile building, and a grim waiting room with a few tattered magazines and yesterday's copy of a free newspaper, which is what I was used to in the Netherlands. But things were different here. The University Hospital in Riga had not had a coat of paint in decades, and there wasn't really a waiting room with an organized take-a-number system. Patients were scattered around the room, sitting on broken-down chairs, some of them moaning, while gurneys carrying sicker patients rattled through the corridor. After a thirty-minute wait a doctor arrive, and I was placed on a bed, rolled into a room where I was put on a drip and given some medication. An hour and a half later I was allowed to leave, but had to pay first. '427,' said the woman at the desk. I didn't understand her Latvian-accented English very well, but thought she meant 427 euro. Not cheap, but I assumed my insurance would cover it. It wasn't until she wrote in down for me that I saw the decimal: the charge was 4 euro and 27 cents.

Things were definitely different here, but the doctor seemed competent and he gave me the right medication (I placed a slightly concerned call to my own doctor the next day). And that is my first conclusion about this category of Youropeans: the hospitals may look different, the circumstances may vary, but doctors are the same everywhere. The 73-year-old Mara, a pathologist from Zagreb, the 28-year-old Austrian Martin, model and orthopaedic surgeon in training Ylva, dermatologist Maria In Bucharest, the Nicosia and Madrid-based cardiologists: they are all highly educated, responsible, and (almost always) hard-working people.

Take Mantas, an orthopaedic surgeon from Vilnius, himself as sick as a dog, but he declined to cancel the appointment, and showed up for the interview at 8.30 in the morning at a coffee place somewhere near his house. He asked for a glass of water with his espresso, and tossed back a couple of pills; he would probably take something stronger later in the hospital. His was not an eight-hour shift, but closer to twelve hours. He started by showing me some photos on his mobile, a whole series of special cases, not all of them his own patients.

'Here, you can see the bone sticking out in this one.'

They sometimes had strange fantasies, some of which you might call sick if they weren't doctors. The surgeon Maria, a petite Portuguese woman, likes meeting her patient, but what really gets her going is hacking and sawing on their limbs. I guess you could call that a form of contact. Hilde, a young paediatrician working in the ER of a teaching hospital in Amsterdam described her love of her work in the same way that many of her colleagues would: 'It's a beautiful profession. The idea that you can sometimes really cure people. The work is practical, requiring a fundamental understanding of why the body isn't functioning, and what you can do to correct that. It is often intense, and difficult if you are not successful and are forced to acknowledge that you have reached the limit and the patient, a child, is going to die. I have to figure out how best to deal with that, and make it is as bearable as possible.'

In general, they think their work is important. According to

Serge, a hand surgeon from Paris, women judge a man on the basis of two things: his shoes and his hands. Nail biters are doomed to strike out on the first date. The Berlin-based dentist Matthias said that women judge men on the basis of their shoes and their teeth. During my interview with Serge, I surreptitiously examined my own gnawed-off fingernails, and after hearing Mathias's words of wisdom I wondered how my teeth were. Not so good, apparently, because he gave me the unsolicited advice to drink less tea as one my front teeth was becoming discoloured. He himself was sporting a black eye he got the day before playing basketball with the German over 55s. Basketball was his first passion, and he had played on the national team until he started university when he was 35, and his sporting career was more or less over.

IT'S A FAMILY AFFAIR

Even more so than with the police, for most the people interviewed, becoming a doctor was a long-held desire, and a conscious choice. It has to be: medical school takes a long time, and that too is true of every country. When he was only three, the Roman psychiatrist Nicolò began pestering his mother with questions such as: 'You're looking at me. But why?' Frank always had a secret desire to become a doctor, but he thought his laziness would stand in the way. He conquered his doubts when he spent several weeks in a hospital with a knee injury when he was nineteen. (He had been a very talented skier, one of the nation's best. Also one of its best runners and a member of the national basketball team. I know, it's Luxembourg, but an achievement nevertheless.)

And for most, it was also a family affair. Mantas's father was a famous brain surgeon. The grandfather of the Polish doctor Filip was a doctor, as were both his parents and his sister. 'No, my family choice of a profession is not very adventurous.' I spoke to him in the doctor's lounge of his hospital, just after he had finished a 48-hour shift. Pale and tired, he was picking at a Chinese takeaway left behind by a colleague. He doesn't have much more energy to spare, but Filip (28) is so anxious to become a gynaecologist that he is doing his specialist training on a volunteer basis, and is only paid for his night shifts. He doesn't care: 'I will be doing what I want to do for the next fifty or sixty years.'

You also have to be extremely motivated to become a doctor in London, where salaries are not at all proportional: during her internship Jeanette earned less than ten pounds an hours, less than the price of the two cups of coffee and two cups of tea we drank during our interview in a lunchroom near Sloane Square. 'The problem is the same for teachers, firemen and police officers. We are not paid accordingly. And because it so unbelievably expensive to live in London, a higher income is not just a little extra spending money, it means being able to afford childcare.' The astronomically high rent in London means that ordinary people are forced to commute two and a half hours. And yet Jeanette is prepared to make the sacrifice. She did not start medical school until she was 35, when she finally had the nerve to quit her well-paid job as a business consultant.

Doctors are wholly committed, and for the rest of their lives. I talked to only one exception: Azadeh, a Danish-Iranian doctor who is no longer quite as enthusiastic. 'It's such a solitary existence, doing my rounds at night. The nurses have each other, their own cosy lounge. I am thinking about switching jobs, maybe working for a pharmaceutical company.'

'What? Joining the devil! What will your friends think?'

'Almost all of them are doctors, and I expect some of them will disapprove. But I think the working conditions are too strenuous, and the pay is not good enough.'

If she switches she'll earn enough to buy beers for all her friends to win them back. Alcohol costs a fortune in Copenhagen, too expensive for struggling doctors.

DOCTORS ARE MIGRATING FROM EAST TO WEST

They recognise one another from a distance. 'I recently spent a month at the University of California, taking a course for a variety of participants, not all of them doctors,' said Toomas, an Estonian and former ship's doctor, 'but it's easy to identify the doctors.' Even without the stethoscope around their neck. They are same type of people, and international experience has made them even more alike. It begins when they are still in medical school, which many of them, especially those from small countries, attend abroad. Almost all Maltese doctors were trained in Great Britain, David said, trained in Cardiff. He is a sport's doctor, having to lick the wounds of the national football team after yet another defeat. The level of medical care is just as high in Malta as in the rest of the EU, but not every specialisation is available. Sometimes David has to send a left back with a bad knee to Italy.

Luxembourgers have to study abroad, and Anistassiades had to leave Cyprus to study at Hadassah Medical School in Israel. 'One of the best in the world, as you know,' the doctor said, standing in front of a wall covered in diplomas and citations. I didn't.

'And then to Johns Hopkins, where I became a cardiologist.' I had heard of Johns Hopkins, one of the most famous medical schools in the US, and Mateja, now 73, had briefly studied there. She was only the second Slovenian to be admitted, and she left her husband and three children behind to study there for seven months. She admitted she had felt a bit guilty about this. 'But they survived.'

Many doctors continue to work internationally, even after their studies. They all agreed that this is inspirational and educational. Mantas told that there is even a kind of Facebook for orthopaedic surgeons. 'It's perfect. You can watch online videos, but also find invitations to seminars. When I post a question there, I get responses from all over the world in no time.'

Increasingly, doctors are also taking actual jobs abroad. Dutch doctor Hilde sees a lot of Germans leaving the *Heimat* because of the explosion of the administrative red tape in Germany. 'They learn Dutch so quickly, it's amazing.' They have to: doctors may all speak English (or German) but not all of their patients do.

Money is usually the motivation for working abroad. Doctors in Croatia earn only a tenth of what they can earn in Western Europe, according to Mara. 'And that is why so many of my colleagues have moved there in recent years.' The same is true in Slovakia, where 80 percent of all medical students want to work abroad. They are trained here but then immediately go abroad Romana explained. It is a tragic development she said dramatically, as she sighed, gestured and rolled her eyes (she originally wanted to be an actress, and it seems she has succeeded, even though her public now consists mainly of patients and her assistant. The worrying trek to the West leaves job openings in Slovakia or the Czech Republic that are in turn filled by Ukrainians and Bulgarians. But not Georgi, for whom things have worked out well in Sofia.

'Why did you come to Bulgaria? Couldn't you find enough interesting people in Europe?' He said, laughing at his own joke.

We were sitting in the cramped office of one of his own clinics. He is one of the country biggest entrepreneurs in the healthcare sector, and spends most of his time running his business, except for Wednesday morning, when he still sees patients. He is cardiologist. 'And a damned good one,' he added. The interpreter he called in – a meek student – looks a bit lost sitting next to him, because of course Georgi speaks English. And French. He learned the latter when he was in the Foreign Legion, the mercenary army the French government sends in when it does not want to risk the lives of its own people. He joined in the early nineties, when he was a junior doctor, because he couldn't support his family. He was a parachutist for as few years; it was an extremely tough environment but it suited Georgi (steel blue eyes, stubbly beard), who was sipping whisky from a mug, which he replenished a couple of times during our interview.

'In this country we earn approximately 1,000 euro a month; in the Netherlands I would earn 30,000 euros a months. At least.' But 'we' refers to doctors in general. Georgi's presumably earns much more and that is why he stays in Bulgaria. András, a doctor/entrepreneur in Budapest is in a similar position as the owner of Swiss Clinic, a chain of private clinics. Which is not Swiss at all. 'One of the co-founders was, but he is long gone.' Well, there's not much difference between a white cross and a red cross, and cashing in on Switzerland's reputation probably makes good commercial sense too. Hungarian doctors normally earn about 500 euro a month, nurses between 200 and 400. 'I pay doctors 2,000 euro,' András said.

PAYMENTS ARE MADE UNDER THE TABLE

The poor salaries in Eastern Europe are to some extent a holdover from the communist era, when doctors, farmers and labourers were all paid the same amount. That is no longer the case: a car mechanic in Prague earns much more than a doctor in Prague, especially if you calculate the hourly rate, Barbara complained; she had taken her car to the garage that very morning. But they're car doctors, I said, trying to smooth over the situation. And I couldn't imagine that the car she took to the garage was some broken-down old Skoda. She is the owner of the country's first private clinic, which employs approximately 100 doctors.

Low pay in these countries has resulted in the widespread phenomenon of doctors being paid under the table. 'We call it the grey economy,' Barbara said. 'It is still happening. Most of the hospitals in the Czech Republic are public institutions where the doctors are excellent but do not have the time to give patients much attention. Patients are willing to pay a little extra, in cash, for that attention.' She doesn't allow it in her clinic, nor does Janis, a very successful plastic surgeon in Riga. But the Latvian plays it down, saying: 'You should think of it as a tip given by a satisfied patient, not as something the doctor asks for.' His clinic looked nothing like the third-world style clinics I would see later that week. A posh receptionist oversaw a quiet waiting room where a mother leafed through a glossy magazine while her two sons played computer games on their mobiles. But he assured me that his prices were not exorbitant, and as a result he had patients from all over Europe. Long live the EU, membership of which had boosted confidence in his country's reliability.

Mantas did not think that the practice of unofficial payments would change any time soon. Patients want a good doctor, one who is given more time in the operation room, and therefore gets a tip of 500 to 1,000 euro extra per treatment. The doctor has little or no motivation to change the situation. It is not a problem for Mantas, who is financially independent.

As I said, I paid 4.27 euro at the desk for treatment, and nothing under the table. I could have got an even better deal in Zagreb, where it would have cost me nothing, according Mara. 'That is not official policy, but in practice foreign guests who require treatment do not have to pay. We are very hospitable!'

OH DEAR, GREEK DOCTORS SMOKE IN FRONT OF THEIR PATIENTS!

Those are some of the similarities, but what about the differences? I was often told that there is a big difference between Europe and America. According to Serge, Europeans are better doctors, more flexible, and Americans are too wrapped up in their rules and protocols. 'They are too technical,' Serge said, 'and they simply don't talk to patients, which is very important. They are afraid to make a mistake and get sued. We are more human. I worked in United States for a while, and I was shocked that my secretary sent people away because they weren't insured.' He would never do that.

And how do doctors differ from one another within Europe? In Belgium, patients prefer to bypass their general practitioner, who is an important filter in the Netherlands. Belgians go straight to the hospital or a specialist. I suggest to the Amsterdam-based doctor Hilde that the Dutch system sounds more efficient, but she is not so sure. There is a danger that certain illnesses will go undetected in the Netherlands, because of the extra step in the procedure. 'It means that patients are sicker when they come in, and that it is sometimes too late,' Hilde said. It was 5 December and St. Nicholas and his Petes had just arrived at the hospital, providing a welcome and festive disruption to the otherwise somber routine on the paediatric ward.

> The EU also influences the work of doctors. The European Guideline of Working Hours limits the number of hours people are allowed to work. 'That sounds good, but it isn't. Many skills are acquired only through endless practice. You just need to have encountered enough disasters. That is why I didn't want to be a surgeon: I would have been ninety before I was any good,' Jeanette laughed. She did not start medial school until she was 35. 'EU rules are good for doctors,' Toomas said. 'They set a reliable standard. I can now understand why a patient who comes to me from Germany or Italy uses certain medications.'
> Ylva thinks it is not worth the trouble. 'I used to have my own method of keeping patient records. Such as: "I did this or that, but I think it is mostly psychological". Or I described a patient as "the man with the strange dog", so that I knew who it was. But that is no longer allowed, because all of the records are to be made public. It means I have to exercise self-censorship, and I don't like it.'

Another cultural difference: the very proper Swedish doctor Ylva (64) worked in Greece for a time on a European research project, and was shocked: 'my Greek colleague smoked all day, right in front of patients!' Things are well organised in Sweden, and she sees only twelve patients a day, taking her time, thirty minutes per patient, which is a far cry from the seven minutes I am officially allotted by my Dutch GP. Ylva is very pro-active: she also treats people in her office. She automatically runs tests on anyone who comes to her surgery, including me. (Walking into a Youropean doctor's office often triggered a nervous reaction on my part: since

I was in a doctor's office, there must be something wrong with me. It was easier to suppress that reaction in the office of plastic surgeon Janis, but in a GP's office I couldn't help asking about my lingering cough. She had all the time in the world, after all. Fortunately, I felt no such urge with that other category of Youropeans, the sex workers.)

Dr Ylva also said people in other countries tend to see GPs as no more than a service hatch. 'Patients from the former Soviet Union immediately say "I want zspecialist".' She is well aware of how lucky she is to have so much time at her disposal, and of the many reasons her foreign colleagues are worse off. In Germany, for example, there are many more general practitioners, most of whom have their own practice. They need to earn money, so they spend as little time as possible on each patient, and encourage them to come back next week, or write a prescription for only a month instead of several months.

FREE HEALTHCARE?

There may not be much difference between European doctors, but there are differences in the way in which healthcare is organised in various countries. Most have some kind of national health service, which provides 'free' care. But of course it isn't free: we pay for it in taxes. In Poland, everyone pays 10 percent of their salary for healthcare. The disadvantage of this system, Filip said, was that people go to a doctor for every minor ailment. He thought the Czechs had the right idea: they pay one or two euros for every visit, which creates the necessary threshold.

Mateja in Slovenia is 72, but as feisty as a terrier and active in many areas, particularly in politics. There is no love lost between her and the current (corrupt) crop of politicians, who are far too liberal: the past was better, when Slovenia was still rich, and the most successful part of former Yugoslavia. 'Our healthcare system was damned good: we had the lowest young mortality rate in Europe. And now? Suicide rates are rising, mortality rates for people between forty and sixty are rising.' Mateja can rattle off all the statistics, and throughout the interview she bombarded me with percentages. 'Do you know why?' asked the old-style communist whom the press calls *Khmer Rouge*. 'It is because people have to work too hard, and put in way too many hours. Another good reason to be a member of the EU: I hope workers will have more rights.'

The British system, the National Health Service (NHS) is said to be very good. The influential Washington Post recently compared all Western healthcare systems, and the NHS received the highest score. 'Canada and the US were the worst,' Jeanette said, 'and the more I see of the British system, the more I value it. Everything is free. Everything. The only drawback are the waiting lists, which can be long in comparison with private care.'

The crisis has had a considerable impact on healthcare. Ireland's system, for example, would be better if doctors were paid on the basis of their performance, like they are in England, according to Margaret. 'That is not possible here, for the simple reason that the country is bankrupt.' It means that working in Ireland is frustrating, particularly in public hospitals. She is fortunate enough to work in a private clinic as well. They function well because they are run by entrepreneurs who are good at keeping budgets in check and responding to new developments. 'They still make a profit, regardless of the crisis.'

Cyprus has been hit even harder and Anistassiades, a cardiologist in a private clinic sighed: 'As a result of the crisis, people have less money for us, and our fees have come under even more pressure. It's a mess.' He has good reason for complaint, because in an effort to save two banks, the Central Bank of Cyprus declared that clients would forfeit savings in excess of 100,000 euro. Overnight Anistassiades, now 72, lost his hard-earned pension.

DOCTOR GOOGLE

Society is not what it used to be, and doctors are all too well aware of this. Patients know exactly what is wrong with them, and what treatment is required. 'Google has changed a great deal for doctors,' Filip said. Hilde sees the upside of this and thinks it is good that patients read up beforehand and are more health conscious. The danger of internet, she said, is that people see too many worst-case scenarios online. 'You type in headache and get a diagnosis of brain tumour or Ebola.' And there is less hierarchy: the doctor is no longer an unquestioned authority, while patients sometimes prefer not to have an opinion. They would rather have someone else decide for them. They experience that kind of equality as an added responsibility, a choice. 'They say "I can't make the decision".'

But there are cultural differences here as well, and sometimes the hierarchy is still intact. Doctors in Mediterranean countries are expected to write out a prescription, because patients who go home empty-handed may question the doctor's skills. It is also a generational question, and during my interviews I met doctors who spoke to me from behind their massive desks in the way I assumed they also spoke to their patients: slowly and very clearly, but above all in a didactic manner that left little scope for questions – which is not necessarily conducive to a good interview.

Vanity is an innocuous illness that many doctors suffer from, and this is clearly evident from the way they decorate their waiting room. At least one wall is always covered in impressive certificates and framed diplomas. Like the room of the Madrid-based cardiologist José. He is a handsome man, like a doctor in a penny romance, although with a slight lisp. He took a heavy book off a full bookshelf and said: 'Last year this was chosen as the best medical book of the year. I wrote it. And this' – he picked up another book – 'has even been translated into Chinese.' But his most important trophy was on his desk: a photograph of him and the Queen Sofia. 'It's not important to me,' he lied. 'What really counts is a patient's laugh.'

No, European doctors — those responsible, hard-working and often stubborn people — are really the same all over Europe. They know what they're doing, and they are all more or less equally good at what they do. But if I had to choose one country, I would say Estonia. Go to Riga and get an eye lift or a boob job from Dr. Janis, who has all of his foreign patients stay in a nice hotel, and may even take you sightseeing in his private plane. And the bill will only come to 4.27 euro, or perhaps 427 for the deluxe package.

MY FAVOURITES

3 Toomas, Tallinn. He said I had a cold coming on and prescribed the following: 1 spoon of honey, 1 spoon of butter, 1 spoon of rum. Light it and let it burn for five minutes. Drink it and you'll be cured. He had been a ship's doctor, which explains it. It works, by the way.

2 Pippa, Helsinki. She is 40 but looks 30, is the director of Finland's biggest private clinic, did an MBA in her spare time last year, has three children, built her own house and is the doctor of the national women's football team. And is a nice person.

1 Benoît, Brussels. He initially wanted to be an artist, a graphic designer or a cabaret performer. I interviewed him at home in Anderlecht, where his daughter played quietly on one of those traffic rugs while her father gave me a fierce, witty and socially aware run-down of the entire European situation as well as of the finer points of the Flemish/Walloon divide. Like most Francophones he was convinced that French was the world's third most important language. It isn't; it is in fourteenth place. Chauvinism, however, is a French word.

5

BECOME AN ENTREPRENEUR IN ESTONIA OR IRELAND, BUT NOT IN SOUTHERN EUROPE

Bucharest. 'And this department deals with bookings,' Dragos said, with an expansive gesture, as if he were showing me vast fields of grain. The king is showing me around; that's what it feels like, and when he appears, his subjects suddenly drop their voices on the telephone or whisper to one another. Tall and physically fit, he looks good in a suit, and he knows it. In a two-storey office just beyond the centre of Bucharest, roughly 100 people work for Dragos's twenty companies, all of them in the tourist and transport industries. 'I would fit into most of your categories,' he said later from behind his desk; I was seated across from him, perched uncomfortably on a small chair. He is an entrepreneur, but he was also once a doctor in Germany, where he emigrated in the 1980s. He returned to Romania in 1995. He is also a national celebrity, because of his role in *Arena Leilor*, the Romanian version of *Dragons' Den*.

Dublin. 'This is Morrigan,' Owen said, showing me a poster of brightly-coloured fantasy figures. 'She is the reinterpretation of the Irish goddess of sex and death. We based this game on her.' He designs video games, and his new company BitSmith is true to type: four fairly unassuming guys are slumped over their laptops, wearing huge headphones. You wouldn't mistake their boss for a banker, either: a great hulk of a man in his early thirties sporting a goatee and earrings. 'We are now going to focus on the Chinese market,' he explained. The games business is booming, that much was clear to me, even though I am familiar in name only with World of Warcraft and Call of Duty. The last games I played were Pacman and Donkey Kong, in a snack bar sometime in the previous century.

Paris. Alexis left a job at Arthur Andersen to set up Causses, a hip organic store with a social objective: to improve the quality of life in the neighbourhood.' The way the *Arabe du coin*, the ethnic corner shop, did at one time. He wanted it to be the shop he would like to have on the ground floor of his own apartment building, not an expensive deli you only visit once a week, but a supermarket for your daily shop. Good, affordable quality. Relatively affordable, apparently, since the honey and tea I bought while waiting for the boss were not exactly cheap. Not expensive, however, by Parisian standards, according to Alexis. I believe him.

What I mean to say is that entrepreneurs are a mixed bag: some of them employ hundreds of people, like Dragos, or Martin (59), who got out of the real estate business just in time and is now the owner of the Burger King franchise in Spain. But they are also owners of neighbourhood stores, like Alexis, or Aarre, whose small business is located in an upscale part of Helsinki: thirty square metres neatly stuffed with everything from bread and vegetables to beer, magazines and even the odd toy.

And there is a new kind on the rise: the social entrepreneuers. Max, for example, who has a restaurant in Ljubljana that is run by immigrants. He is an immigrant himself, having travelled from Zimbabwe to Yugoslavia as a student in 1982. Or Claudio's company Ecodoma. He is also an immigrant who left his native Italy and moved to Latvia, for love. His company provides advice about renewable energy. And Patrick, whose Funds for Good raise money by trading shares in support of two charities: the Red Cross, and micro-credits for start-ups in Belgium.

ROBIN GOOD

It was interesting to talk to the entrepreneurs, particularly because they are committed, optimistic, and bold. For many years I was one of them: my company was called Robin Good, and its objective was to help other companies make their own social involvement more tangible, and turn their words to deeds. Activities included events and employee volunteer projects. Unilever employees, for example, built a small football stadium for a shelter that houses problem teenagers, in just two days. A large insurance company supported different local projects throughout the year. When I set up the company in 1999, it was a new phenomenon, but by the time I sold it in 2007, the concept was widespread. My company was instrumental in helping leading businesses to adopt socially responsible policies.

I sold my company because I wanted to write, but I still miss being an entrepreneur. The clear objectives and the structure provided by turnover figures and liquidity prognoses. The kick you get from landing a new client. But what I miss most is working with colleagues, clients and other entrepreneurs. Now I sit in a room by myself, typing all day. Guy, a savvy silver fox from London, explained it this way: 'The great thing about being an entrepreneur is the fact that your fate is your own hands, that you can do what you think is right. There is no place to hide, because you're the one who has final responsibility for what happens. So if things go well, you can pat yourself on the shoulder, but sometimes it's awful, like when my company when tits up.' He has owned Go Native since 1998, a short-stay apartment rental service that employs approximately 200 people. None of whom were working particularly hard during our interview: it was Friday afternoon, and their energy had been diverted to drinks, table football and ping pong. Every now and then a stray ball bounced off the meeting room door. Our interview ended at 6.00 and the boss finally got to join his staff for a drink. I felt a pang of envy....

Most of the entrepreneurs I spoke to were men, but there were a few women, including Barbara, a hotel owner in Vienna, Inez, who owns a temporary employment agency for students in the Netherlands, with offices in Amsterdam and Utrecht, and Brigitte, who with her Scottish husband has created a brand of chocolate in Copenhagen called Chocolate and Love. Most of my Youropean entrepreneurs were also slightly older, with an average age of 40. But some of them were very young. Tomek is only 25, but he is fast becoming the Jamie Oliver of Poland.

'Order something,' Tomek said when I met him in his restaurant.

'I heard the food here was terrible,' I said.

'It is. That's why people keep coming back.'

It was lunchtime in Kitchen. The boss had just returned from a run and was wearing sweatpants and running shoes. 'I'm training for a marathon.' Not his first. He said he has to stay fit in order to run a restaurant, open two new places and do a TV cooking programme.

TWITTER'S OFFICE WAS JUST AROUND THE CORNER AND LINKEDIN ACROSS THE STREET

I talked to entrepreneurs in every sector, from the highly educated to the streetwise, good and bad. Impossible to find a common thread. In order to draw any conclusion at all, I talked to them about the business climate in their country, asked about government support, their status as an entrepreneur, and about the European Union's influence on their company.

That climate was not so good In Denmark, to pick a random starting point. According to Birgitte, of Chocolate and Love, they're just not that entrepreneurial. Danes are extraverts and good at languages, which helps, but boldness and business acumen are not part of their genetic makeup.

'Not part of the Viking heritage?'

'Well,' she said, 'the funny thing is that there are a few major multinationals here such as Maersk, Novo Nordisk, Carlsberg and Lego are Danish. But it is not so easy to start a company and grow it, partly because of the high wages.' Apart from that, Denmark is the ideal place to start a company: if it goes under you can always fall back on generous unemployment benefits, free healthcare and training, while in other countries you might lose everything. 'The paradox is that this soft cushion does not help; it tends to encourage laziness. A lot of people are not hungry enough.' And that is a self-evident fact: setting up a business is 99% transpiration and 1% inspiration.

The devil is in the detail, apparently. While I was waiting for my interview, Birgitte and her husband were skyping with their New York-based designer, discussing the packaging of one of their chocolate bars. 'I think the green of that little corner should be a bit greener, can you do that?' As the shared screen of their Mac became increasingly green, Birgitte and Richard took a step back and studied it intensely, as if it was an important painting in a national museum.

'Yes, much better. And if you drag it a few millimetres to the right? Yeah, like that.'

Their wrappers wins prizes, it has to be said.

And the entrepreneurial climate in Belgium? Not the worst, but certainly not the best, according to Patrick. To begin with, you lose any claim to social benefits when you start a company; in France, for example, you keep them during the start-up period. But the biggest issue is cultural. Having a good job at a big company is considered cool, but starting your own business isn't. If you go bankrupt, you're a loser, while in the US, that's when people start to take you seriously, said Patrick.

In Malta, losing face is also something to be avoided at all cost, said Chris, who owns an advertising agency. It is typical of a small community, especially an island, and means doing everything you can to avoid going belly up, but it also makes people reluctant to start a business in the first place. In terms of the business mentality, Malta seemed surprisingly northern for a country that is just a stone's throw away from Sicily. People are on time, and a deal is a deal, thanks to the British influence — Malta was a colony for almost two centuries — and English is still an official language, in addition to Maltese (which is derived from Arabic).

There are interesting developments in Greece, where the Dutch embassy is involved in encouraging Greek start-ups. The Orange Grove project helps young entrepreneurs to find workspace, often in collaborative office buildings, and organises networking events and contacts with potential financiers. I learned this from Yiannis, who has long progressed beyond that stage: although he is only 32, he is a serial entrepreneur who was getting ready for the launch of Covve, an online network service ('LinkedIn, but better'), and before that he owned a bar and a theatrical production company. He earned his stripes as a consultant in London. Young, highly educated, lots of experience abroad and internationally oriented, Yiannis is a citizen of the world who has more in common with entrepreneurs in Hong Kong or San Francisco than with his fellow countrymen. And yet, he prefers to live in Athens, even though so many of his friends have already jumped ship. He sees a light at the end of the tunnel, and believes that the business climate is rapidly improving. The Greeks have let things slide over the past few decades, but that is about to change. 'Take something really Greek like olive oil. For us, it was always just a commodity: we sold it to the Italians and they put in nice bottles, stuck a fancy label on it, and sold it for a fancy price. Now we are branding it ourselves,' Yiannis said in fluent business-ese.

Finally, the Irish, home of the game-giant Owen. He has been making money out of programming since he was fifteen, when the IT Boom hit Dublin in the nineties. There was a huge shortage of computer experts, and he recalls how teenage friends were hired to set up entire networks for legal firms. 'Strange times. And it had a strange effect on the city. Suddenly guys in their early twenties were rolling in money while the rest of the country was still relatively poor,' Owen said during lunch in the canteen of a hip, high-tech collective business centre. I ate something non-organic, and he had a small gluten-free snack (the giant wanted to downsize). Ireland had been smart, and early investment in a good infrastructure made it attractive to technology-based companies. Low taxes were an added bonus. Amazon, Apple, Dell, Facebook, and Microsoft all have their European headquarters here. 'Twitter is just around the corner, and LinkedIn is across the street,' the Irishman said.

As I left the canteen I noticed that it is sponsored by Apple, Google and IBM.

FROM AUSTRIA TO FINLAND, PERSONNEL IS BECOMING TOO EXPENSIVE

What about the government – does it help or hinder businesses? As an entrepreneur, Western Europe is your best bet, preferably the Northwest, and specifically in Estonia, despite its recent history as part of the former Soviet Union. Setting up a company there is a piece of cake. 'You can do it online, in fifteen minutes,' said Karoli, who narrowly missed being named Europe's young entrepreneur of the year, and whom I met on a bus. She was getting ready to launch her new company Jobbatical. 'We do everything online. I can't remember the last time I actually saw an information counter. Oh, yeah, when I applied for a new passport.' It has also become easier to fire employees, and severance pay is only a month's salary. Start-ups are everywhere in Estonia, especially since the money from Skype was freed up for investment. That was an Estonian company.

Neighbouring country Latvia is also doing well. The tax rate is acceptable and the government communicates openly, is pro-active and responsive to questions, which is typical of northern countries, but not what the Italian Claudio is used to. Finland? Not too bad. The government helps start-ups because unemployment is so high. But that applies only to start-ups without personnel, Aarre explained. And personnel is the problem: way too expensive. Once you have hired someone, it is extremely difficult to get rid of them. Staff can be fired for economic reasons, but then no new people can be hired for the next six months.

It is easier to do business in Austria, which has made an effort to stimulate entrepreneurship by cutting some of the cost and red tape involved in setting up a new company. But here too, personnel is becoming too expensive: net salaries are half of gross salaries. 'In my hotel I pay the cleaning staff 1000 euro a month,' Barbara said. 'I would like to pay more, but I have 24 maids, and room prices in Vienna have fallen, while water and electricity have gone up.'

According to Owen, the situation in Ireland is favourable. The government provided a starting capital of 65,000 euro so that BitSmith could become a real company instead of a couple of guys with laptops. In addition, if investors can come up with 1,000 euro, the government will match the investment via Enterprise Ireland, a body that was set up expressly for that purpose.

Finally, Luxembourg. Although small and medium-sized companies (SMEs) are somewhat looked down upon, the country rolls out the red carpet for the big players, who are actively encouraged to set their European headquarters here. They have managed to land Amazon, which pays Luxembourg 15 percent VAT on all of its European transactions. And it is more than just a postal address: Amazon employs several hundred people. The country wants to break with the past, with the tradition of bank secrecy, and because this has been a major blow to the banking industry, it must find other ways of keeping the economy afloat. In that respect, there are some advantages to being a small country: in the US even a big company is just one of many, while in Luxembourg it is much easier to get access to the right people, including the Minister of Economic Affairs, said Mike, the owner of the biggest independent publisher in Luxembourg, with 8 titles and 72 employees. The biggest? What about RTL? Well, RTL is German owned, through Bertelsmann.

Even I was able to speak to him, that minister: it was that easy as he was handing out election flyers in the market. His party's stand, of the Socialist Party, was located between a sausage seller and a flower stall. The stand the minister broke up himself at the end of the day, after an afternoon of handing out flyers, probably some of them to people he knows personally: there are only 300,000 eligible voters in the entire country.

Southern Europe is a different story. 'The government does absolutely nothing,' the Cypriot hairdresser/entrepreneur George complained, an otherwise calm and reasonable man. 'The only thing they do is raise taxes. They make it next to impossible to hire and fire personnel. You know, in my family we are religious, and we try to be good employers who treat our personnel fairly and pay them very well — we haven't cut salaries over the past two years, despite the crisis. But the government should give us something in return.' What? He suggested that they could, for example, offer free training for entrepreneurs and help them to improve their productivity.

Luca in Rome: 'Do we receive help?' He laughed scornfully. 'What do you think? When they're taking 57 percent in corporate tax?' He thinks this is stupid, because it encourages the black economy, and he has nothing good to say about the banks either. They borrow from the ECB at 0 percent and charge entrepreneurs 13 percent.

On the other hand, an entrepreneur who is worth his salt doesn't need the government. Roy doesn't, in any case, and he thinks their role is greatly exaggerated. His fellow countrymen have a bad habit of waiting until help arrives from above or from an external source, according to the Hungarian hospitality industry mogul. Not him, of course. 'I get that from my godfather, an American hotel operator,' he says rather full of himself, and very America-minded. 'I see challenges, not problems. Also something I learned from my godfather.'

Inez has never felt the lack of Dutch government involvement. By her own admission, she was ignorant but enthusiastic when she started her company, and she never expected any help from official sources. She is however pleased with government efforts to facilitate exports, for example, via trade missions. She has been to Spain, Turkey and China, and these trips generated useful contacts. 'And great experiences: I remember that in Turkey I was heavily pregnant and was given the seat of honour next to the minister. A real circus, but a lot of fun.' She is convinced that everything is possible in the Netherlands, provided you have a plan. Yes, it has been her experience that the banks have been less cooperative over the past few years. When Inez set up her temporary employment agency LinQ, when she was thirty, she had no trouble borrowing money, but now banks want her to accept personal liability.

For the rest, this is something that almost all European entrepreneurs agree on: the banks have abdicated their responsibility and can no longer relied upon. They operate on a 'don't call us, we'll call you' basis: if your business is going well, they set their asset managers on you, but if you get into trouble they're not answering the phone. I know that much from my own experience with Robin Good. The bank refused to lend me a cent when I was short of cash after a year and a half, and they predicted the rapid demise of my business. Seven years later, I had sold my company at a profit and the bank, Fortis, had gone belly up.

Those commercials in which banks portray themselves as business-friendly always make me laugh, unless they make me angry. Surprisingly, the European Commission shares that view, at least where Dutch banks are concerned. The Commission recently investigated how easy it is for SMEs to borrow money from a bank. The situation in the Netherlands was the least favourable, while companies looking for a loan were best off in Malta and Luxembourg, where banks never turned down a request.

Perhaps that is because banks in Luxembourg almost never get a request. 'It is a country of civil servants, that is the norm, the tradition. Parents prefer to see their children become a doctor or lawyer. Entrepreneurship is risky,' Mike said.

ENTREPRENEURS ARE POPULAR IN ITALY BECAUSE THEY CREATE JOBS

The status of entrepreneurs varies. It is low in Luxembourg, and in Portugal, it is still better to work for a multinational. Antonio doesn't think so, and he has always had his own business, varying from a communication consultancy to a raspberry farm. He has also written two books – not bad for someone has just turned thirty. He told me something very odd, which is that hard work is not really valued in Portugal. A person who achieves something without much visible effort is considered more successful than someone who works hard. Don't tell Calvin.

And in the Netherlands? According to Inez (and me) business had an imagine problem in the seventies and the eighties, when entrepreneurship was a dirty word. 'Now all students want to get their hands dirty,' Inez said, and she knows what she's talking about: her company finds jobs for them. They may be mistaken about the amount of work involved, but the popularity of television series like *Dragons' Den* is proof that entrepreneurship is sexy again.*

Entrepreneurs are what drives the economy, and they are especially important in a country that has been hit as hard by the crisis as Italy has. 'People appreciate our courage, but above all the fact that we create jobs,' Luca said. 'I am going to take on twenty people next week for my new venue. He is referring to Baccanale, a café/restaurant hybrid where they serve excellent prosecco ('better than most champagne') and delicious antipasti, all of which I am required to sample, which makes the interview much more pleasant.

Of course status is also dependent on the sector. In Helsinki, shopkeepers are respected, Aarre said. I can understand that in

---

* *In my Robin Good days, I briefly coached students taking a business course at a secondary school in Amsterdam. They were all wildly enthusiastic: in their minds being an entrepreneur means an easy ticket to big bucks and a shiny Mercedes.

his case. Both the shop and the good-natured Finn have a social function. Many of the neighbourhood residents leave a spare house key with him, and have their post delivered to his shop. During the hour I spent with him on a bench in front of the shop, countless people greeted him or waved. 'But,' he sighed, 'they all say they need a small shop like mine, but most of them shop at bigger, cheaper competitors.'

Entrepreneurs working in the real estate sector do not score well, according to Oliver in Berlin. They are in it for the easy money, for a Porsche and a Rolex. He is not like that, as I found out when I went looking for an apartment for myself in Berlin, and he generously helped me without expecting anything in return. No, you are better off designing games, like Owen. 'People think it is so cool. The only mild criticism I ever get is from people who wonder why I don't move to California. I could get an offer of a half-a-million dollar investment in two weeks. Or be hired by companies willing to pay me 150,000 a year. But I like it here.'

The situation is different in Eastern European countries like Lithuania. Gedas knows that the right mentality is a crucial element in the success of a company. He definitely has what it takes, and the franchises he operates for the Dutch-company Suit Supply have been highly successful. Lithuanians, however, are not by nature entrepreneurs. That is the legacy of the Soviet Union, where people were civil servants or employed by state industries. 'Fruit stands were really the only privately owned companies. Nevertheless, it is good country for businesses,' Gedas said. Big international companies use it as a kind of testing ground for new ideas they want to try out in a small, safe environment before rolling them out in the rest of the EU. Juraj in Slovakia also confirmed that entrepreneurship was not an option in the past. Risk took a different form in those days, usually as (covert) resistance to communist power. That is why there is still not much entrepreneurship in his country, which means there is all the more opportunity for those who are smart and willing to work hard.

The fall of the Berlin Wall unleashed a lot cowboy-capitalism in Eastern Europe, which Dragos, a leading Romanian businessman, defined as a combination of the entrepreneurial spirit with a healthy lack of respect for the law, even though the government was providing a lot of the money. And corruption. It is now much less prevalent, according to the Romanian, partly as a result of Romania's accession to the EU is 2004.

LONG LIVE OPEN BORDERS!

Most entrepreneurs agree that the EU is a good thing (more about this later), especially those who are internationally active (with the possible exception of Barbara, who was suddenly forced by EU rules to improve the fire safety of the stairwell in her hotel, which cost 250,000 euro). But most agreed that trade had become much easier, and the administrative burden has decreased as there is no VAT charge within Europe. Dragos acknowledges the advantages, because his branch—international bus transport—faces fewer national laws, and there is less pressure to look for loopholes in those laws. The open borders have changed everything. After 1995 the Romanians were free to travel, provided they had arranged a visa, a return ticket and travel insurance at least thirty days in advance. That was a good situation for Dragos, who then knew exactly how many busses he needed. Later, a new rule required travellers to carry at least for 500 euro for expense abroad. For many Romanians, this was an insurmountable barrier, but Dragos's smaller competitors got around the rule by simply selling passengers a receipt proving they had the required amount. As a result he lost a lot of passengers in 2005 and 2006. 'Now that the borders are really open, the market has opened up. If you can provide value, you survive; if not, you go under,' was King Dragos's conclusion as he glanced at his expensive watch. He had another meeting, with a man who was waiting somewhat nervously close by. The boss walked me to the door, but not before instructing a flunky to take me to wherever I wanted to go, and telling me that if I needed anything—anything at all—during my stay, I should come to him.

WHAT WOULD YOU DO IF YOU WERE THE CEO OF EUROPE?

Countries are led by politicians, most of them at least. Singapore was an exception: Lee Kaun Yew, who died recently, ran it as a business for decades. Its civil servants and administrators were excellent and well paid, and the city-state was a success. Its universities were among the best in the world, it was safe, etc. A country, or a European Union, is an organisation too, like a company. And entrepreneurs who have experience running an organisation often have outspoken ideas about how their country could be run more effectively. And so my question was, what would you do if you were CEO of Europe?

Barbara, the owner of large private clinic in Prague: 'I would start by improving communication, so that people really understand what goes on in Brussels. For the rest, I think we have a good life in Western Europe. I would try to hold on to that. You know, whether socialists or conservatives are in power, 95 of the budget is used for infrastructure — streets and so forth. At least it is in the Czech Republic. In the meantime, they keep talking nonsense, just to make a point. Politicians should be much more aware that they are there for us, not for themselves'

Dragos, a successful entrepreneur in the tourist branch: 'More flexibility, less bureaucracy. There is way too much of it in the EU. Schengen, the euro and solidarity funds are all well and good, but I am waiting for a new EU directive on package travel. They have been working on it for five years.'

Inez, owner of temporary employment agency LinQ: 'I would encourage the exchange of talent. We already have a single market, and we are starting to notice that now. In the Netherlands, for example, there is less tolerance of the old culture of academic mediocracy. Talented people should have equal opportunities, and that is not the case now. In new Europe — in the East — there are more than enough people who want to participate but do not have the opportunities that spoiled students have here in the Netherlands in terms of self-development and financial support. Take my au-pair, who is Romanian. Because she grasped every opportunity she see saw, she was able to start her own au-pair agency three years ago. Now, all of my friends have someone they found through her.

> Martin, the owner of all of the Burger King franchises in Southern Spain: 'The first thing I would do is fire all of the civil servants in Brussels. And put a stop to their privileges and tax benefits, for example. Why should a representative in the European Parliament be paid more than a representative in the national parliament. People don't understand it. And Europe should be a good leader; it should embody the European dream.'
>
> What would you do if you were Mr Tusk, the leader of Europe? Tomek: 'Oh, he has a lovely daughter, she has lunch here sometimes. She is a fashion blogger.' Tomek had a habit of not answering the question.

MY FAVOURITES

3 Gedas, Vilnius. Owner of a number of Suit Supply stores in the Baltic States. As far as I could tell, he was a good entrepreneur with a well-organised business. He was also an intelligent man, one of the few Youropeans who was able to give a coherent answer to questions about European identity.

2 Barbara, Vienna. Her Hotel Beethoven was my home away from home in Vienna. A good hotel with a charming, sociable and hard-working owner.

1 Inez, of course, Amsterdam. For many years we were both members of the same organisation for young entrepreneurs. It was not a networking club, but a small group of people who met every month to help one another become better entrepreneurs. I owe a lot to them, and to Inez in particular: an optimistic, intelligent powerhouse.

6

THE WISDOM OF EUROPE'S HAIRDRESSERS

The hairdressing business lost me as a client a few years ago. Since my thirtieth birthday, hair has tended to grow everywhere except on my head. A well-known Dutch fashion designer is the reason why I stopped getting my hair cut. He saw me in the dressing room of a sports club, desperately trying to re-arrange the few remaining strands of my hair, and advised me to get a pair of electric clippers, set them on low and shave it all off.

And now I was walking into one hairdressing salon after the other, trying to get an appointment, not for my hair, but for an interview. Sometimes I sat in a hairdresser's chair to conduct the interview, because I looked terrible, according to some of them — that was the annoying part of talking to hairdressers; I could feel their pitying gazes wandering to my poor, shorn skull. So I sometimes asked my questions while they held a razorblade to my throat. At Chop-Chop in Riga, for example, a very masculine place with manly music and table football. No women allowed, 'no matter how persistent or pretty they are'.

It wasn't until I started looking for hairdressing salons that I noticed just how many of them there are in Europe. Three in a row sometimes, each of which has its own clientele: one for seniors, one for bizarre, fashion-forward hairdos, one for Afro hair. Of course there are not many of the latter in, say, Estonia, but lots of them in Brussels, Lisbon and Paris, and they were always packed, and definitely the most fun. The women there were probably not even all clients; it was more like a clubhouse where they came to chat, laugh and call their friends on their mobiles. It was little wonder that the hairdressers in these jam-packed salons didn't have much time for me.

So, lots of hairdressers, and if my Youropeans had their way, there would be many more: those who were still working for someone else wanted to open their salons as soon as possible. They were entrepreneurial and anxious to stress that their own salon would not be as boring as where they now worked, although they hastened to add that it could not be too eccentric since people in Warsaw or Zagreb weren't used to much. Eastern Europe is hopelessly conservative, they said. Paris is great, but the real Mecca of the hairdressing world is London. 'They don't follow trends there,' Peijc in Zagreb said dreamily, 'they have their own individual style.'

Yes, London. That is the home of the God of Hairdressers, Vidal Sassoon. It may be a coincidence, but almost half of the people I interviewed had been trained by Sassoon. Not by the maestro himself, of course, but by one of his followers, or more indirectly via an often pricey training course. 'He was the greatest. Do you know what his breakthrough was? Doing Mia Farrow's hair for Rosemary's Baby, Polanski's 1968 masterpiece,' said Fred in Brussels, placing the master in art-historical perspective. It's what you'd expect of him; his salon, located above a brown café, is reached via a rickety staircase, and is more of a studio than a salon, and he seemed more of an artist than a hairdresser as he welcomed me into a room lined with old film stills. Classic jazz was playing in the background, and hair clippings were swept into a dog house. Instead of looking into a mirror, clients watch closed-circuit television footage of the passers-by on the street. 'My fans love it,' said Fred, who sports a wild beard. Fans, not clients.

I don't know much about hairdressers and hairstyles. I'm not a woman, but someone who styled his hair with spit as a teenager, and whose hair was so straight when I was child that the hairdresser suggested a permanent. Although they were fairly common in the seventies, my mother nearly choked on her tea, and responded with a firm no. So when the Youropean hairdressers grew starry-eyed and enthused about Vidal's revolutionary techniques, it took a while for the penny to drop. I learned that he introduced the bob line – short and angled, like the mini-skirts that were in fashion at the time. It was new and different. After Vidal, women wanted hair they could wash every day, and style themselves, instead of having it set in a salon. 'Women now come in once a month to have their hair cut and coloured, but they wash it themselves,' Lionel said in Luxembourg.

Vidal Sassoon's hairstyles are not accepted everywhere. Even 46 years after Rosemary's Baby, short and angular is too modern for the Romanians. 'I told you,' Diana said glumly, 'people here are rather conservative.' Péter, a Hungarian, was the only one who dared to criticise Vidal. 'I think it is boring. It looks like a helmet.'

I liked the hairdressers. They are of course sociable: they are talkers who are used making contact with people. That is the same everywhere. They also tend to be people who like their work because it is what they have wanted to do since they were young. Like Joni, in Helsinki, who began practicing on his sister's hair when he was seven. He still does her hair, and his parents as well. 'They're difficult clients, though,' he said. Markus, from Vienna, didn't practice on his sister, but on her Barbie dolls. And since Barbie's hair never grows, his sister was often angry. Some of them practiced on themselves. 'it's possible if you use two mirrors,' said Merje in Tallinn.

Becoming a hairdresser was not everyone's childhood dream: like most boys Abi wanted to be a professional football player, and he might have been if he hadn't broken his leg when he was about to sign with an English club. And so he, who is Moroccan-born, and his Slovakian wife left London and started cutting hair in Bratislava. Sean from Dublin was lazy at school, and his results were poor, so he had only three options: become a hairdresser, a photographer or a cook. The latter seemed like hard work, and photographers have too little work, and so when he accidentally walked into a hairdressing school and saw only women, he immediately knew what his choice would be. Somewhere along the way things went wrong, because in his shop, located above a pub called The Bleeding Horse, he has only male colleagues and clients.

Hairdressers cut hair, but I quickly learned that not all hair is created equal. 'Men's hair is boring, you can't do anything with it. Latin hair is thicker than North European hair. And Afro hair is completely different to 'European' hair, which is what Madame Paule, who is from Martinique, calls white people's hair. In Malta, humidity is a problem, and hair gets frizzy very quickly, so a good blow dry is important. But according to Marcus, cutting is not difficult. 'And colouring can be learned as well; it's almost like chemistry. The hardest part is knowing what the client wants. If she says "I want blond", what does she actually mean? The trick is to understand what she wants, to see what's possible, and then combine the two.'

Yes, what does 'she' want? Am I a male chauvinist pig to assume that men are easier, that they just plop down and say 'give me a nice, short cut'? Yes, women are more difficult, Abi confirmed. 'They say they want a different style but what they really want is a different life. They don't always think about how it will look the next day. But you know, no one is 100% satisfied with their own hair. Not even me,' he said with false modesty.

Knowing what the client wants can be difficult, but they all agreed that talking to clients was the best part of the job. And the most important. Clients come rushing into the salon in a cloud of stress, and they need to be put at ease. How do they do that? Valium in the tea? No, they start by massaging the scalp while they are shampooing their clients' hair. Nice warm water in the winter, and cool in the summer. Then the clients start to talk. 'No, they don't listen. It's one-way traffic,' Elena said. She runs the oldest hairdressing salon in Madrid; it has been open for a hundred years. 'They just want to tell someone their story; all I have to do is say yes or no occasionally.' And when you get home your partner starts talking. 'That's right,' said Salvatore, an Italian hairdresser in Amsterdam. 'My wife starts talking to me when I get home, and since I have been listening all day, it doesn't always register. That makes her angry. Can you imagine?'

What do they talk about? Holidays, love, children. About problems, according to Madame Paule. Her clients say she should have a sign on the door that says hairdresser/psychologist. 'I listen. And when they leave they are calm and serene.' Some hairdressers even go one better than a psychologist. 'My clients tell me things they wouldn't tell their priest,' said Sabrina, who cuts hair no more than 300 metres away from the Vatican.

And what subjects do people avoid? The crisis: people come to relax. George in Nicosia has banned his staff from talking about it. 'It is taboo. Some of my clients have lost millions.' He himself has discussed the crisis with international journalists. His business is just around the corner from the Cypriot National Bank, which saved two banks in 2013 by ruling that clients would forfeit deposits in excess of 100,000 euro. The financial term for this practice is a *haircut* and a journalist from Reuters News Agency thought it would be amusing to ask a hairdresser what he thought about the situation.

I know things. Natalie said this at least five times during our interview, sometimes in jest, sometimes in all earnestness. And it's true: she knows things about food, about countries where she's travelled, about Sweden where she lives, about Serbia, her parents' country. We sat in the waiting room of the salon while her colleagues continued to cut, colour and blow dry in the back. Every now and then her boss stuck her head around the corner, looking amused, but possibly also slightly worried that the most colourful member of her staff (26, jet black hair, black glasses, a nose ring and red lipstick) might be making wild statements.

'Politicians should ....' She is searching for the English word when it becomes clear that a client is not quite as absorbed in her magazine as we thought. 'Cooperate?' 'That's it. *Tack*.'

I have to admit that I underestimated the hairdressers. Before I met them I would have placed them where most people do: 'Low, much too low,' Angelique in Berlin complained. 'People think it is easy, but you really do have to know a lot, including chemistry, to be able to mix colours properly.' Joni, who like Angelique is only 21, is happy about becoming a trainer. He will travel all over Finland and then all of his friends — most of whom have a university education — will see that Joni is not dumb, and that he has a real career.

Pavlina in Prague, who is also a part-time bass player, is even more decided: 'So-called intellectuals are disdainful of us, mostly because they think we are uneducated. But most of my colleagues had years of training before they started. No, we are not intellectuals, but we learn from people and from life.' The university of life, so to speak. Some of them have in fact studied, for example Vytas from Lithuania, who studied forestry, then public administration and is now planning to start on an MBA. Mauro from Lisbon was originally a computer programmer with a degree in mathematics before he started doing what he really wanted to do when he was thirty two. 'Are you gay now?' his astonished friends wanted to know. That is another prejudice, but only five of the eighteen male hairdressers I interviewed were (openly) gay, and the others had wives and children.

The low opinion of hairdressers, their limited social status, varies per country but is also dependent on other factors. There are of course celebrity hairdressers. Like Stevo, who regularly does shows in London's Albert Hall, and who has therefore been awarded a medal of honour by his own country, Slovenia. I walked with him through Ljubljana, and watched him shaking hands left and right on our way to a lunch restaurant where we got VIP treatment and our sausage sandwiches were compliments of the house.

Some have their own business, and earn a good living from it, like Lionel, the Luxembourg-based hairdresser who has the looks of an aging French playboy, and whose tanned face looks incomplete without a Gitane stuck between his lips. 'In the past,' he grumbled, 'you could get a job at a bank if you could write your name three times. And if you could only write it once, you could be a hairdresser.' Now he employs 140 people and drives a Porsche. 'I am no longer a hairdresser, but an entrepreneur, and people take me seriously.'

Speaking of money, the average haircut and dye job costs a fortune, and when they're finished your hairdresser will also sell you

Price for women's or men's haircut
(in Euros)

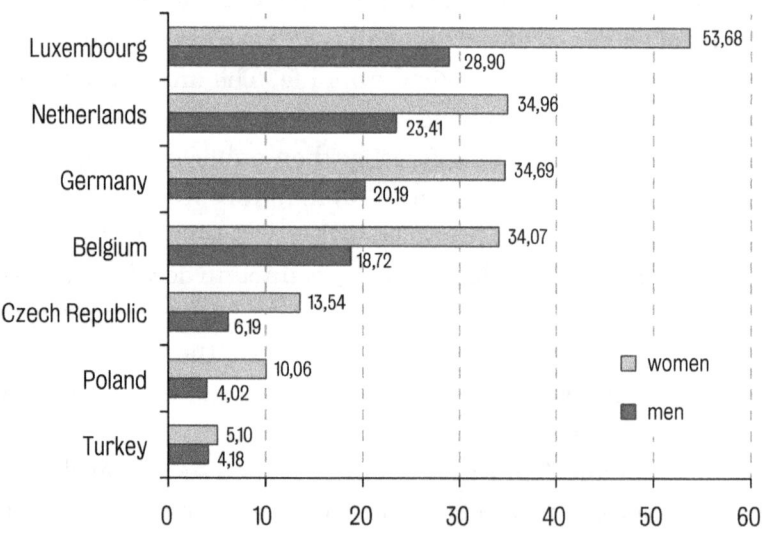

The differences in a number of European countries. Mind you, it's only cutting (data: Eurostat)

a lot of expensive products, emphasizing that you absolutely have to use them if you don't want to end up with limp, lifeless hair. A good hairdresser is expensive. Does that help their status?

According to Natalie, their status is improving. 'Certainly in Stockholm, because people here are fashion-conscious. The link between hairstyles and fashion is a good thing. That is true in Paris, but also in London. Péter thinks it is his mission in life to improve the status of hairdressers. According to him the key factor is how the salon looks. His is located in a monumental building on Budapest's prestigious Andrássy Avenue, and it looks like a museum. Diana, who is just 23, owns a salon in Bucharest called Le Chateau. It has two storeys and is decorated with white leather chairs, chandeliers and modern art displayed on black walls. She is a charming woman who proudly showed me around her salon. 'Do you see that painting?' She pointed to vague orange nude. 'I modelled for it.'

MY FAVOURITES

3 Natalie, Stockholm. Yes, the one who knows things. Funny and cheerful. If I had any hair I would definitely go to her salon.

2 Joni, Helsinki. Very androgynous: I wasn't sure when he or she walked in. Disarmingly open, intelligent and ambitious.

1 Madame Paule, Paris. Her beautiful art-deco style salon is like a film set. The reading material she provides includes not only women's magazines but also actual books. I spotted a Guy de Maupassant novel on top of a stack of books.

7

NOBDY KNOWS A SEX WORKER

'You should do something about your site. The design is all wrong, and the optimisation could be much better.' Nika is no one-trick pony: she builds websites, has a degree in engineering, plays the piano (she says), and she is an escort. You wouldn't know from looking at her. With her hair in a bun, wearing glasses, faded jeans and sneakers, she looks more like a librarian. I would guess she's is in her late forties, but her website puts her age at fifteen years younger. Her site is good, and it includes an extensive photo gallery. Whether it is optimised or not, I couldn't say.

'They've done a good job of fixing it up,' she said, looking around my hotel room with an approving glance. It was an absurdly large room: even struggling journalists sometimes get an upgrade. She was familiar with most of the good hotels in the city — Slovenia is small. We spent the next three hours talking about corruption, former Yugoslavia, and above all about her profession. That was why she had agreed to an interview: 'I read the interviews with my colleagues on your site, and I hope that your blog will help me to reach a lot of people, so that I can show them that we do difficult work, but that we're strong.' She wanted to do something to break the stereotypes.

I found Charlottte in London in the newspaper. Not in the advertising section at the back of the paper, which used to be filled with 'personals', but on page three of *The Times*, in an article about protests against restrictions being imposed on British porn films. Face-sitting, for example, had been banned and so Charlotte and a group of supporters were going to face-sit (albeit fully clothed) in front of the Houses of Parliament: exactly the kind of protest the press loves. A few weeks after our interview she was planning to take part in the Sex Workers' Opera, a kind of educational musical about her branch of industry, and she was already looking forward to it. In 2013 she had been named London's Sex Worker of the Year.

'What are the criteria?' I asked. I found it hard to imagine that they had polled all of her clients. 'The organisers of the Sexual Freedom Awards look at things like professionalism, the services offered, and the way in which you present yourself. For example, whether you are handicapped-friendly.' Charlotte is: during our interview on a drizzly Tuesday morning in her apartment overlooking the Thames a client telephoned her (she was wearing an oversized cardigan and slippers) to ask about wheelchair access to her place.

My interview with Elizabeth in Zagreb was also an interesting experience. When the lift door opened I saw that one of three doors on the third floor was opened just a crack. I cautiously pushed it opened and stepped inside. The lights came on revealing a tall dominatrix — at least 1m 80 — dressed in a black leather cat suit and a hood that covered her entire face, with just a slit for the eyes. 'So,' she said, 'are you sure you just want to talk, or would like an SM session?' I chose the former. Elizabeth is also very open about her work. 'My friends know that I do this, it's nothing to be ashamed of.'

As you can see from the photos in this book, Charlotte, Nika and Elizabeth are the exceptions. They were the only ones who agreed to be photographed for the Youropeans project. The other 25 said no, and it was extremely difficult even to get them to give an interview. I found most of them, and their telephone numbers, online. But they usually hung up as soon as I mentioned the words 'interview' and 'journalist'. My best bet was to pretend I was a client and not reveal myself (figuratively speaking) until my incredibly trustworthy demeanour had persuaded them that my intentions were entirely honourable. Sometimes it worked: 'Really? I've never met a writer' and she went on to tell me about the books she had read, but other times all I got was silence and suspicion and I had to go back my hotel room and start my search all over again.

Whatever the outcome, I paid them. Not the full price, but usually half, which varied between 25 and 100 euro. The interview also cost money when it took place in a coffee bar instead of in their 'office', when it was clear in advance that I wasn't a client. On the one hand this seemed odd, since I didn't pay the hairdressers, entrepreneurs or artists for their time. On the other hand, there wasn't much in it for the sex worker, as Eva in Amsterdam said: 'I can't show the interview to anyone, can I? Even though it's a good thing.'

TWO NAMES, TWO TELEPHONES, TWO LIVES

The sex workers were a colourful group, ranging from 21 year-old Rosa in Dublin, an Indian girl, and 22-year-old Nicola in Bratislava – both of whom work out of fairly luxurious apartments – to Bojanna, a 55-year-old streetwalker in Warsaw. From escorts to erotic masseuses, cheap or expensive, I interviewed 27 women and 1 man, although Melissa, a Brazilian shemale working in Prague identifies as a woman. What they all have in common is the need to keep their work secret, not necessarily because it is illegal (more about that later) but because of the harsh judgment of the outside world.

Sometimes their sister knows, sometimes their mother, but usually no one does, not even their lovers. Most of them don't have one, because as Anabela said 'if he loves me, he's probably kind of weird.' She is from tiny Luxembourg, where she sometimes runs into a client on the street. Some of them greet her, but most of them don't. She understands, especially if they are with their wives.

They make up respectable jobs as an alibi. Jojette laughed when she told me that the outside world thinks she is a babysitter. Masseuse is a popular choice, as is bartender, which neatly explains the late working hours. Maria in Malta told me about the elaborate cover stories she has to invent when her family visits from Greece. They do not know what she does, but 'I am on very good terms with them, and they have already visited three times. It's so hard to have to lie to them.' She gazed out of the window, fidgeted with her iPhone cover and said, almost as if she was talking to herself: 'It's a lonely life, I can't even remember the last time I had sex,' she said, meaning the last time she had made love with someone other than a client.

Bojanna's daughter also believes her mother works in a bar, and so she always calls her during the day. Because she lives 40 kilometres away from the city, too far away to come over and visit unexpectedly, her mother is free to work the park near the Marriott Hotel. She agreed to talk to me, sitting on a bench in the park, but the cars cruising slowly past us were clearly her priority, as she smiled at potential clients.

'Are you never afraid?'

'Yes. Some clients are completely crazy. They want to beat me or have kinky sex. They sit in their cars dressed as women, for example, in full make-up. Some of them force me to give back the money afterwards. Especially young boys. Bojanna, 55, is blond, small and sturdy, and wearing white boots, a thick turtleneck sweater and a denim jacket on this cold October evening. A red Mercedes stops and Bojanna gets up and leans towards the open window on the passenger side; she negotiates briefly, waves apologetically to me and gets in the car. End of interview.

Diana in Sofia also has to keep her job a secret from a child, but hers is still young — too young to be suspicious. She finishes work at seven every day, and as soon as she closes her door behind her she forgets everything that happened that day. We were sitting on two chairs near her bed in the room she works in.

'My astrological sign is Gemini.' She laughed. 'During the day I'm all sexy and *oh la la*, but after that, I'm normal.' It is a common strategy.

Budapest: 'Is Vikki your real name?'

'No, my real name is Judit,' she said. 'I have two lives. Two names. Two telephones.'

'Two apartments?'

'No, just one. I live here too.' Glancing around the faded studio I saw that there were indeed signs of normal occupancy: a few jackets on the coatrack, a big TV at the foot end of the bed and a bottle of Coke on the kitchen counter. Not exactly homey.

Amsterdam: 'They are two different worlds, and I can block the other one out,' Eva said. In one world she is a 30-year old who has an advanced secondary school diploma, and who is setting up her own line of clothing. In the other world she works in an erotic massage parlour, 'I am a perfectly normal girl. I may do this work, but I'm not slutty. I don't go out much, don't do drugs or smoke. I don't even drink.' Above her head, in the corner, a porn film is playing on a television set, but fortunately the sound is turned off. The setting may be strange, but she is convinced that 'we are very normal girls. It's just that the outside world doesn't know it.'

'Why do you think they don't know?'

'Well, nobody knows any whores. Yeah, my friends do, but they don't know that.'

TRIPADVISOR FOR SEX WORKERS

The sex industry could do something about the lack of understanding, at least it could if it was better organised. But even in Amsterdam, which is famous for its liberal attitude towards prostitution, efforts to improve organisation never really got off the ground, and *De Rode Draad*, a union for prostitutes, went bankrupt in 2012. There are nevertheless a number of networks and organisations, some of them at the European level, such as the International Committee on the Rights of Sex Workers in Europe. These organisations were not interested in me, or in my Youropeans Project, and they refused to cooperate. Some of them objected to my use of the word 'prostitute' in my correspondence with them. I learned that the politically correct term is sex worker. Others did not approve of my approach, which they felt was not serious enough or too focussed on my own interpretation of the circumstances in which sex workers find themselves. In short, most of them were publicity-shy and suspicious of journalists, and therefore not in touch with the people who are in the best position to get their message across to public. Charlotte and Nika are better at this.

'They are forced to do it.' 'They are dumb.' 'They cannot possibly enjoy their work.' These are just a few of the commonly held prejudices about sex workers, which meet with very little resistance.

Well, Romanian Laura studied law, Rosa in Dublin is taking an accounting course (although she admitted that she preferred shopping to studying), Maria was planning to be a teacher, Kira, a Ukrainian in Cyprus, teaches English to Russians and Elizabeth in Croatia works in a good restaurant. As a chef of course; you wouldn't expect anything else from a dominatrix.

I saw little evidence of coercion, at least in the group I interviewed. The majority of them were independent and did not work for a pimp — again, to the best of my knowledge and insofar as they were honest with me. The women set their own boundaries. 'Coercion? Nonsense. I do this work because I want to and I choose my own hours and my own clients. I'm in charge,' Kira said in Nicosia.

According to her excellent site, she is a stylish woman, caring and well educated, a good talker and an attentive listener. 32 years old, slight, blond hair and brown eyes, full lips and long legs: she sure knows how to position herself. When I met her in person in the lobby of the local Holiday Inn, she said she gets the highest ratings. On what? It sounded like TripAdvisor. 'Do you ask your clients to leave reviews?' I asked. 'No, they do that themselves.

Nika, whose age I would put at about fifty, is the most expensive escort in Slovenia. It's all a matter of pricing, she explained. She has read up on the subject and she knows it's never a good idea to sell yourself cheap. Marketing-minded with a strong sales pitch, well-presented, psychologically sound and extremely independent: if you look at them that way, these are enterprising women who are running their own business. Some of them even have staff. Like Nicola and Claudia in Denmark who have joined forces with colleagues to employ a receptionist in their brothel. The Danish girls have chosen this line of work, but Claudia suspects that many Eastern European and African women, like the Nigerians at the station, have been coerced. But, 'Who is really free? Most office workers are ordered around all day by their boss, while I can determine my own hours and let you pay for it,' Charlotte said, demonstrating a fine sense of nuance.

HYGIENE ÜBER ALLES IN GERMANY

A substantial number of women are more or less forced to do this work in the sense that they have to support themselves or pay off debts. European sex workers have that much in common with one another (and with the rest of world): 99 percent of them do it for the money. Not for reasons of personal development, secondary benefits or the chance of a promotion. 'The week before I started doing this,' Nicola said in Bratislava, 'I could only afford to eat rice. I used to think that girls only did this so that they could go shopping, but that is not always true; sometimes it is bitter necessity.' She is saving up for an eye operation and her Finnish colleague works to pay for groceries: food is so expensive in her country, especially the organic food she needs because of an allergy.

Isabella works in Calle Montera, an almost posh shopping street in Madrid during the day, but after six, prostitutes congregate there, particularly around McDonalds. (That's where street walkers gather in many other cities as well, like Vilnius. What is it with McDonalds?) She is from Romania, Europe's single biggest supplier of sex workers. Eastern European women in general are over-represented in European prostitution.

'Why did you leave?'

'*Porque no tengo dinero*, hombre! It was impossible to get a job there.' She is visibly cold, which is not surprising since it is November and she is wearing a mini-skirt. She has two children at home who are being raised by her mother. She saw them the day before, on Skype, and she plans to go home for Christmas.

'Do you ever enjoy your work?'

'No,' most of them say. 'It is sex between two strangers, and there is money involved.' Leila, 26, whom I spoke to in a dismal Finnish bar at 3 in the afternoon, left little room for doubt. 'No, because this work is not normal, it's not good for my soul. I want to grow, and this job prevent me from doing so.' She fell silent. Seated one table away from us a thin man took a big swig of beer. His hands shook, his eyes bulged.

'What do you think about your clients? Are they abnormal too?'

'Yes, because why else would they pay for sex? Nobody dies without it,' she laughed unhappily.

'Have you ever had a nice client?'

She thought about it and then remembered one who had taken her dog to vet, and another who had helped her hang some curtains.

'It is so exhausting,' Diana in Sofia complained. 'All that sex, all day, every day. I'm OK right now, but sometimes I get really tired,' she said in her high-pitched voice. A yellow and red dragon is crawling out from under the short sleeve of her T-shirt, and a name is tattooed on her ankle in Cyrillic letters. The apartment she shares with two other women reminded me of student housing when I came in and saw the other two women talking to each through their open doors; one of them was making her bed in her underwear and the other one was lying on her stomach on her bed watching television. 'I have to be mentally and physically fit,' Diana said. 'No drinking or smoking. Well, maybe once a month when I go out. I spend an hour in the gym every day, and sleep ten hours a day.'

> ### PRICES FOR SEX WORKERS
>
> The amount of money a sex workers earns is dependent on several factors. Prices are lower on the street than in an upscale nightclub; attractive sex workers earn more than those with green hair and a humpback. But prices are also a reflection of the economic situation in a country. In Fylis Street, a long, narrow street in Athens, just a few hundred metres from the famous Omonia Square, pedestrians slalom between gaping sacks of rubbish, and it smells of pee and faeces. Anna works there in a 'studio'. She asks 20 euro for normal sex, but refused to tell me how much of that goes to the fat, bad-tempered old woman — a slipper-shod madam — who was shuffling back and forth on the other side of curtain.
>
> When Rosa in Dublin worked as a beauty specialist she earned 50 euro a day, but as an escort she earns that in an hour. In Amsterdam's red light district, clients pay 50 euro for twenty minutes. On the Oranienburgerstraasse in Berlin, clients pay 80 euro up front just to accompany a girl to a room. The bra comes off for 150 euro, and the client is allowed to touch and kiss. Sex costs 250 euro. She will however always keep her tights on, which have an opening in the crotch for the sex act. It may not sound very enticing, but in Germany, *hygiene über alles* is the guiding principle.

Fortunately, there are exceptions. Eva in Amsterdam, for example. 'I think it's great. Mainly because of my colleagues; they're a lot of fun, and all very different. Maybe it's also exciting because it's a secret.'

Between five and seven women work in her salon, and they spend most of their time sitting in a room together, waiting to be introduced to a new client.

'And the work itself?'

'Yeah, it's good too. Mostly because I get to meet so many different people. Crazy, isn't it, to like doing this? It's not even the about the sex, which usually doesn't last all that long. I don't think that men come back because they like being inside of me. That's the same with every woman. They often say: the sex was good, but it was also nice being with you. That kind of appreciation helps.'

MALE PROSTITUTION IS ALMOST ALWAYS ILLEGAL

Prostitution is not illegal in most EU countries. Croatia and Malta are exceptions. The minimum age requirement in countries where it is legal is 18, except in the Netherlands, which is due to raise the age to 21. Pimping is allowed only in Germany, Greece and the Netherlands. There are brothels in these countries, an organised form of prostitution that is not permitted in other EU countries.

There are of course many ways of getting around the ban on brothels. In Athens, clients are introduced to only one girl at a time. Anna was introduced by the slipper-wearing madam, who is to all intents and purposes, a pimp.

Male prostitution is absolutely illegal in Athens, which is odd since 'Greek love' is enduringly popular here, and in other Mediterranean countries, according to shemale Melissa (and other male prostitutes I have spoken to). This popularity is also seen in the number of online advertisements for this genre on Southern European sex worker sites. Melissa, who was wearing a bikini, explained it in her apartment in Prague: 'Those men want to be taken, but they absolutely do not see themselves as homosexuals. So when they look back, they want to see breasts.' Melissa got hers a year ago: she took off her bikini top and encouraged me to admire her ample C-cup.

'Yes, very nice,' I said, quickly trying to think of a serious follow-up question.

Melissa urged me to touch them but when I politely refused she crawled onto my lap a few minutes later and, without missing a beat, continued to discuss Europe and the EU, stressing how important he/she thinks it is. Apparently a shemale combines the seductiveness of a woman with the aggressiveness of a man.

Although the trend in Europe is to restrict prostitution, the mayor of Rome planned to create a red light district, arguing that it would be safer and more manageable. Would you want to work there, I asked Carolina. Of course not, she replied, rolling her eyes: she's no streetwalker. Street prostitution is the most widespread form here: Italians have an uncomfortable tradition of having sex in cars because it is cheaper than an escort.

Prostitution is legal in some of the streets in Luxembourg — as is often the case, those near the train station. Anabela is not a fan. 'It is bad; bad publicity for the city, not an attractive sight. It shouldn't be encouraged.'

Elizabeth thinks it is a good idea that her profession is forbidden in Croatia. 'Yes, because if it was legal, they would want money from us.'

'Who?'

'Politicians, of course. That can't happen now, because officially, it does not exist.'

In Berlin, everything is very official: even street prostitution is regulated in Germany. All of the girls are registered, and they pay taxes and see a doctor every three months. They are lined up along the Oranienburgestrasse, a street with a busy nightlife, alone or in pairs. It is all out in the open, but they are dressed fairly conservatively because the sex worker and her client first have to pass by the many sidewalk cafes along the street before they reach her room in another street. 'Some of them follow ten metres behind. I understand. But it's a pity, since we could use the time to get to know one another,' Marie laughed. She laughs a lot, even when something isn't funny.

The police keep an eye on things. I asked if she had a pimp. 'No,' she said firmly,' the only person I pay is Frau Merkel. 40 percent, which is pretty steep. But she only pays over the first 80 euro, and Aunt Angela sees nothing of the rest. She takes a bottle of water out of the refrigerator in the room where she works, in a house shared with other working girls, and asks me if I'll pay for the drink. 'You don't have to, but a real gentleman would.' Twenty euro, she said, so I decide not to be a gentleman.

The law is different in Sweden (and Norway and Iceland). There, paying for sex is illegal and the client can be prosecuted. Julia thinks this is unnecessary and says she doesn't need the protection. And in her view, the law might just as well not exist as it doesn't deter clients. But the law has its advantage; if the market was entirely open, too many girls would want to become prostitutes, and she would have fewer clients.

DON'T LET ALLAH SEE!

In addition to a fluctuating number of sexual partners, sex workers also have international contacts. You might say that an intimate knowledge of their neighbouring countries.

'Who are your favourites?'

'The English,' said Daniela in Riga. 'Germans are nice and polite, and so are the French. I also like Italians and Greeks. Preferably no Turks—they're rude. And I really don't like clients from India, because they're dirty.' She laughed scornfully. 'They can wash themselves for hours, but it makes no difference.'

Anna, who is Romanian, works in Athens, but she is not fond of the Greeks. 'They're bastards.'

'Why?'

'They stink and they always want to do it without a condom.'

Diana from Sofia does not like Germans, or rather, they do not like her. 'They don't like my body; I don't know why.' As far as I could tell, there was nothing wrong with it, but then I am not a German. The Bulgarian also dislike the Turks. 'And I don't like men with a moustache. It's bad for my skin. Hair belongs on your head, not on your lip.'

Muslims are not popular. According to Julia from Stockholm, they always make strange requests. They want it to be pitch black in the room, for example, so that Allah can't see. Claudia, who works in the Nørrebro district of Copenhagen, which has a large Muslim population, is not a fan. 'They call me names in the street but they visit me anyway, in secret, even during Ramadan.'

The Slovenian Nikki seems to have made a thorough study of the question. 'The English are gentlemen; it's in their genes. Italians want Barbies, young girls no older than 25. Look at Berlusconi. Austrians are nice, German too.'

'But the Dutch are the best, right?'

She has to think about it. 'No, they're normal, OK, but I think I've only had two or three of them.'

MY FAVOURITES

3 Eva. I ran into her again in the city. She was with two friends and I stopped myself from greeting her just in time.

2 Nika. A few days after our interview she sent me an email with the title of a book that explained why the EU was a mess. Just saying.

1 Charlotte. I still get emails from her too: I'm on her mailing list. That's how I know when there is going to be another face sitting protest, and that she now has a radio programme called Charlotte Rose Talks Sex. It's airs between the slightly unexpected hours of 9 and 11 on Monday mornings.

8

ARTISTS ARE ALWAYS HARD UP, EXCEPT IN THE SOVIET UNION

Berlin was one of my first cities and the artist I was scheduled to meet was Suzan, an actress. A friend of a friend put me in touch with her and we had communicated via email, agreeing the week before to meet on Monday evening for the interview. I was to contact her as soon as I arrived in the city to discuss the exact time and place, but when I called her the appointment seemed to have slipped her mind. 'Bad timing: I actually don't have time tonight, because I'm going to the premier of a film I was in. It's no big deal – it was only a small roll in a minor film – but I have to be there.'

'Good timing,' I said, 'what you need is a Dutch journalist to accompany you.' I thought it would be fun, and a good opportunity to take a closer look at the German film industry.

She agreed, and asked me to meet her at half past seven in the lobby of a hotel close to Potsdammer Platz, where the film was being screened. In Amsterdam I had once been to the premier of what passed for a major film in the Netherlands. Guests were picked up around the corner and driven the last few hundred metres to Tuschinski Theatre in a slightly dilapidated limousine. I remember that it was raining hard and four tourists were taking pictures. So much polder glamour. I had also been to a few smaller premiers, where after the director gave a short talk about the film, the twenty or so guests were treated to warm beer and peanuts served at the bar from plastic containers. I was not expecting this evening to be much different.

At half past eight Suzan, who was dressed to nines, sailed into the Ritz Hotel; we quickly downed a cocktail before leaving for the screening. We went out the door, crossed the street and turned the corner onto a red carpet that stretched between two rows of crowd barriers for approximately a hundred metres. Fans were on the right, camera crews on the left. Suzan obligingly signed autographs, and struck an appealing pose for the cameras every few metres, sometimes with me in the shot. She smiled mysteriously when the press asked her who the handsome man at her side was. The following week I saw my picture in some of the gossip magazines. The film was not bad at all, especially not for a German comedy, which I had been led to believe is not a very extensive genre. A little film in a big country.

WHO DO YOU THINK YOU ARE?

The size of a country is the determining factor in its artistic climate. In a small country, people are quick to label artists as slightly crazy. '*Stramba* is what we call it here,' said Celia, who is a painter in Malta (or is *on* Malta?). These days Malta has an art school, and there is certainly no shortage of Sunday painters, but according to her, the general public has fairly conservative views when it comes to art. Although Celia has a 'normal' family life, with children and a lawyer husband, she is regarded as being a bit 'different'. 'It's a good thing my work is not experimental or contemporary,' she laughed.

On Cyprus, a slightly bigger country, Stalo finds it increasingly difficult to deal with the narrow-mindedness of her fellow islanders. She designs bags and jewellery, and is something of a living artwork herself. Her hats and heavy make-up were not a problem in London, where she had lived for years, but in Nicosia they attract the wrong kind of attention.

Estonia is not an island, but it is at the edge of Europe. Kiwa. 39, is an interdisciplinary artist: his work is both experimental and contemporary. He was the first Estonian to produce this kind of art, and he felt misunderstood and not taken seriously. People were not sure whether he was an artist, a musician or a writer. I was very impressed with what I saw and heard of his work, and it was not hard to imagine that he would have been more successful in London. Or at least that it would have been easier for him to find acceptance, with his dayglow yellow shirt and post-punk, bleached hair 'When I walk around in the city I can feel people staring at me, and I see that they think I'm dangerous. Not because I look like a terrorist, but because they think I'm creepy and they don't understand. In Tallinn, public perception of artists, especially contemporary artists, is very negative. They are seen as money-wasters.

In Amsterdam Pierre Bokma, one of the country's best actors, confirmed that artists are viewed with suspicion. 'At least in the countryside, where people fear and distrust the unknown. In the city, the status of the artist is much higher.' He also works in Germany, in Munich, and he believes that Germans have a much greater sense of culture.

The way that artists are seen depends on a number of factors. Generally speaking, both traditional and contemporary art can find an audience in an urban area, while the more challenging forms of modern art are less accepted in smaller communities. However, the artist's persona also plays a role in the level of acceptance. Celia in Malta has an ordinary family and is therefore not regarded as all too *stramba*. X's situation in Zagreb is quite different. His art is accepted, and has been shown in American museums, and it is not unconventional art: it is modern and colourful, but figurative, a bit like Van Gogh's work if I had to make a comparison, and we stopped being shocked by this kind of work at least a century ago. But X himself is both Jewish and gay (a double whammy in Croatia) and after reading my interview with him on the Youropeans site he asked me to make his photo unrecognisable, and to call him X. He said with embarrassment that friends who read the interview had warned him that it could cost him his job at the art academy.

Luxembourg is proof that small is not always a disadvantage in terms of art appreciation. According to the photographer Bruno, art follows money and so things were pretty good in his country. That has not always been the case, because before the rise of the financial industry over the past fifty years, Luxembourg was poor. 'Art used to be something you bought to match the sofa, or an oil painting you won at a fancy fair. But tastes have evolved; the middle classes have travelled abroad and seen art in New York, Paris and London, and people who are better educated buy more art.'

THE IRISH HAVE EARS, THE ITALIANS HAVE EYES

There are marked differences in the art forms that individual countries prefer. For the Irish, it's music. Ireland is small and sparsely populated, but everyone knows U2, Van Morrison, Sinéad O'Connor, the Corrs and Snow Patrol (as well as the writers Oscar Wilde, James Joyce, Jonathan Swift and W.B. Yeats). The singer Ollie Cole has an explanation: 'The Irish are poetic. We're good with language. And almost everyone in Ireland can sing. Last week I went to a family gathering where almost every guest sang a song. My six-year old niece came in, sang something lovely and then went out in the garden to play.' Unlike the Italians. 'They've got a good eye, but no ear.' Nothing but lousy music from Italy.

In the seventies, Greece had Demis Roussos, Nana Mouskouri and Vicky Leandros, three world famous pop stars, but now the Greeks mostly listen to *bouzouki*, traditional folk music. Which is unfortunate for Bob, who plays heavy metal. He looks the part: black clothes, leather jacket, boots, the odd tattoo and long, black hair. At the same time he is a very friendly guy, who gave me a lift to my next appointment after our interview and confessed that he thinks Jennifer Aniston, who is also Greek, is cute. I've seen this before with heavy metal rockers: on stage they belt out numbers with titles like 'At War with Satan' and 'Welcome to my Nightmare', but when you meet them in person they turn out to be soft-voiced, tea-drinking vegetarians.

People often ask him if he can make a living out of his art. 'I have a nice apartment, I don't have to give lessons, and I earn 3,000 euro a month with the band, my video productions and solo projects. And I'm happy with my music, unlike most of my friends, who play in bouzouki clubs.'

The question is not irrelevant: almost every artist has trouble making ends meet, and most of them are on the brink of poverty. Kiwa earns a little money as a teacher at an art academy, Pedro in Lisbon reluctantly rents his apartment to tourists via Airbnb, and Ferenc does a little shady dealing on the side to help finance his Anarchists' Theatre in Budapest. 'Everyone has their own dodges,' the Hungarian said with a grin while we standing outside the cold because he really wanted to smoke a joint.

And what about Christiania, the free state located in a former military barracks in the centre of Copenhagen? It was once a social project set up by hippies, many of whom still live there. It is now a top tourist attraction, a kind of hippie safari featuring the studios of real-live artists, vegetarian snack bars and the chance to smoke a joint on a square while a Doors cover band plays. The buildings are picturesquely run-down, with walls that are painted as colourfully as the skin of the residents, but there are rubbish bins everywhere and ATMs spitting out cash for space cake and souvenirs, of course, because anarchy may be fun, but practicality also has its virtues.

Finn (72) is a painter and has been a resident since the early days. 'Most of us can survive only because of the dealers,' he said. They now rule the area with an iron fist. Christiania's main street is known as Pusher Street, surely not named after Øle Pusher, the inventor of gluten-free muesli. 'Some of them sponsor us with canvases, paint and free drugs,' said the Dane, who created the main entrance to the area a few years ago: a big wooden entry arch formed by two gigantic totem poles, linked by a sign. On one side it says 'Welcome to free town Christiania', and on the other side 'You are now entering the EU'.

Every artist has his or her own way of surviving. Bruno in Luxembourg gets by because he is clever: he has managed to secure a place on the committee that evaluates public art. And he is thrifty. He and his wife, also a photographer, live and work in a small but pleasant apartment — a studio really — in Grund, the medieval centre of Luxembourg. During our interview their new-born baby slept peacefully in a cot while its mother worked at her computer. It was all very Bohemian, especially since Daddy Bruno looked disconcertingly like Jesus (or possibly John Lennon).

Maša, who is 28 and from Ljubljana, told me honestly that she could only survive with help from her parents, because she can't live on the proceeds of her art. 'Not yet, anyway. I'm giving it five years.' It seems unfair to me: the average bank employee earns many times what a good poet can earn from a successful bundle of poems (which means selling 500 of them). Maybe the world doesn't value artists enough?

Maša agreed, but at the same time she thought there were too many artists, or people who think they're artists.

Or, as Pierre Bokma said: 'If you can't make a living out of it, you should give it up, or do something on the side. That is the problem with the Netherlands. Everyone moans about their problems and expects someone else to solve them.'

THE STATE COFFERS

But there is help, and not only in the Netherlands. Hanna in Helsinki is a playwright and choreographer who has a subsidy for three years, the maximum period, of 1300 euro a month. She does not have to explain what she does with the money, but it isn't enough to support her four children. Certainly not in Finland, where a beer costs eight euro, and where children's clothing is presumably also not cheap either.

This is Europe

In Austria Coco Wasabi (not her real name of course; her name is Valentina, but only her parents call her that). 'It works. I stuck 4,000 stickers that say "who the fuck is Coco Wasabi?" all over Vienna.' She receives the maximum possible subsidy of 670 euro a month and is happy with that, but still has to work in a bar two days a week to make ends meet. Vienna is expensive, and she has a car, a studio, a flat screen, a dog and she smokes enough for two. Coco has a tattoo on her arm of her parents, who have reluctantly accepted her decision to become an artist. As a thank you.

Els Moors is another example. She is a renowned poet who represented Belgium in last year's Poetry World Cup, a two-day festival held in a beautiful hotel in London. A limousine picked her up from the airport. It was quite a contrast with her biannual visit to the unemployment office, accidentally one day before the festival. It has become something of a ritual. She brings her books with her, and a folder containing the most recent reviews of her work; the staff at the unemployment office are almost apologetic, she said. They do not actually expect Els to start actively looking for a job. A third job, that is, because her second job is teaching a creative writing class.

'What are you working on right now?' I asked Anouk in Paris during lunch at a very noisy restaurant near Place de la Bastille. 'Nothing,' she laughed unhappily. 'We actors are always on the dole. Waiting for a new role, preparing for auditions. To be honest, it's a nightmare,' she said somewhat dramatically — you're either an actress or not. 'To survive as an actress you have to come from a rich family, or marry a rich man, which is what many of my friends have done. Not me, not yet.' The economic crisis has not been kind to artists — I don't think there is a single EU country that has not decided to cut back spending on the arts in recent years. To the dismay of almost every Youropean I spoke to, including Anouk: 'The minister of culture is a nitwit. *Qui est-ce*, has he ever written a novel? Performed in a theatre?' she grumbled. 'We should just stop everything for five years: no music, museums, cinema, nothing, we should stop all art. Then we would see what it's really like, and realise that society cannot exist without art.'

There are more than enough grounds for complaint, for example, because the government subsidizes the wrong people. 'Enormous budgets go to obscure projects. To connections,' Dilma said in Bucharest. Or the money is spent on beginners, said Celia in Malta. 'Which comes at the expense of established artists, and there is a reason why they are established.'

'Because they are good.'

'Exactly.'

Does the Danish government help the freebooters in Christiania? 'No. Nor do we want them to. We are anti-establishment. But, make no mistake, Christiania is Copenhagen's biggest tourist attraction. A million visitors a year. More than Tivoli.' Stranger things were said at that table in Finn's studio that afternoon, as several conspiracy theories were floated, particularly after the second joint. But also during my visit a perky tour guide led a group of tourists into the studio to see a real-live artist in action. The thick cloud of hash smoke added an authentic touch to the hippie experience.

'The government paid me well for the wall hangings,' said Ieva, a fifty year-old textile artist and teacher from Riga. 'They always spent a lot of art. Many of us made a good living out of it. That all ended in '91.' In other words, the past was better.

'During the Soviet era, artists were organised in unions – it was compulsory so that Moscow could keep an eye on us. But in order to control us, they had to feed us. We may have forfeited something in terms of originality, but we were polite about it.'

'And now you're free, but poor?'

'Yes, nobody is interested in textile art,' she complained quietly in an office that was hidden away in the catacombs of a beautiful art academy.

> The European Parliament chooses a new Capital of Culture every year. Athens was the first, in 1985. These days, there are two capitals every year: Wrocław and San Sebastian are the choices in 2016. Cities outside Europe are also eligible: Reykjavik, Istanbul, Bergen and Stavanger have all taken a turn. The title sounds impressive, but the reality is somewhat less remarkable. Studies indicate that it costs cities an average of 357 million euro, while it produces only a 12.8 percent increase in hotel bookings.[4] In the Netherlands, Leeuwarden, which is not exactly famous for its cultural heritage, beat The Hague and Eindhoven for the honour in 2018. Maybe it is an incentive prize.
>
> Riga was the Capital of Culture in 2014, Did it help artists at all? Absolutely, Ieva said. Much more attention was paid to art and culture in general. 'And I was asked to produce a big tapestry marking the event.'

200 kilometres to the north, in Tallinn, Kiwa told me a similar story. I talked to him at a sidewalk café right next to the art academy. 'The cellar here was a club.' He gestured towards a door next to the academy entrance. 'It was only for members, for artists. If you could manage to write one book a year you could party here for the rest of the year.' Art had a clear purpose then, he said. 'People went to exhibitions to find the colour that was lacking from the grey, day-to-day life of the Soviet Union.'

A POT OF GOLD IN BRUSSELS?

Most artists get little support from their national governments, and they can expect pretty much the same from Brussels. Romas, a filmmaker from Vilnius, is only 24, but he has already made a name for himself. Like me, he has tried to access European funds for his projects. But then it would have to be a European co-production, he said, with an artificially inflated budget. But that's not how he works, and not how I work.

Celia once had an exhibition in Brussels. 'It was Malta Week, and a sort of fair had been set up near the European Parliament buildings. They bought one of my paintings for their permanent collection.'

'Did they pay well?'

'Yes, not bad,' she laughed. 'But I had to wait a long time for my money.'

They probably then had to buy art from Slovenia, Estonia and Germany as well, because there are bound to be rules governing the composition of the permanent EU collection. How would that work? 200 German paintings for every painting by a Maltese artist? I did see art from all over Europe when I was wandering through the building one afternoon. The whole circus had just decamped to Strasbourg, and it would have been easy to mistake the parliament building for a museum: long white corridors and almost no visitors.

Europe and the arts. When I first asked Bob, the Greek heavy metal musician, in English what he thought about Europe, he assumed I was referring to a band.

'Aren't they shampoo rockers?' I can see how Bob might find his Swedish colleagues a little bit on the girly side.

But no, not at all. 'You probably only know *The Final Countdown?* They've done some great work.' Swedes are good at metal, Bob told me, but the European centre of heavy metal is Germany. They have the cheapest music instruments, the best festivals, the whole package. 'They are even the capital in that respect,' the Greek said with a bitter laugh. Like many of his fellow countrymen he was not happy with the tight German grip on his country's purse strings.

Now that I live in Berlin, I sometimes run into Suzan, the actress I accompanied to the premier. We live in the same neighbourhood, Prenzlauer Berg, and we have coffee now and then and she offers advice about places to eat. Simple restaurants, because struggling artists can't afford anything else. Berlin is crawling with them, and even my cleaner is actually an artist, as is the carpenter who helped me build a bookcase. But also because glamour is not really Suzan's thing, and red carpets events are few and far between. She prefers to stay home with her son and a good book. 'All that fuss: my hair alone takes three hours.' I don't doubt it, having waited an hour for her to arrive at the Ritz that evening. She is a popular actress, but even she doesn't work every day. She is only paid for the 55 or so days a year she spends on a film set. 'The problem is that the government treats actors like ordinary people with an ordinary job, but that isn't true. You cannot register for unemployment unless you are filming for 180 days a year. And that is impossible, unless you're in a soap opera.'

'You could go on strike!'

She gave this some thought as she took another drag on her Gauloise Blonde. 'No, that wouldn't work: there is no solidarity among us. I could write something on my body and throw myself naked at Angela Merkel's feet.'

Sounds like a plan.

EUROPEAN ART CHAMPION

Which European country treats its artists best? Based on my own research, the Czech Republic would win that title, at least where writers are concerned. I watched a literary talk show in a jam-packed Prague hotel, which was part of the *Of Love and the Low Countries* event, a two-day presentation of Dutch-language literature. They had flown in a whole passel of writers, including Esther Gerritsen, Annelies Verbeke, Auke Hulst and Peter Buwalda. They had been selected by the *Letterenfonds* (the national fund for literature in the Netherlands) either because their books had been translated into the Czech language, or might be at some distant date in the future. I had been passed over yet again and had not been invited – it was the charming wife of the ambassador who called my attention to the event. (The *Letterenfonds*, the sugar daddy of many a Dutch writer, was located just across the street from my apartment in Amsterdam, but the only thing I ever got from them was the inconvenience of yet another costly renovation.)

'*Kdo to čte je blázen,*' said the presenter Igor from the podium. Hahahahahahaha.'

'*Smrdíš a jsi ošklivá,*' said co-host and writer Jaroslav. Hohohohohohoho.

The audience of three hundred, three quarters of whom were women, was screaming with laughter.

'*A nyní hloupý belgický,*' Igor and Jaroslav introduced a shy Flemish writer, and even he got a laugh, although it may have been more like an encore for the Czech duo.

But when the Fleming read a passage from his book, the audience was silent and attentive, following the translation on an overhead screen. They applauded, and clapped even harder when Verbeke gave her reading, and laughed appreciatively when Igor told a story about a trip to Amsterdam and a cousin in Heerlen. Buwalda read from *Bonita Avenue*, which seemed to be a much slimmer volume in Czech. It is hard to say whether this is because Czech is a more succinct language or because the translator decided to omit the superfluous passages. Two hours later the literary ladies wandered out of the auditorium and into the night, their cheeks glowing, ready for one last glass of wine. Or possibly a pilsner; after all, this is the Czech Republic. Have you ever been to a literary evening? Would you turn out for Czech-Dutch cultural festival? I thought not. But this is Prague. *Of Love and the Low Countries* was the one-off theme of a programme organised by EKG, a literary talk show that always attracts a capacity audience.

In the Czech Republic, art is cherished, and everyone is either already an artist or wants to become one, including my Youropeans: immigrant Egor is a singer (currently working as a receptionist in a hotel), hairdresser Pavlina plays the bass guitar in a band, and clothing designer Klara prefers to think of herself as an artist rather than an entrepreneur. 'Is it like Hollywood, where all the girls work as waitresses and the boys in gas stations, waiting to be discovered?' I asked Jaroslav a few days after his performance. 'Yes, it is like that,' he said, pointing to a building further along the street. 'That was the insurance company where Franz Kafka worked during the day. He wrote at night.' Artists have even reached the highest office in the land: Václav Havel, the first post-communist president was a writer.

MY FAVOURITES

3 Kiwa, Tallinn. He lives in the wrong country, if you ask me. In Western Europe, he would not be stared at like he was an alien. Post-punk, but vulnerable all the same.

2 Coco, Vienna. Fresh, provocative, ambitious and hard-working. And extremely sociable. I gave the Roma boys begging at our table a dirty look, but she fished a euro out of her handbag, thus also explaining why she needed an extra job as a barmaid to make ends meet.

3 Els, Brussels. (This was a difficult choice, because I liked all of my artistic brothers and sisters.) Funny, original and a very good poet. 'Speaking of European differences: in Romania they have a saying that there is something of the poet in everyone. In Germany, poetry has to be intellectual and challenging, and Belgium expects its artists to be commercially savvy enough to go on tour, take to the stage, and promote their art.'

9

FAMOUS SWEDES ARE LISTED IN THE TELEPHONE BOOK

Local celebrities. My golden opportunity to take an Austrian playboy model to lunch or to interview the recently retired head of the European Council. Of course I also included this category because of the enhanced publicity value that celebrities tend to have, as publicity was a vital part of this project: my objective was to ensure that as many people as possible would get to hear about Youropeans so that the project would have the maximum possible impact. The celebrities were a motley crew, which could be roughly divided into five groups, starting with politicians. Not too many, however, since they have a tendency to waffle, or to do exactly the opposite and say what they think people want to hear.

POLITICIANS

1. Brussels: Herman van Rompuy. The Belgian boss of Europe until 1 December 2014. It was clear that he had just retired from office: he no longer felt obliged to mince his words.
2. Amsterdam: Felix Rottenberg. Leader of the Dutch Labour Party between 1992 and 1997, and the reason I decided to join

the party (a decision that was quickly reversed following a disappointing visit to a party meeting in Amsterdam). He is now mostly known for his work as a political commentator on TV and in the newspaper.
3. Luxembourg: Xavier Bettel. He was the mayor when I spoke to him, and was elected president two months later (the interview was apparently good for his career). Just turned forty, a liberal, who embraces all aspects of his freedom and is openly gay.
4. Madrid: Cayetana Álvarez de Toledo. Her full name is Cayetana Álvarez de Toledo y Peralta-Ramos (long names are the curse of the nobility; she is a marchioness). A former journalist, she is now an important protégé of the minister president. She is active in the think tank of her party, the right-wing Partido Popular. She stands a chance of becoming a minister in Spain, even without the help of this interview.

SPORTS STARS

5. Nicosia: Konstantinos Charalambidis. Captain of the Cypriot national football team. Was more interested in training than in doing an interview; he would rather let his feet do the talking.
6. Riga: Kaspars Daugavins. Latvian ice hockey player who signed with the American National Hockey League (NHL) and now earns 700,000 euro a year in Switzerland.
7. Ljubljana: Tina Maze. The most famous woman in Slovenia by a long shot. She won two gold medals at Sochi, for downhill skiing and the Super G. She was also world champion in 2015.
8. Copenhagen: Henrik Larsen. Former football player, top scorer in Denmark's legendary 1992 team, that became European champion as a complete surprise. He is manager of Brøndby, a big Dansh club.
9. Budapest: Judit Polgár. By far the best women's chess player ever, she was a grandmaster by the age of fifteen. She beat Karpov and Kasparov and was ranked fourth in the world. She retired in 2014, but is still revered in Hungary.

ARTISTS

10. London: Omid Djalili. One of England's most famous stand-up comedians, and that is saying something. Look him up on Youtube. Has also acted in several films, including *The Infidel*, a film about a Muslim who finds out he is actually Jewish. He is neither: Omid's parents are Iranian and Baha'i.
11. Stockholm: David Batra. Swedish stand-up comedian and actor with Indian heritage on his father's side. Also happens to be married to a well-known politician.
12. Dublin: Ollie Cole. He was a singer with Turn, a band that had hits in England and Ireland and was nominated best Irish Band in 2005 and 2006, but lost to U2. Snow Patrol used to be their support act. Now a solo performer.
13. Bucharest: Andrei Rosu. He was also a well-known singer, albeit in the background, with Gaz Pe Foc, the Romanian Back Street Boys. He is now more famous as an ultra runner who runs marathons in place like the North Pole. That's right, the North Pole.
14. Vilnius: Romas Zabarauskas. Talented and successful Lithuanian filmmaker, only 24 but already a vocal advocate for LGBT rights.
15. Rome: Sara Ricci. Acted in the soap opera *Vivere* for seven years. 'My show is seen not only in Italy but also in Canada. So I'm very popular!' She doesn't mind saying so herself.
16. Vallette: Ira Losco. Singer. Without realising it I had already seen her on so many posters and advertisements that she looked familiar to me when I met her at the end of my week on Malta: she is the face of the island. Came in second in the Eurovision Song Contest in 2002, and that counts for something on Malta.*
17. Zagreb: Lidija Horvat Dunjko. She came in sixth in the Song Contest in 1995. She was then, and still is, one of the stars of

---

* She took part again in 2016, and finished 12th. Not bad.

the Croatian opera.
18. Tallinn: Piret Järvis. Yet another participant in the Song Contest. Her band Vanilla Ninja was representing Switzerland for some reason, and they came eighth. She is now a well-known TV journalist.
19. Paris: JC de Castelbajac. The Frenchman designed a jacket made of teddy bears for Madonna, and Lady Gaga's provocative glove bikini. He dressed the Pope, 500 bishops and 5,000 priests in rainbow vestments.
20. Helsinki: Stefan Lindfors. Finnish designer, celebrated in many international exhibitions. He is also a sculptor and film clip maker, because doing just one thing would be boring. His clip for Finnish rockband HIM was chosen Best European Video in 2004.

TELEVISION PERSONALITIES

21. Warsaw: Maciej Orłoś. As the presenter of Teleexpressu he has had between four and six million viewers in Poland every day for the past 23 years. For years, he has also been the person who calls in the Polish points in the Song Contest.
22. Prague: Lenny Trčková. TV and radio presenter. For nine years she hosted the popular Óčko; she is the face of the Czech MTV generation.
23. Vienna: Cathy Zimmerman. Newsreader, model and the second Austrian to pose for *Playboy*.
24. Sofia: Merlin Konstantinova. Realty star known for taking part in the TV programme *Survivor*. Bulgarian model and fitness champion.

OTHER CELEBRITIES

25. Lisbon: Salvador Mendes de Almeida. He ended up in a wheelchair after a motorcycle accident. He is now a source of inspiration and a spokesperson for the handicapped in Portugal

with his own TV programme and a foundation (and also manages a family business).

26. Athens: Peter Economides. Four million Greeks have seen his YouTube film. Does it show him jumping over burning cars or singing a duet with Robbie Williams? No, it is a 30-minute speech about rebranding. Rebranding Greece to help Zorba improve his faltering image.

27 Berlin: Luise Neumann-Cosel. The green face of Germany, the young (28) leader of BürgerEnergie Berlin wants the company to take over the energy network from the Swedish corporation Vattenfall, which delivers the wrong kind of energy: coal, or worse, atomic energy. The price? Approximately one billion euro.

28 Bratislava: Anton Srholec. Performs at rock festivals before thousands of people. No, he is not a singer or a rock star. Anton is an 85-year old priest and communist resistance hero.

It may not say everything, but the number of likes on Facebook is one indication of fame:

Tina Maze	500.000
Herman van Rompuy	39.000
Judit Polgár	32.000
Xavier Bettel	26.000
Omid Djalili	18.000
Peter Economides	15.585
Maciej Orłoś	10.700
Cathy Zimmermann	7700
David Batra	7600
JC de Castelbajac	7500
Andrei Rosu	6700

'Where are you from?' is usually the first question taxi drivers all over the world ask, just after they have turned down the radio a bit and flicked a cigarette butt out the window. 'Ah, Holland!', they exclaim before launching into a complicated anecdote about a wild trip to Amsterdam, a Dutch person they once met, or an enthusiastic story about football heroes Cruyff, Gullit and Van Persie.

But what if you have to confess that you're from Malta? A country with zero famous painters, writers or scientists. Never won a single Olympic medal. If the Maltese national football accidentally ties a game, the opponent's coach will be fired the next day, which is what happened to the Bulgarian Penev. As noted above, Ira Losco, the most famous woman in Malta, owes her celebrity to a second place position in the Eurovision Song Contest. Her Wiki entry proudly proclaims that she has opened for Elton John, Katie Melua and Ronan Keating.

How does that feel? What is it like to come from a country no one knows much about, a country whose teams never win? A country where coming second is a big deal? In Malta I felt that it encourages modesty: people who do not identify with the athletic, musical or fine arts skills of a fellow countryman they don't know, even though they themselves have no athletic ability whatsoever, cannot sing a note or have the artistic skills of a three-year old. It apparently helps to create a very homogeneous society, where 90 percent of the population turns out to vote in an election (even a European election), where there a few criminals, and the police know who they are, and where corruption doesn't stand much of a chance. There are only eight hundred surnames in the entire — which on second thought may not be healthy either. It's a good thing a plane or a boat occasionally arrives bringing new blood to the island.

Ira's local fame has not gone to her head. She travels abroad often enough to realise that her celebrity does not extend very far beyond Valletta. She even promised to drop off a book for me at my hotel — it was either by her or about her, I can't say for sure — but then promptly forgot about it, so she does have a bit of the diva in her.

I wanted to know what it is like to be famous, whether the experience varied from one country to the next. As it turns out, there is north-south divide here. There is little celebrity hysteria in Sweden, where famous people do not even have unlisted telephone numbers. Comedian David Batra does not need bodyguards. The only people who bother him are drunks, who are hard to shake off after he has had his picture taken with them or exchanged a few words. When he's out with his friends he doesn't want to be bothered with that kind of thing. It is sometimes difficult to be a comedian. 'People always want to tell me jokes. And I have to stay friendly – if I don't it will be all over social media in no time.'

'Does it bother you that people recognize you?' I asked designer Stefan Lindfors. We were sitting at a sidewalk cafe near his house. He had greeted nearly every passer-by for the past twenty minutes. 'A little,' the Finn said, 'but it would bother me more if they didn't recognize me.'

Tine Maze is so famous in her own country that she feels the need to escape now and then. That's why she trains just over the border in an Italian ski resort instead of in Slovenia, which is where we met for our interview, but I was told not to mention the name of the village anywhere. We were to meet in front of the church at twelve o'clock, and I had been standing there for five or ten minutes when a motor scooter pulled up. It stopped right in front of my nose, the helmet came off, and there she was, on a vintage Piaggio: the fastest women in the world.

I had already noticed that Salvador Mendes de Almeida was a celebrity in Lisbon: the policeman I talked to before him insisted on driving me to my appointment when he heard who I would be interviewing next. He accompanied me to the door of Salvador's office, and lurked there, hoping to catch a glimpse of him. 'People always want to talk to me,' he said, 'especially if a member of their family is handicapped.' He is happy that his celebrity gives him the opportunity to help others, which he does on TV and in the street, except when people get flustered and ask him for an autograph. The man is capable of so much: he manages a company and a charity organisation from his wheelchair, using a joystick to operate his chair and a keyboard, but he cannot write.

'The countryside is different from Warsaw,' TV presenter Maciej Orłoś said. 'In the city they are more used to seeing famous people, but I get stared at everywhere. It's better when I'm abroad, although last month in London people constantly approached me.' Not surprising, roughly one million Poles now live in the United Kingdom, and they are the second largest nationality in Ireland, Sweden, Lithuania and Iceland.

And the dark side of celebrity? I asked if fame also had its disadvantages. 'I hadn't expected that posing in *Playboy* would create such a stir in Austria,' Cathy Zimmerman said. 'People were endlessly judgmental: they talked about it for two months.' She is a very attractive woman, dressed in a short, tight leopard print dress — but unlike her countryman I quickly forgave her for that. 'If a photographer catches Kate Moss using cocaine, she can still model for Gucci the next day. That wouldn't be possible here. This is a very conservative country.' And yet, Europe saw a very different side of Austria in May 2014, when its entry in the Eurovision Song Contest was a bearded woman (who won).

In Estonia the press is relatively reserved, and according to Piret Järvis, there is no paparazzi culture. Unlike Germany, where her band Vanilla Ninja was very popular in the noughties, and she was therefore hotly pursued by the tabloid press. She had her own stalkers, too, like the man who thought he was her father.

Lenny Trčková said the paparazzi had become lazy, at least in Prague. 'Instead of taking them themselves, they wait for Czech celebrities to send in their own photos. And believe, they do it!'

MY FAVOURITES

3 Maciej Orłoś. Friendly, intelligent, and very modest. For the past 23 years he has had a daily audience of close to six million Poles, but during our interview in an otherwise empty lunchroom he had to waive frantically to attract the waitress's attention. Sometimes even a celebrity struggles to find an audience.

2 Father Anton Shrolec. I met him in his house, a tiny apartment in a massive grey apartment block in the suburbs of Bratislava. In his kitchen he treated me to a cake he had baked himself, wine served from a two-litre Coca Cola bottle ('bottled by my brother') and, above all, to his words of wisdom. Still robust at 85, he drove me back to the city centre after our interview because it was raining hard and the tram stop was a long way off. Without glasses.

1 JC de Castelbajac. I met him in his office in Paris, which looked out over a department where his top-notch employees, most of them women, are working at big Apple computer screens. JC kept interrupting me: 'Do you know Roxy Music's *Song for Europe*. No? Let's listen.' He found the number on YouTube and turned up the volume. A few of the girls glanced up, but they had probably seen their boss do stranger things. 'And this one?' A Kraftwerk song, also about Europe. 'You know, I designed a beautiful flag for Europe. I don't like the current one, the blue and gold thing with the stars. This is what mine looks like.' He started to draw. 'Voilà. It is like a rope — the Eu-rope. Every part of the rope has a different colour; this bit is the German flag, yellow and red, and there are the French colours. Maybe you can use it for your project.' And that is what I did: it is now part of the Youropeans logo.

10

IMMIGRANTS, REFUGEES, ASYLUM SEEKERS, EXPATS: THE NEWCOMERS

An immigrant is, quite simply, someone who settles in another country. It is the eighth Youropeans category, added because I wanted to know how newcomers viewed these countries and their social structures. I was looking for the outsider's point of view. But added also because immigrants are the subject of what is Europe's most heated debate. Every day, Europe's newspapers are full of them; in the past they were reported on in the foreign news section, now they are everywhere, most often in bold type on the front page. First it was mainly the Italian, Greek and Maltese newspapers, then England and France and now everywhere, from Romania to Estonia. Whenever boats full of refugees are found adrift in the Mediterranean, or refugees are discovered hidden in lorries heading for the Channel Tunnel, or train stations are overrun. Whenever there is trouble at an asylum seekers centre.

The EU has been tackling the problem for years, in a number of ways. They have tried to strengthen the external borders by diverting refugees into local crisis centres in buffer zones, and by trying to deter people smugglers. Italy – and to a lesser extent – Greece (Malta's voice is less audible) have been complaining for years that their fellow member states should be more Involved. Now that the dam has burst, and Europe is being flooded with refugees who want to settle here, something may finally be about happen. The EU has assigned members states a quota for the number of refugees they are expected to accept. This in turn has sparked protests, since every country thinks their quota is too high, or thinks that they should not be forced to accept refugees: solidarity is of course a fine European principle, but there's no need to get carried away with it.

In the spring of 2015, the headline in *Die Zeit* was: WIR WOLLEN NICHT DASS SIE ERTRINKEN. WIR WOLLEN NICHT DASS SIE KOMMEN. WAS WOLLEN WIR TUN? (We don't want you to drown. We don't want you to come. What should we do?). I asked the Youropeans about this complex issue, but first let me introduce you to the people in question: the immigrants.

'WHITE PEOPLE ARE EXPATS, THE REST ARE IMMIGRANTS'

Saturday afternoon. The coach stops and noisy children pile out, followed by mothers, some of them with strollers, unaided by fathers: they light a cigarette as soon as they set foot on the pavement. This is not Euro Disney or some fairy ground, but a small park near Oranienplatz in the Berlin neighbourhood Kreuzberg. No roller coaster, but there is a bouncy castle, a table football game, and a corner where children can paint. It doesn't take much to make a child happy, certainly not these children, who are all asylum seekers. They've come to spend an afternoon with their fellow asylum seekers here in what they've dubbed Lampedusa Village. Although it temporarily resembles a mini-theme park, this illegal tent camp smack in the middle of a respectable Berlin neighbourhood has for almost a year been home to close to a hundred refugees, of whom only some actually started their journey from that Italian island, about an hour's swim away from Africa.

For most of them, many of whom are West African men, becoming a European was not their life's dream: they had a good life in

This is Europe

Gaddafi's Libya. He was fond of sleeping in a tent, but preferred to do so with five virgins rather than fifteen unwashed men. There were eight tents in Lampedusa village: seven for sleeping and one information tent, manned by a very unhealthy looking Nigerian. UNITED AGAINST COLONIAL INJUSTICE screamed a banner above a blackboard full of newspaper clippings, pamphlets and a picture of Ulrike Meinhof, the RAF terrorist whose connection to these asylum seekers was not altogether clear to me.

There were a few Germans there as well. One of them, a woman of maybe 25, maybe 50, wore a T-shirt proclaiming SOLIDARITÄT MET DER FLÜCHTUNGSBEWEGUNG. She was raking gravel with the help a man whose knobby shoulders carry the weight of the world (and tatty linen bags). The children were enjoying themselves, jumping up and down in the yellow and green castle. Their mothers sat in the shade with the strollers, the fathers gathered in small groups to smoke. Two Malinese men were playing a game of draughts, using stones as pieces. Four friends stood watching, which seemed to be an indication of their level of boredom. Lampedusa Village, Berlin.

I met Joe here, who fled from Nigeria, because they were trying to kill his family. That is his story, but somehow I don't believe him. He had already claimed to have been a professional football player. Either way, he is not likely to have left Nigeria because he had such a good life there. Things were good in Libya, his first destination. 'Boss, I'm telling you, I worked in construction, had a house, a car, the sun. But when the Europeans began their bombardments, I had to leave.' On Lampedusa the Italians gave him 500 euro and told him to leave. Now he was not allowed to work, and since he spent all day twiddling his thumbs in this camp he was willing to sit on a park bench with me and talk, but he didn't want his photograph to be recognizable. Every now and then, when the children's football rolled in our direction, he jumped up and kicked it with his left or right foot or put a spin on it, perhaps to convince me that he was in fact a pro.

When I started the project I thought it would be easy to find people for my immigrants category. Like hairdressers, entrepreneurs and artists, there are a lot of them, and everyone knows at least a few. It turned out to be much harder than I thought, partly because most people do not want to be called an immigrant. By that I don't mean Yonous in Athens or Stephen in Malta, both of whom reached Europe illegally by boat: they had no objection to the term.

But Mohammed, a policeman in Stockholm, who was born in Eritrea and moved to Sweden when he was three, did object. When I found him through a friend of a friend I thought it was a lucky stroke, two birds with one stone, since he was both a policeman and an immigrant. Especially when, in addition to talking about his work with Interpol, the subject of immigration kept coming up during our interview. Mohammed, who is a dark-skinned, bearded Muslim, sometimes talked to groups of young people of non-Swedish origin, for example, at schools. 'How many of you are immigrant?' he often asked them. Half of the class would raise their hand. 'But you were born here, weren't you? Then you can't be an immigrant, because immigration is something you *do*,' he told them. But when I emailed him a month later and told him I was putting him in both categories, he felt stung. He was a police agent, not an immigrant. So I asked him if he had stopped being an immigrant at some point, but he declined to answer. I am assuming the answer is yes. He was integrated, successful. No longer an immigrant.

The immigrant I had in mind for Estonia felt the same way. The EU agency there had given me the name of someone who had immigrated from Great Britain, and was now a member of the city council in Tallinn and a former Estonian candidate for the European elections. It sounded like an interesting story, but when I approached him he was offended. 'I'm not an immigrant, I'm an expat,' he wrote in his email, 'because I moved to a country that is poorer than my own.' That is a peculiar definition of the term expat, which I thought referred to anyone living temporarily in another country. I later came across an editorial in *The Guardian*, entitled 'Why are white people expats, while the rest of us are immigrants?"[5] Being an expat depends on the country of origin, and on social and economic status, the writer argued. By this definition, Africans, Asians and Arabs are always immigrants, Europeans are not. The British /Estonian council member was black, which apparently automatically made him an immigrant, but maybe he doesn't read *The Guardian*.

It is a complicated issue.

I found them in the end, the immigrants/expats/foreign-born/ refugees, but after I had interviewed them all I realised that I needed to divide them into sub-categories. I was looking for the outsider's viewpoint, but Joe's experiences were so different from those of, say, Andrea, a university professor working in London, as were the ways in which their new countries — temporary or otherwise — had welcomed them.

But I wasn't sure what system to use to divide them into categories. In the Netherlands, instead of immigrant, we tend to use the term *allochtoon*, which is officially defined by the Central Bureau of Statistics as someone who has at least one parent who was born abroad. And *allochtonen* are either Western or non-Western, the same distinction as the expat/immigrant divide mentioned in *The Guardian*: people from Africa, Latin America and Asia, except for Japan and Indonesia (the latter is an odd exception, probably based on our colonial past, but then why not make an exception for Surinam as well?) are non-Western.

There is another relevant distinction in the Netherlands, based on who is exempt from the obligatory citizenship test. EU citizens, as well as those from Norway, Iceland, the United States, Canada, Australia, New Zealand, Japan and South Korea do not have to take the test. I have used the same system for purposes of this book, dividing those interviewed into 'the West' and 'the rest', even though José, a construction worker who left Portugal to work in Luxembourg in the late nineties, is a typical immigrant, and Max, who had a university education when he moved to the relatively underdeveloped Slovenia from what was then Rhodesia, is more of an expat.

Immigrants, refugees, asylum seekers, expats: the newcomers

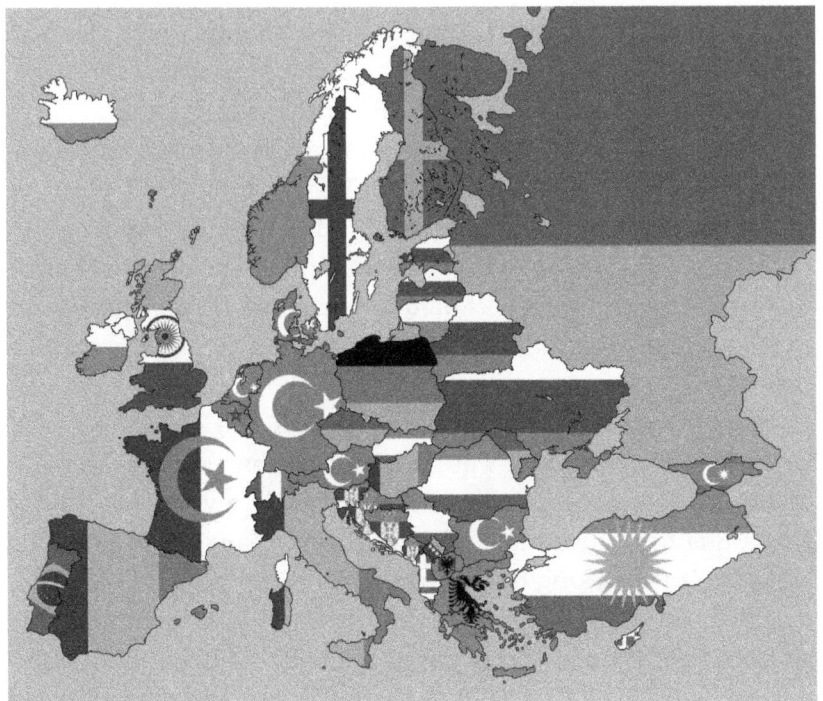

The second most common nationality in each country.

IMMIGRANTS DO THEIR BEST – AND EXPECT OTHERS TO AS WELL

'They tried to make me vomit by forcing me to drink soap and water. They hung me up by my feet; oh, they tortured me in so many ways. I thought they would kill me, but my stethoscope saved me. When they found it in my backpack they thought I was someone important. They let me go and I fled to Turkey. The United Nations High Commissioner for Refugees (UNCHCR), wanted to send me to Canada, but I chose Greece.'

'Why?'

Because of all the Greek names and terms found in medical and philosophical literature. And I thought it was far away, but it turned out to be just next door. My family thought I was crazy, but I paid the smuggler 2100 dollars for a false passport and boat passage. And I was so afraid.'

'Afraid of being caught the Greek coast guard?'

'Yes, I practiced my new name all night. But mostly of the water, it was my first time at sea.'

Yonous: his life reads like a book. It deserves to be made into a film; I could see Bruce Willis in the lead role. The torture chapter was written when he was 24, and he is now 40. He no longer practices as a doctor, but is the head of a large refugee organization in Greece.

Stephen also came to Europe by boat. He is a 27-year-old Zimbabwean. After his father was murdered, he feared for his own life. The boat he was travelling on from Libya to Italy was diverted to Malta due to bad weather. He works as a cleaner in a hotel and when he isn't working he is studying, because he wants to be an engineer. He is allowed to work and study: that's something anyway, but he is not exactly a carefree student. It will be another five years before he is fully qualified, and until then he can be deported at any time, because his asylum application was rejected.

'At any moment?'

'Yes,' Stephen said, staring at the floor. Tired, dulled, ashamed. The airco zoomed, and down below us hotel guests rollicked in the pool he cleans every night. He has already spent 18 months in a kind of prison, his punishment for trying to enter the country illegally.

PARIS AT WAR

Paris, March 2014, somewhere on the Boulevard Barbès, not far from the Gare du Nord. The provocation started at the stoplight: he brushed past me, narrowly missing my front wheel and looking daggers at me. A hundred metres along the street, he finished the job. I was struggling with the lock on my rented bicycle, when the young North African approached and spit disdainfully right next to my shoes.

> **ONE-WAY TICKET TO EUROPE**
>
> The journey from Libya to Lampedusa (or Malta) covers a distance of a roughly 200 kilometres, and takes about 12 hours. It costs approximately 1500 dollars to secure a place on a jam-packed boat where there are not nearly enough lifejackets for the passengers, most of whom cannot swim. Boat refugees want to reach Italy because from there they can travel to other Schengen countries by public transport. Greece is less popular, because although it is also party to Schengen, it is surrounded by countries that are not, and refugees therefore need smugglers to help them reach Hungary, for example, via Serbia and Macedonia. Malta, a small island, is not at all a convenient destination.
>
> In Italy they can catch a train, because refugees are placed in camps, where they can easily walk out: the police do nothing to stop them, and do not ask for identification. There is a reason for this: refugees can apply for asylum in only one country, and if they were asked for identification in Italy, they would have to apply there. Italy has no intention of doing that, and most refugees would rather claim asylum in a Northern European country where there are more facilities for them, such as asylum seekers centres and opportunities for study, and where they often also have family. Once they reach a Northern European country they are asked where they entered Europe, but no one admits to having entered via Italy because they would be sent back there. The standard answer is; 'I don't know. We arrived at night in a boat and then travelled here in a lorry.'

I still had two interviews to arrange: with an immigrant and a hairdresser. It should not have been difficult. Although Amsterdam is the world capital of immigration, with 170 nationalities (more than in Antwerp and New York), this says more about the passports than about the number of immigrants (or ethnic minorities), and my impression was that there were more immigrants in Paris. Dominique Strauss-Kahn (Tunesia), Patrick Bruel and Bernard-Henri Lévy (Algerian), David Guetta and Edith Piaf (Moroccan), Albert Camus and Louis de Funès (Spanish), Charles

Aznavour (Armeian), Johnny Hallyday (Belgian), Nicolas Sarkozy (Hungarian/Greek) and René Goscinny and Roman Polanski (Polish) are all of foreign ancestry. As is the current mayor, Anne Hidalgo, who was born in Spain, and two of my Parisian Youropeans: JC de Castelbajac from Morocco, and doctor Serge from Algeria. I remember the 1998 World Cup, which was played in France. The right-wing politician Jean-Marie Le Pen declared in advance that it was going to be a disaster, as almost the entire team was made up of 'foreigners'. A few weeks later, captain Zinedine Zidane, who is Algerian, raised the world cup.

But I was looking for a real immigrant, someone who had not been in the country very long, and I hoped to find one in are around the Gare du Nord. They were undoubtedly out there, but how long they had been in France (newly arrived or for generations) I had no way of knowing because they apparently preferred spitting to talking. There were also a lot of hairdressers, most of them for Afro hair, like Obama Coiffure, which had a big image on its window that was meant to look like that Kenyan president. There were shops offering *spécialités Africaines*, lots of people on the street, women talking animatedly to one another or chattering into their phones, men offering goods for sale, stolen or otherwise, like the car radio and the bicycle a toothless West African tried to sell me for five euro. The neighbourhood is black, except for the police. Their vans are stationed at various corners, parked right up on the pavement, and every now and then they jump out to patrol the area, always in threes. They are big, heavily armed, and very white.

If you ask me, Paris is at war. It is a quiet war, without many weapons.* The foreign troops are launching an attack on the city from their stronghold in the *banlieus,* the suburbs. They are gaining ground, and have now reached the *périphérique*, the ring road, and are advancing on the city centre. The Paris where the tourists

---

* I made this observation in Paris in March 2014, before the Charlie Hebdo attack, and the attack at the Bataclan on Friday 13 November 2015.

look at art, the rich buy art, and where jeu de boules is played on the Place des Invalides on Sunday afternoon, and a cup of coffee costs eight euro. Boulevard Barbès in a stone's throw from the Place de la Bastille, once the starting point of the revolution that cost the Parisian elite their heads.

I bicycled through the neighbourhood, slowly because most people refused to make way, despite the big pictogram of a cyclist on the asphalt. Further along the street three policemen hopped out of their van for another patrol. Two teenagers contemptuously sized up the trio, and as soon as the police had turned their backs, they spit on the ground. Disdainfully.

I found the hairdresser Madame Paule in a quiet side street, and Abdel, an immigrant, sells chestnuts on one of the boulevards near the Place de la République. His can't be a very profitable business: most of the chestnuts on the grill are charred. He is from Bangladesh. 'Why France? Pourquoi? Perché? Por ché?' I tried, but he didn't seem to speak any of the languages his clients might understand, which also can't be good for business.

'It is better here.'

'The weather?' I ventured, pointing to the sky. It was raining.

'No.'

'More money?'

'No.'

'Political reasons?'

'Yes.' He laughed. He fished a carefully folded piece of paper out of his coat pocket. It was in a protective plastic sleeve, and it had his name on it, his religion (Muslim) and his status: he had been given asylum.

'It is good here. I receive 1300 euro a month.' Plus the three or four euros he makes from his chestnut business, of course.

BOB MARLEY IS NOT BIG IN LJUBLJANA

There are different reasons for moving to another country. Whereas Stephen and Yonous were forced to flee, and Abdel's motive was a little vague, Hamid simply chose a country where he could earn money and pay for his brother and sister's schooling. He travelled from through Turkey to Sofia, where he works in a supermarket. Monique left the Ivory Coast, also for a better life. She is a sex worker in the area around the Noordstation in Brussels. Which is where I also found Rachid, a 31-year-old Moroccan who had entered the country from Italy on a tourist visa. Christina, a tiny Filipina came for the money too, but Cyprus was a disappointment: she works 70 hours a week as a cleaner even though she is a trained nurse. She lost her job when the crisis hit, and she misses the hospital, where she was doing the work she is qualified to do, but can no longer afford to do. Pay for foreigners has been reduced to only 500 euro a month.

A third group of immigrants came to Europe to study, and stayed on, which was harder for some than for others. For example, Rido (27) from Nigeria, is now unemployed in Zagreb; Thierry (32) from Cameroon earns a good living as a team leader for the car rental agency Avis in Budapest; Aimée (45) moved from the Congo to become a successful building contractor in Bucharest; Max (54) from Zimbabwe is an influential social entrepreneur in Ljubljana, and Sandra (30) from Uganda is an artist-slash-cleaner in Amsterdam (as it happens, she is my cleaner).

I wanted to find out how they pictured Europe before they arrived. What did they expect to find here? Sandra thought that everything would be clean, rich and modern. 500-storey-skyscrapers and incredibly fast cars. And in most respects, London did not disappoint when she arrived there in 2002.

Max, who grew up in what was then Rhodesia, learned at school that Europe was the centre of the world. 'The British taught us this. The land of milk and honey; you could get anything in Europe. So when I moved to Yugoslavia when I was nineteen, in the early eighties, I didn't take my records with me. I thought I could buy them there.'

'What kind of music?'

'Like Bob Marley. But man, the only Marley record I could find was a compilation, not even sung by him, but some tribute to him.' He also noticed that people's general education was inferior. At home everyone knew the name of the American president, but here they didn't even know their own prime minister's name. They were very interested in Africa, but as soon as Max told them that his capital city was much bigger than theirs, and that they also had banks and a parliament, they lost interest. They wanted to hear about wild animals.

Monique, from Ivory Coast, was curious about whites; she wanted to see them in the flesh. 'Yes, really,' she said irritably when I looked as if I didn't believe her. She was annoyed with me anyway, having peered through her lace curtain and seen at least three potential clients walking past during our interview.

MIKAEL ERICSON IS FROM KURDISTAN

And had Europe welcomed them? It depended on where they had ended up. In Western Europe, people are used to immigrants, especially in the urban areas. In some places, like London, they are the norm; it was hard to find a Youropean who was entirely English — only Guy, the entrepreneur and Charlotte the sex worker qualified as such. Many nationalities have established huge communities: there are over 200,000 Bengalis, and London is the six-largest French city. I found it easy to imagine that you could live in London and remain a 'foreigner', living, working and marrying within your own community.

Others live in cities where there are few immigrants, and so they are more noticeable. Sometimes that is an advantage. Rido and Thierry, for example, have performed on television and in commercials because there isn't much competition where dark-skinned actors are concerned. But more often than not, being an immigrant has its drawbacks. Hamid had been beaten up a few months earlier when he was walking down the street with his Bulgarian girlfriend. 'Just because I am black. Of course, we went to the police, and I was even able to identify the people who did it, but they let them out the next day.' He was the only black person in the coffee bar where we met. Foreigners, including Albanians and Arabs, congregate in a street a few hundred metres away, which is where I found Hamid, in a phone shop.

Christina in Nicosia was paid less than Cypriot nurses. It apparently doesn't matter how good you are at your job, she concluded, because if you do not speak or write Greek you're automatically relegated to the B category. That is particularly galling, because it is the Filipinas who taught them the finer points of nursing. 'You know, they call us *mavro*. It means black. But now, when someone insults me, I speak enough Greek to be able to tell them that I am not dumb, that I speak English and have travelled, while they only know their own stupid country and can only speak Greek. I like my colour; my heart is white but theirs is black,' she said quietly, but sounding fierce all the same.

In the labour market, people with different names or a different skin colour are at a disadvantage. Mohammed has a friend named Mikael Ericson who also speaks fluent Swedish. But he is from Kurdistan, and he looks Kurdish, and he feels this when he goes for a job interview.

Sandra also feels she has to work harder than a Dutch person to get a job. 'It's my surname. And, Ok, my Dutch is not all that good,' she admitted, in English. 'But that is normal,' she said, as if she is talking to herself, 'every country puts its own people first.'

'How xenophobic are the Hungarians?' I asked Thierry.

'In the street, they're OK,' said the Cameroonian, a giant of a man wearing a leather jacket and sporting a neatly trimmed beard. He brought his girlfriend along to the interview; she is also foreign, a Romanian.

'Yeah? I don't see many friendly faces,' I said. This was something that really struck me in Budapest.

Thierry found this unsurprising, since most people have to live on no more than 100 euro a month. What he meant by this was that while people did not discriminate in the streets, companies and government institutions did. For example, he had recently tried to buy a television set, and pay for it in instalments, but the saleswoman said that wouldn't be possible as he was not Hungarian. Clever of her to know this without having seen Thierry's passport; he told her that he had been paying taxes for seven years, and that he was fairly sure that his salary was higher than 75 percent of the staff in the store. But there was no getting around it; he could not buy the television.

Athens is perhaps the worst place in Europe to be an immigrant, especially since the rise of the extreme right party Golden Dawn. Yonous talked at length about the explosion of xenophobia, and the fact that the police were often guilty of unnecessary violence. He was no longer able to go everywhere, and felt he always had to be looking over his shoulder. After the interview, when I was leaving the building where the Refugee Forum is located, on the second floor of a tatty apartment complex in the city centre, I passed a trembling junky on the worn-out staircase and saw three police agents around the corner. One of them was masked, the others were armed with sticks and they were in the process of arresting a terrified black man. Sunday afternoon, two blocks away from Omonia Square.

IMMIGRANTS ARE MAKING HEADWAY

Of course some Youropeans, like Andy in Copenhagen, have never experienced racism or discrimination. The cheerful hairdresser from Trinidad, dressed in a shocking pink polo shirt, is convinced that it all depends on your own attitude, if you're positive and greet people with laughter, you get laughter in return. I laughed back at him, and wondered if it only worked that way in the tolerant northern part of Europe. Or maybe it is the south that is more tolerant, because, as Lolo, a Cape Verdian said: 'The Portuguese themselves are not exactly white.'

You can't give up, let them make you a victim. You have to make something of yourself, according to the successful immigrants. Take Aimée who immigrated from the Congo to Romania. His story was so interesting that it made it into *The New York Times*: he is a coach, the only black one in the country anyway, of a football team that has a one-armed goal keeper. 'There were camera crews on the touchline, and now everybody recognizes me,' he said. Except in the MacDonald's on the Piata Unirii, so at least we could drink our coffee in peace. He said he was fully integrated: married to a Romania woman, he has children and he pays his taxes. He manages a construction firm, but also has some souvenir shops on the beach. 'I work hard, and make a good living, but everything is above board, which is not often the case in my branch of work. Because sooner or later, you'll be caught out.' Aimée also looks like a football coach; legs spread wide, he was wearing a shiny blue shell suit and big white sneakers, and he had a fancy telephone. Be like the Romanians, he preached, work, integrate. Take a language course, they're free. Don't rely on social services for too long. 'I am proof that you can achieve anything if you work hard.' Not everything, apparently, but more about that later.

Moroccan-born Rachid, who now works in a gift shop in Brussels, was another straight shooter. It wasn't busy, so he had time to talk, and said he could chat and unpack copper water pipes at the same time: it wasn't that complicated. 'This is not the right place for me,' he said, as he produced a copy of his CV for me: he always has a few on him. 'I have an education; I even have a Microsoft certificate,' he said. 'I want to leave this job, it doesn't pay enough, and I have to work under the table to make ends meet.'

'Is that so bad?'

'Yes, it amounts to stealing from the government.'

They don't come any more honest than that. If you're hiring, I'll send you his CV.

These newcomers owe their success to hard work, to having done their best, and they expect the same from others. Madame Paule, one of my favourite Youropeans, who served me fresh mango juice in her beautiful art-deco style hairdressing salon, put it this way: 'I come from Martinique, but I will always respect France, the country that welcomed me. And I think that all newcomers should do the same. But many of them live off France, take everything, but still criticize. Why don't they leave? Take same boat or plane they came and go back home!'

But Thierry thought that native Europeans should also make more effort. A Hungarian friends was complaining to him about being unable to find work in Budapest. But he spoke English, didn't he? And German? Why not go to Vienna? Oh no, that was not an option; he would miss his family, he couldn't go to Austria on his own? The Cameroonian thought this was typical Hungarian behaviour. People move all the way from Africa to find work, and his friend could have found a job a two-and-half-hour train journey away.

PASSPORT

No, Aimée did not have everything. He did not have a Romanian passport, for example.

'Didn't you want one?'

'Of course,' he said, and he told me how his passport request is denied every time, and said there were new requirements every year, and that he had to renew his temporary status every year. And that irks even the very calm and collected Aimée. I can't blame him: a month would be enough to make me angry, let alone 23 years. He is not afraid that they will send him back: this is his home. But he would appreciate a little respect.

In Sofia, Hamid also does not have the papers he would like to have. According to him, no black person has ever been given a residence permit; they are all here illegally. 'I have challenged the decision, but if it's negative again, they will deport me. And I am not ready for that,' said the young Ghanaian despondently.

I had learned from Sandra, my Ugandan cleaner, just how complicated and nerve-racking the process is. For starters, the procedure lasts too long – about two years. 'I reached a point when I thought I no longer cared whether it was yes or no, as long as I had an answer. Then at least I could get on with my life.' The fact that her son has Dutch nationality did not constitute grounds for letting her stay. I heard a string of stories about hearings at the Dutch Immigration and Naturalization Department (IND) in Rijswijk, rejected applications, letters from lawyers, meetings with education officers. The rules were unclear, complicated at best, the application fees expensive, sometimes 1,000 euro a pop (too expensive EU law according to one judge handling Sandra's case). At one point I tried to help her write a business plan, because if she was able to demonstrate that she was a promising business start-up she would be allowed to stay. It didn't work although in all honesty I couldn't blame the IND: her plan to promote tourism in East Africa did not seem very solid.

In the end, she was allowed to stay, on humanitarian grounds – and based on EU law.

'They no longer had any reason to refuse.'

'Were you happy?'

'No, I didn't have the energy to be happy, I was simply relieved.'

In Valletta Stephen thought that people should be told within three months whether they would be allowed to stay.

'How would you solve the problem?'

'If I were the government of Malta, I would ask the citizens what they thought of foreigners and immigrants. And if they said they didn't want them, they should stop letting people in, and send everyone back to their own country. But they should leave them in detention centres for eighteen months.'

Fair enough, you might say.

MY FAVOURITES

3 Rido, from Nigeria. He was a charming scoundrel. He admitted to using his looks to his advantage, acting in commercials whenever a dark face was required. 'That means you're against immigration, because more of your kind would mean more competition,' I said. He thought about it, but then decided that his African brothers would be welcome in Zagreb.

2 Hamid, from Ghana. He endeared himself by saying he had come to work in Sofia so that his brother and sister in Ghana could go to school, ('They are more intelligent than I am'). That kind of sacrifice may be unexceptional in Africa, but I was deeply moved.

1 Sandra, of course, from Uganda, whom I know best. She was my cleaner in Amsterdam (she liked to call herself my assistant manager): a sweet, funny woman, and I missed her when I moved to Berlin.

11

BUT YOU'LL ALWAYS BE A FOREIGNER (EVEN IF YOU CAN SING THE NATIONAL ANTHEM WHILE STANDING ON YOUR HEAD)

Expats. Foreign-born westerners who did not have to undertake a dangerous journey to reach Europe. They usually arrive by plane, and enter through the front door. They come for a variety of reasons, for example for love, which may be the best reason of all. Helvia moved from the Netherlands to Italy when she was 28. Claudio left Italy and moved to Latvia for his girlfriend. Sometimes both lovers move to a new country: Anna, who is Russian, accompanied her Australian ex-husband and lived with him in Kazakhstan and Ukraine before ending up in Prague, where she has been managing an elegant jewelry store for the past sixteen years. Illah followed a similar path from The Hague to Slovakia, where she works as a photographer. Some, like Egor from Siberia, followed their parents: 'My mother was a TV show presenter and my father a magazine editor. They wanted to emigrate, and they had to choose between the US and the Czech Republic. They made the wrong choice,' Egor said. He is nineteen, wears two big black earrings, and works at the reception desk in a hip hotel, although he sees his main job as that of lead singer in a hard rock band. Then are those who move mainly out of curiosity: your laptop works everywhere, and so you can work everywhere. That's what I did: In in May 2015 I exchanged my apartment in Amsterdam for one in Berlin. Religion can also be a driving force. The evangelist Michael was convinced there were enough sheep behind the Iron Curtain who could be tempted back into the flock. He and his family moved to Poland, where he now runs a big volunteer organization distributing food and clothing to the poor.

Or love of music: Minori, who is Japanese, is a soprano who was invited to study in Vienna, the capital of classical music. That was five years ago, and now she's waiting tables in a sushi restaurant, mincing her steps and wearing a traditional long, narrow Japanese skirt. Andrea meets the textbook definition of an expat: an Italian invited to teach at London's prestigious Imperial College for a few years.

You might be more inclined to think of José as an immigrant: he joined the huge Portuguese community in Luxembourg when he was twenty-five. 100,000 of Luxembourg's total population of 600,000 are of Portuguese origin. They now have their own political party, and more importantly, clubs supporting their football teams back in Portugal. I found José one Sunday morning in the Sporting Braga clubhouse. A group six or so men were seated at the bar watching a rerun of a Portuguese football match. José, who is short and stocky, with a weathered face, joined me – a Campari on ice in his hand – at my table for the interview.

'What do you for work?'

'I'm the chairman,' he said proudly.

'But what do you do for a living?'

'Oh you mean that. I work in construction,' he said quietly.

He is like so many other Portuguese *gastarbeiders,* brought in to do the heavy work. But now they also work for banks and the ministries, like real Luxembourgers (this a country of office workers and civil servants, not entrepreneurs).

Cecilia is Argentinian, but she now lives in Madrid, which she reached circuitously via Paraguay, Bolivia, Sudan, Chad, Sweden and the Netherlands.

'How did that happen?'

'I wanted to see Europe and my university in Argentina had an arrangement with a Dutch university. I thought, that's a nice centrally located country to use as a basis to see the rest. I ended up in Leiden, but it was boring, so I moved to Amsterdam.'

An alumnus of Leiden University, I wisely decided to ignore the insult.

LANGUAGE IS THE KEY TO A COUNTRY

So there were all kinds of reasons for wanting to move, but for expats, the threat of war or some other emergency situation were not among them. I wondered if that made a difference, if it was easier then to make your way in a new country. Apparently it is, especially if you move from a rich country to a poor one, instead of the other way around. Linda, Michael, and Mark came from English-speaking countries (Ireland, Australia and England) and now live in the Baltic states. Linda and Michael teach English.

Illah from The Hague told me that people simply couldn't understand why on earth she wanted to come to Bratislava.

A waitress asked what we wanted to have for lunch, Illah ordered in Slovakian.

'Sounds good', I said.

'People sometimes think I'm Slovakian. And if not that, maybe Czech, but definitely not Dutch. And that's what people appreciate most, the fact that I've learned their language.'

She thinks that language is the key to a country: language brings with it another way of thinking, a greater understanding of a country's culture.

CAZZO! MANNAGGIA! CHE STRONZO!

Helvia is definitely fluent in her new country's language, as I learned when sat down next to her in her Fiat. She swore, sound her horn, and parked in the middle of the street on a small square.

That's what I thought at least, but it turned out to be the *seconda fila*, a second row of cars parked behind the first; if you want out you have to sound your horn until someone hurries out of a shop or café to move their car. When in Rome ... 'Yeah, I have heard that I've become too Italian. Too exuberant, and not prepared to live by all those dumb rules.' But you never really become one of them. She has noticed when she picks her children up from school that other mothers are allowed to complain, but not her. They look at her as if to ask: 'Then what are you doing here?' Sometimes she loses her temper and reminds them that she has been paying taxes for fifteen years, and has also had to swear on the flag of their damned country.

Laura also moved here from the Netherlands, as a child.

'When does someone become Italian?'

'My sister's son and daughter are Italian. So are my sisters. I am not, but that is because of what I do for a living: I am an artist.' Every region in Italy has its own identity — the country hasn't existed all that long. She said that she had worked a lot with Italians from the south a few years ago, and that they were also regarded as foreigners.

You can become British, according to Mark. Second-generation Pakistanis, for example, go to cricket matches and speak with the accent of the city they come from. But you can't become Lithuanian. 'Technically, yes,' the Englishman in Vilnius said, taking a big swig from his pint. He could renounce his British citizenship and apply for a Lithuanian passport (double nationality is not allowed), but even if he fought in the army, he would still be a foreigner. Lithuanians of Russian origin, who account for approximately 10 percent of the population, are still seen as Russian. Like Mark's girlfriend.

Anna, who manages a jewelry store in the Czech Republic, is also a Russian, or strictly speaking, a Kazakh.

'Does it create problems for you, the reputation of your fellow countrymen?'

'There are different kinds of Russians — two types really,' she told me in her office/private showroom above her shop, which has showcases full of rings, necklaces and other expensive items. 'You have those who are really poor, and you have the newly rich. And neither of them has a very good reputation, I know that. But I am neither.' Her parents were university professors in Alma Ata, and she herself looks like someone one of her clients would rather give a beautiful ring to than to their wives. There are probably people who hold her personally responsible for the invasion of Czechoslovakia, but there is nothing she can do about that, she said. People are unfriendly to her in the streets, and at first she thought it was personal, but she now knows that the Czechs are simply a bit morose.

Egor, a young compatriot, found it more difficult to adjust. 'It didn't help that I'm a metal head with long hair, wearing a Sepultura T-shirt.' Later he showed me a map if Russia on his iPhone, and told me he came from Novosibirsk, in Siberia. It has a population of over a million and a half and is the third largest city in Russia.

'You are actually an Asian,' I said.

'Russia doesn't care whether it's Europe or Asia. It's just Russia, and it occupies a third of the world's land mass.'

IT'S HARD TO TELL PEOPLE APART IN TALLINN, WHERE EVERYONE HAS BLOND HAIR AND BLUE EYES

Irene, a red-haired Ukrainian, manages the breakfast room in my Dublin Hotel; her guests are her audience and she pours coffee and clears plates with a song and a great sense of theatricality. In 2000 the Irish government encouraged large number of foreigners to come to Ireland to work on farms and in the hospitality industry. And if your new country needs you, they are inclined to give you a hearty welcome. 'From the minute I landed here, things went well. I never felt uncomfortable,' Irene told me. She speaks English with a heavy accent, but carefully, as if treating it with respect. She is happy to be where she is, and her life here is easier.

Her daughter attends a good (and expensive) international school, and the bank gave her a sizeable loan for her house. 'I would never have got that in my country,' she said.

'My country, you said, but you meant Ukraine.'

'Oops,' she said.

José, the Portuguese Luxembourger, also came as a *gastarbeider*, but an uninvited one.

'Are you fully accepted here?'

'Almost, but sometimes you notice that it's better not to make waves.'

He lit a cigarette, poured himself another Campari, and glass of port for me. It was half past eleven on a Sunday morning and I hadn't had breakfast yet, but I don't want to be rude. 'There is a good Portuguese-Luxembourgish football team, which reached the cupfinal a few years ago. *We* were much better, but the referee was – how can I put this – blatantly unfair.' He also notices it more now that unemployment has risen; Luxembourgers favour their own people over newcomers.

Being married to a local also speeds up the integration process, said Claudio in Riga and Michael in Tallinn. Michael mentioned the genetic homogeneity in Estonia, something which I had noticed too. Everyone is blond or dark blond, and blue eyes are predominant.

'Because of my work as a teacher I have met a lot of people. I keep running into people in the street, and thinking I know them. But I'm not always certain, so what can I do? Not say hello? That would be unfriendly and rude. So I greet them with the wrong name. Or somebody greets me and I don't know who they are: they might be my former students.'

'Are you getting better at it?'

'No. I understand that your brains are programmed to a specific society, and mine is Australian society, with all its different types and races. The homogeneity here means that people, locals as well, seek eye contact with one another. If you recognize someone you should give a little nod, and if they nod back, then you know it's alright.'

How hard was it to get the right papers in a new country? Not that hard, apparently. Illah's story was typical. She was asked to bring her rental agreement and employment contract to the most hard-to-find office building in Bratislava, on the far side of the Donau where the busses don't run. The lack of customer service there is legendary. No toilets, no coffee. You have to fill in your forms there; nothing is available online to download. And when it is finally your turn they ask you: 'Do you have this stamp?' Of course you don't, so you have to go back to post office. Illah first got papers for three years, and then for five years, after which she can apply for a passport. She recently noticed that things have improved slightly. There are now two departments, one for Europeans and another for non-European applicants. The European one has a toilet and a better waiting room.

'The first time I applied for residence permit, sometime in 2004, Lithuania had just joined the EU. The only form they had was in Russian. The civil servant began to ask me all kinds of difficult questions, and was reluctant to cooperate at all until I explained that I wasn't submitting a request, I was simply collecting a permit he was obliged to give me.' Mark, 36, hip round glasses, is an artist/music producer, whose Facebook page describes his profession as 'Immigrant in Lithuania'. His letter to the president of the country, thanking him for joining the EU and giving him a wonderful new life, ended up on the front page of a national newspaper. The publicity took Mark by surprise, but he is proud of it. 'But, let's be honest here,' he said, 'the result of this European freedom of movement is that it is not really immigration anymore. I just moved to a different city: I could just as easily have moved from London to Leeds.'

The same is true for me. The difference between Amsterdam and Berlin is not that big, nor is the actual distance. The more important factor is that Berlin, like so many of the world's big cities, is international: I'm not exactly the only foreigner here. And the city is geared to that. Internationally, people's requirements are more or less the same everywhere in terms of food, clothing and house furnishings, and the people who provide those things are also international. Of course, it took me some time figure out the most efficient way to use public transport, where the nearest gym was, and it took a ridiculously long time to get an internet connection. (To get one I had to 1) be registered in Berlin, so that 2) I could open a German bank account, and only then could I 3) enter into a contract with a provider. And each of those three steps took time – a lot of time – because banks and internet providers are officious here too.) But it took me no time at all to get acquainted with my neighbours. Those on my floor, who had lived there for 41 years (they were real *Ossies*: my apartment is in East Berlin), showed up on the first day, and I heard my downstairs neighbours before I met them, late at night when I was ready to go to bed. They are three students and I only had to stomp on the floor once to get them to turn down the volume. They invited to dinner the next day.

MY FAVOURITES

3 Cecilia. There is not much in this chapter about the Argentinian, now resident in Madrid, but that is not because she had nothing interesting to say. We talked about her work as well as about Europe. For example, about the fact the Argentinian do not get as worked up about a financial crisis as we do. They have one every ten years, and in 2020 the country was bankrupt.

2 Mark, from England. Lithuania's Best Immigrant. National champion, and I had no trouble believing that he could compete the European title.

1 Helvia, who is Dutch , and who in addition to being an expat/immigrant, was also my guide, precariously navigating the streets of Rome in her beat-up old car.

YOUROPEANS!

DOCTORS

Hilde Amsterdam

Kostas Athens

Matthias Berlin

András Budapest

Maria Bucharest

Romana Bratislava

Benoît Brussels

Margaret Dublin

Pippa Helsinki

Azadeh Copenhagen

Maria Lisbon

Mateja Ljubljana

Jeanette London

Frank Luxembourg

IMMIGRANTS

Sandra Amsterdam

Yonous Athens

Joe Berlin

Thierry Budapest

Aimée Bucharest

Illah Bratislava

Rachid Brussels

Irene Dublin

Egor Prague

Omnia Helsinki

Andy Copenhagen

Camila Lisbon

Max Ljubljana

Andrea London

HAIR-DRESSERS

Salvatore Amsterdam

Nikos Athens

Angelique Berlin

Péter Budapest

Diana Bucharest

Abi Bratislava

Fred Brussels

Sean Dublin

Joni Helsinki

Andy Copenhagen

Mauro Lisbon

Stevo Ljublajana

Emile London

Lionel Luxembourg

ARTISTS

Pierre Amsterdam

Bob Athens

Suzan Berlin

Ferenc Budapest

Dilmana Bucharest

Els Brussels

Oliver Dublin

Hanna Helsinki

Finn Copenhagen

Pedro Lisbon

Maša Ljubljana

Nicky London

Bruno Luxembourg

Ferran Madrid

LOCAL CELEBRITIES

Felix Rottenberg Amsterdam

Peter Economides Athens

Luise Neumann-Cosel Berlin

Judit Polgár Budapest

Andrei Rosu Bucharest

Anton Srholec Bratislava

Herman van Rompuy Brussels

Ollie Cole Dublin

Stefan Lindfors Helsinki

Henrik Larsen Copenhagen

Salvador Mendes de Almeida Lisbon

Tina Maze Ljubjana

Omid Djalili London

Xavier Bettel Luxembourg

 **Cayetana Álvarez de Toledo** Madrid
 **Konstantinos Charalambidis** Nicosia
 **JC de Castelbajac** Paris

 **Lenny Trčková** Prague
 **Kaspars Daugavins** Riga
 **Sara Ricci** Rome

 **Merlin Konstantinova** Sofia
 **David Batra** Stockholm
 **Piret Järvis** Tallinn

 **Ira Losco** Valletta
 **Romas Zabarauskas** Vilnius
 **Maciej Orłoś** Warsaw

 **Cathy Zimmermann** Vienna
 **Lidija Horvat-Dunjko** Zagreb

ENTRE-PRENEURS

Inez Amsterdam

Yiannis Athens

Oliver Berlin

Roy Budapest

Dragos Bucharest

Juraj Bratislava

Patrick Brussels

Owen Dublin

Aare Helsinki

Birgitte Copenhagen

Antonio Lisbon

Guy London

Mike Luxembourg

Martin Madrid

POLICE OFFICERS

Verona Amsterdam

Spiro Athens

Frau Jabukowski Berlin

László Budapest

Mariana Bucharest

Christian Bratislava

Nancy Brussels

Dennis Dublin

Delphine Frontex

Joanna Helsinki

John Copenhagen

Paolo Lisbon

Igor Ljublajan

Serge Luxembourg

SEX WORKERS

Eva Amsterdam
Anna Athens
Marie Berlin
Vikki Budapest
Laura Bucharest
Nicola Bratislava
Monique Brussels
Rosa Dublin
Leila Helsinki
Claudia Copenhagen
Lolo Lisbon

Kira Nicosia
Angie Paris
Melissa Prague
Daniela Riga
Carolina Rome
Diana Sofia
Julia Stockholm
Serena Tallinn
Maria Valletta
Kim Vilnius
Bojanna Warsaw
Jojette Vienna

Nika Ljubljana

Charlotte London
Anabela Luxembourg
Isabella Madrid

Elizabeth Zagreb

12

HOW ABOUT THE NEW NEIGHBOURS?

154 A random news item in June 2015, when I was writing this article: 'Sixty people have been arrested during an anti-immigration protest in the Slovakian capital Bratislava. They attacked people watching a cycling race and destroyed police cars. The march was a protest against the European Commission's plan to distribute 40,000 asylum seekers over European countries. According to the allocation system, Slovakia is required to accept 785 migrants. People were urged via Facebook to take to the streets. Approximately 5,000 protestors were present, shouting slogans such as "Stop the Islamization of Europe" and "Europe for the Europeans". Towards the end of the march, incidents occured.'*

---

* This was the situation at the end of June 2015. Before the train stations in Budapest and Vienna were overrun with refugees, before Slovenia and Balkan countries built high walls along their borders, before even Sweden decided to close the bridge connecting the country to Denmark to refugees. This was the moment the term 'mini-Schengen' first appeared. It was before all the other things that have happened, and are still to come.

STATISTICS: THIS IS WHAT WE THINK ABOUT IMMIGRATION

Immigrants come from inside the EU (intra-communal) or from outside (extra-communal). According to Eurostat the two categories accounted for equal numbers of immigrants in 2013: 1.3 million. The number of people from outside the EU is rising sharply, but it is not clear by precisely how much. Germany expects 800,000 in 2015 alone, and the UNHCR is constantly adjusting its estimates upwards.

This is what the 2014 Eurobarometer said: a very small majority of Europeans favours intra-communal immigration: 52%. The most positive attitudes can be found in Sweden (82%), Finland (76%), Denmark (69%), Luxembourg (72%), Spain (64%) and Portugal (63%). Germany and Great Britain are the favourite destinations: in 2013 they welcomed 354,000 and 201,000 immigrants, respectively, from other EU countries. Estonia reported fewer than 1,000 immigrants, and the Netherlands 52,000.

Inter-communal immigration is viewed favourably by a majority of those in the most privileged social and economic categories: 64% of the students, 56% of those who never, or almost never, have trouble paying their bills, and 71% of those who see themselves as upper class.

According to the Eurobarometer, the majority are against extra-communal immigration: 57%. That was in 2014, when this type of immigration affected only Southern Europe. People have a negative view of extra-communal immigration in 23 member states, especially in Latvia (79%), Slovakia (74%) and the Czech Republic (74%), and in the southern countries Greece (75%), Cyprus (75%), Italy (75%) and Malta (73%). Only five countries are in favour of extra-communal immigration; Sweden, where 72% of the population approves of extra-communal immigration is the extreme outlier.

Great Britain and Germany took in the largest number of immigrants in 2013 (250,000 each), but Italy also accepted 201,000 immigrants. Most countries receive fewer than 10,000 immigrants a year. Only Austria, Belgium, France, the Netherlands, Poland, and Spain took in more than 25,000 immigrants.

> These are the most recent figures, but it was in 2015 that the influx began to swell alarmingly. The figures for the first quarter of 2015 show that 185,000 people requested asylum in the EU, an increase of 86% over the first quarter of 2014. 40% of them requested asylum in Germany, 18% in Hungary. Taken as a proportion of the total population, Hungary receives by far the most refugees: 3,000 per one million residents. Austria receives 1,100, Germany 900, Malta 800 and the Netherlands 144. Portugal (17), Romania (15), and Croatia (9) are at the bottom of the list.
>
> Conclusion: the countries on the front line of the immigration crisis are the most negative. The exception is Slovakia: 74% are against immigration even though the country takes in fewer than 500 immigrants a year, only 9 per one million inhabitants. However, that striking ratio may reflect the fact that because immigrants are unpopular, almost none are admitted, and almost no one is given a residence permit. A similar situation prevails in Japan, which has an extremely strict immigration policy: only 6 out of a total of 5,000 applications were honoured in 2014. That is however a 100% increase over 2013, when 3 applications were approved. Worldwide an average of 32% of all asylum applications are accepted.

It began in the Canary Islands, where the first immigrants landed, but when the Spanish marines stepped up their patrols, the influx stopped. Ceuta and Melilla, Spanish enclaves located on Moroccan territory, have long been the preferred route for immigration into the European Union.

But the Lampedusa route is by far the most popular, although those who are unlucky end up on Malta. As mentioned earlier, Greece is less popular because although it is part of the Schengen area, it is surrounded by non-Schengen countries, and most refugees want to travel to a Schengen country. That is why Hungary decided to erect a 4 metre-high wall along its 150 kilometre border with Serbia in the summer of 2015.

Syrians have also long preferred the Lampedusa route even though travelling overland through Turkey was the more logical choice. The Turks, however, long maintained very tight control over both its land and sea borders. At the time of writing, in the autumn of 2015, roughly 5,000 immigrants a day were attempting the 10 kilometre journey.

Feeling runs high about immigration. Barely recovered from the financial crisis, Europe faces a new challenge. And according to many of those who, like Chancellor Angela Merkel, understand the issues, this is a greater challenge than the financial crisis. She is convinced that Germany could rise to the challenge: *'Wir schaffen das'*, (the German equivalent of 'yes, we can') is what she said many times during the autumn of 2015. The refugee problem divides countries, as well as people. It is not something that can be shrugged off. Everyone has an opinion, including the Youropeans I spoke to.

POLICE OFFICERS: OPEN BORDERS ARE A BAD IDEA

'Do you know how many Luxembourgers are in prison here?' Serge clearly did not expect a reply from me; he answered the question himself: 'Not many.'

One group of people who oppose further immigration from either within or outside of the EU are the police. John, a canine police officer from Copenhagen – the big friendly giant – thinks that it was not wise to eliminate all border controls, especially not so quickly. European legislation is too different: in Belgium, for example, it is easy to buy guns of a certain calibre, but in Denmark you have to be a member of a gun club for two years before you can buy the same weapons. Anybody can drive to Belgium, buy a weapon and bring it back to Denmark. He and his colleagues have seen an influx of weapons from Eastern Europe, and pepper spray purchased in Germany. He has also noticed that some newcomers are so cut off from the rest of society that they turn to crime: they are overrepresented in crime statistics.

Police officer Nancy works in a difficult neighbourhood in the northern part of Brussels. She also thinks that the free movement of people is problematic: it makes it too easy for criminals to come to Belgium, the promised land, and do whatever they like there. She thinks there is too little control. Airports have tightened controls, but many, many people from poorer countries arrive by bus. 'And if I stop them in the street and ask them for their papers', they say "sans papier". And if we do not know where somebody comes from, we cannot send them back.'

Serge is even more blunt. He worked on the street in the centre of Luxembourg for a long time, where black immigrants aggressively muscled their way into the drugs business in 2003. The problem, according to him, is that these young men have nothing to lose; often they're better off in a Luxembourg jail than they are on the streets of West Africa. He even knew criminals who wanted to be arrested. They would do a minor break-in – a bus or something – just enough to secure room and board at the state's expense until the spring. He has very outspoken ideas (and not only about immigration, which is great for a journalist, and unusual for a policeman). 'The EU was once a good thing. The open borders are the problem; that's when we lost control. And European legislation makes it damned hard to do anything about it. Twenty years ago, if we had a problem with a Frenchman or an Italian, we put them on a train and turned them over to customs control. That's no longer possible. Luxembourg has an extremely mixed population: 52% is foreign-born. A good thing, except when those new cultures try to force us to live according to their norms. When I'm in another country, I adjust. My wife and I like to travel, also to Arabic countries. We take our shoes off in the mosque, my wife doesn't sunbathe topless. But we accept too much. When you're here you should respect our rules and laws and behave accordingly.'

THE BACKDOOR TO CYPRUS IS WIDE OPEN

Theognossia does not look like a police woman. She is pint-sized and not wearing a uniform but jeans and instead of a severe haircut, has unruly curls hiding a pair of sunglasses.

'Are there more immigrants these days?' I asked as we were driving through her beat, which borders the Turkish part of Cyprus. It was not even an official police car, but her dented Renault-whatever, with a bunch of magazines on the back seat. We had just had lunch at a place where she is a regular — a fairly bohemian restaurant close to the wall that dissects Nicosia in much the same way as the Berlin wall once divided that city.

'Yes, and it makes our work more difficult. I am not a racist and I like people from all different cultures, and I don't want to generalize…'

'But?'

'But, having said all that, we do not exactly get the best people from those countries. Romanians do a lot of breaking and entering. And Cypriots do not pull a knife in a fight; Romanians and Georgians do.'

'The loss of innocence?'

'We were not prepared for this.'

She talked extensively about the occupation and about the border — it touches the life of every Cypriot. I wanted to see for myself so I set off walking through the centre of Nicosia. At the end of a shopping street I strolled past a small booth used by the Greek-Cypriot police and continued down a narrow street along a blind wall approximately one hundred metres long. I passed through the UN zone at the mid-point and approached the Turkish Cypriot customs post. They were alert: a customs officer checked her computer, saw that my criminal record was not all too alarming, looked me over once again and ordered me to remove my sunglasses before flipping through my passport looking for a page to stamp. She did so begrudgingly and with the angry face that seems to come with the job. I was allowed to pass and enter the Turkish zone, where there are a large number of mosques, all with loudspeakers subversively blaring out the call to prayer across the border into the Greek zone. An hour later I had seen enough and I returned to the other side but I was not checked by the Greek Cypriots, nor were cars travelling into the country. This may seem strange, but the explanation is that the Greek-Cypriots do not acknowledge that this is a real border. This border crossing is one of Europe's open back doors: from Turkey it is possible to fly unimpeded to Turkish Cyprus, and from there simply to stroll into the EU.

It is a bizarre situation. Imagine what it would be like if the main shopping street in your own city had a border control post right in the middle, next to your favourite fashion outlet, and just beyond that a boarded up no-man's land controlled by the UN. And that once you passed the next checkpoint you would be entering another country, which is in fact a province of an occupying force. That is what it is like in Nicosia. One of the few the crossing points into North Cyprus is located in the middle of Ledras Street, the city's main shopping street. North Cyprus is recognized only by Turkey, which has occupied the territory since 1974. In recent years, the border has been less hermetically sealed, and Turkish Cypriots sometimes come to shop in the more prosperous Greek Cypriot neighbourhoods, or take advantage of their neighbours' free education and medical facilities.

But not all Greek Cypriots have taken the opportunity to visit the other side since controls were relaxed. 'I refuse to show my passport to travel in my own country,' some of them say. Or they are reluctant to see what has become of the family homes they abandoned in haste. Many, like the home of Youropean doctor Anastassiades, were taken over by Turkish Cypriots or by one of the 200,000 Turks who have come from the mainland over the past few decades. They are sitting at Greek Cypriot tables, sometimes still surrounded by their family photographs.

The once elegant seaside resort of Famagusta, whose famous guests included Elizabeth Taylor and Richard Burton, is now a ghost town. The Turks conquered the city, built a fence around it and denied entry to everyone except the UN soldiers who have been keeping the peace here for decades, patrolling the empty streets. From the beach it is easy to see how over the course of forty years nature has started to encroach on the hotel: here and there a tattered curtain flutters behind broken glass.

I heard this version of the story from my Greek-Cypriot hosts in Nicosia. The Berlin of the Mediterranean. Maybe the Turks see things differently, you never know.

Ana, the attractive Croatian police officer ('they select on the basis of looks'), works for the customs police at the airport in Zagreb, where she has seen the increase in immigration with her own eyes. She has noticed a big difference since 1 July 2013, when the country became a member of the EU, even though Croatia is still a transit country for immigrants hoping to reach other, richer countries. The chance of finding illegal immigrants trying to enter the country is greatest on flights from Turkey. 'But also from Brazil and Columbia.' She sits in her booth scanning the incoming passengers (particularly the good-looking men; she and her female colleagues in the next booth rate them).

'And finally, once they're standing in front of me, I have to judge whether they are legitimate. Do they have the right passport? Is it false? Are they Syrian, not Turkish? It's very difficult. And someone who's here illegally may refuse to have their fingerprints taken, or to request asylum.'

'Why?'

'Because you can only do that once in the EU.' That is the consequence of the Dublin Regulation, and refugees are now well aware of this.

'What happens then?'

'We have to lock them up for six months to a year. After which they try again to cross the border illegally. And if they get caught again, we lock them up again. Right now we have sixty of them here in Zagreb, a lot of whom happen to be Somalis.'

NOT IN MY BACK YARD

The Italian psychiatrist Nicolò is familiar with the immigrants because his brother-in-law has a holiday home on Lampedusa, and Helvia had seen busloads of refugees being dropped off at an empty building across the street her house. It was a crazy situation, she recalled. The neighbourhood gathered at the front of the building to gawk at the Africans, most of whom went straight out the back door with their bag in hand, climbed over the fence and disappeared, on their way to some other place in Europe.

In addition to police officers, the other group of Youropeans who object the most to the arrival of the immigrants, are those who are directly in contact with them because their country is a main port of entry to Europe: the Italians and the Maltese. And possibly the Greeks, but I did not ask Athenian Youropeans about this when I was there in March 2014. At the time, the Troika was the most important source of concern in Athens, and the refugee route through Greece was not as popular as it later became.

Nicolò and the other Italians who had first-hand (or maybe second-hand) experience of the problem took a measured approach: 'We have to ensure that these people become part of society as soon as possible. It is not enough to say "we don't want them", or to send the boats back. If we do that, the problem will not go away.'

Artist Laura felt that the behaviour of the people in Sicily and Puglia was exemplary, despite all the problems and the horrors they were experiencing. 'Just think of the fishermen who find bodies in their nets. But they are really helping.'

'What should Europe do?'

'If the African countries were as rich and as politically stable as European countries are, the people would not have to flee; we should help them achieve this.' She also knows immigrants, in Prato: some 300,00 Chinese work in the textile industry there, close to her previous house in Florence. They came illegally, like the factories they work in. They have 'stolen' jobs from Italians. According to Laura, their presence has changed the city much too rapidly. 'People did not have a problem with African immigrants, but the Chinese? They spit on the ground, kill their cats and hang the skins out on the wash line.'

'How artistic,' was my slightly misplaced comment.

'No, because it stinks. People tried forge a relationship with them, but it was difficult because they do not speak Italian.'

'Have there been any incidents?'

'No. It was all very polite, and limited to verbal complaints on the part of the Italians.'

That this shouldn't be Italy's problem is something everyone agrees on, but not always for the same reasons. Stefano, who is Italian and a police officer (so his opinion counts double) thinks that if they do nothing Italy will end up with a Muslim president, and he's not having it. 'Yes, the most worrying consequence of mass immigration is that in twenty years there will be more Muslims than Christians in Europe. 'The autochthon populations of France, Italy and Germany all have zero population growth, but the Muslims have a high birth rate,' he said. 'Don't get me wrong – I don't hate Muslims, but I am an Italian, I am European, and I do not want to be ruled by Muslims.' This happened to be the plot Michel Houllebecq's latest novel *Submission*, but I doubt that this is where Stefano got the idea.

'How should Europe solve this problem?'

'Help people there! Afghanistan, Egypt, Syria. Of course people flee if they are in danger. But what can we do? We can't shoot them, or send the boats back like Australia does. No! We have to make a deal with their government – if they have one. And we need to transfer some of our wealth to these countries, to these people.'

Luca, who owns a restaurant and food export business, is even more decided. He thinks they should only be admitted if they have a job.

'Should Europe help?' I asked.

'Absolutely,' the Roman said angrily. 'But they do nothing.'

Or maybe Europe does help, if we are to believe Sara, local celebrity. Seated at a table in a popular cafe, where she definitely doesn't mind being seen, she tells me what many people know, but which she discloses in a conspiratorial whisper (she is an actress after all): 'Italy receives a lot of money from Brussels to deal with these people. And I suspect that much of it ends up in the pockets of politicians. They give the refugees food and water for a few days, and then let them go. Politicians… it won't be long before they try to sell the Colosseum too.'

'What is the solution?'

'I think they should have a place somewhere in the middle of Europe that is devoted to the care of foreigners. Paid for by all of us, not just Italians.'

'But where?'

'I don't know. Maybe Germany?' Sara smiled, fairly pleased to have come up with what she thought was such an obvious solution.

On Malta, doctor David placed the influx of immigrants in an historical perspective by noting that the island has for centuries been influenced by foreign cultures. Its location is strategic, and it was where crusaders from all over Europe gathered before starting out on their crusade. 'But, how should I put it… not everyone comes with best of motives.' A bit like the crusaders, actually.

'Is it easier to accept someone who arrived by plane from Germany than someone who came on a leaky boat?'

'Yes, I think it is, and that has nothing to do with racism.'

The Maltese are in fact racist, at least where Libyans are concerned, said the forthright artist Celia. 'You don't want your daughter marrying an Arab,' she said a little more quietly. They are seen as second-class citizens. 'And all those refugees. Of course they have to be saved. But the island is small.'

Kira is a Ukrainian on Cyprus, Isabella a Romanian in Madrid. Julia a Pole in Sweden, Rosa an Indian in Dublin: immigrants are over-represented in the sex industry. And you will see very few Dutch women sitting in the windows of Amsterdam's famous red light district. This is not surprising: sex workers ply their trade in places where they can remain anonymous, and where the clients are the richest. And that is almost never in their own country. I do not have the percentages, but based on my own limited empirical research in 28 cities, I noticed that most sex workers come from Romania and Bulgaria.

But if sex workers are local, they often live and work in less prosperous neighbourhoods, the ones that have been most affected by immigration in recent decades. Claudia's comments were similar to those I had heard before: 'Nørrobro my neighbourhood in Copenhagen was the nicest place in world ten years ago. Now it is Little Turkey. The Danes have fled the neighbourhood. And the immigrants do not respect women. Or show any respect for Denmark. They visit the sex club, the Muslims. Even during Ramadan, and even though it's against their religion. No, I don't like them. There's probably nothing wrong with Islam, but there is something wrong with those people. They are the reason that there is so much war in the world.'

'THE EU COULD DO A LOT TO PREVENT MASS IMMIGRATION'

There are those who have fewer objections to immigration. Immigrants themselves, for example. Like Yonous from Afghanistan and Max from Zimbabwe, both of whom work to improve the lives of their fellow immigrants. Yonous, the head of the Forum for Refugees in Athens is particularly active in this area. The Afghan pointed out that only a small fraction of the enormous number of refugees – 60 million around the world – reaches Europe: three percent. And only four percent of Syrian refugees.

'But the actual number can still be high,' I said to Yonous.

'The problem is not nearly as serious as in Turkey. I know that when you see Lampedusa on television it looks terrible, but in reality it's not that bad.' But there is still more than enough work for him. He was scheduled to meet with the European Commission for Migration and Asylum Seekers the following week. 'Look, this immigration problem really is a European problem. And it cannot be solved if the European Union does not function properly.'

'You get around, don't you?' I said.

> **PERCENTAGE OF REFUGEES IN EUROPE**
>
> The percentages that Yonous quoted are not often mentioned during debates about immigration, but they are correct, and they place the issue in a different perspective. Not a single European country is included in the UNCHR's list of the top 10 destinations for refugees. Turkey and Pakistan are the uncontested frontrunners (1.5 million each), but tiny Lebanon and Jordan also receive huge number of immigrants, mostly as a result of the war in neighbouring Syria. Lebanon has 1.15 million refugees even though its own population is barely 4 million.

'Well, yes. Cecilia Malmström, who is the Swedish representative on the Commission, visits Greece every year to monitor immigration policy. She talks, looks, listens, and visits detention centres. The last time the Commission congratulated me because everything looked so good. 'But you don't think it always looks like that?' I asked. "I know, I know." She sighed.'

'What should we do? Create an even stronger Fort Europe or allow people to come in?'

I asked in Ljubljana. Grey hair, 54 years old, serious eyes behind the round frames of his glasses. Did Max, the calm Slovenian Zimbabwean, have the answer? He did. According to him, we need to change the policies that leads to mass immigration. Immigration is usually the result of conflict. Most of which is unnecessary, and the EU could play a role by ensuring that these wars do not take place. For example, by ensuring that the money multinationals earn in those countries does not flow untaxed back to Europe and the US. Multinationals are able to avoid paying taxes simply because they have better lawyers than African countries. And subsidy policies: The EU heavily subsidizes its farmers, who dump their products on African markets. At the same time, when an African country asks for a loan, the International Monetary Fund (IMF) demands liberalisation of their agriculture market, and says they are not allowed to subsidise their farmers. The result is poverty in Africa and more movement of people. 'So yes, the borders should be opened on humanitarian and socio-economic grounds, and I have not even mentioned the fact that the ageing European population could use some new blood.'

Well, there's that sorted then.

FULL IS FULL? BUT FOREIGNERS IN YOUR FOOTBALL ARE OKAY

A lot of entrepreneurs would agree that fresh blood is needed. Barbara, who manages Hotel Beethoven in Vienna, which I highly recommend, would not know what to do without immigrants, certainly in the tourist industry. 'Austrians cannot be persuaded to clean rooms or wash dishes.' And I also know Dutch entrepreneurs who would give preference to a refugee, who might offer them a job on assumption that they would be more invested in it, and having already taken so much risk to secure a better future, would be excellent employees.

The staff of British entrepreneur Guy is probably fairly representative of London society. 'All colours of the rainbow' he said. 'A wide range of languages is spoken here. 50 percent are British, most of the rest are European. A few Asians, but mostly Europeans.'

'Was that the intention?'

'No, it was not a selection criterion. When we hire new people, we always choose the best, and we don't care where that person comes from.' He is not a supporter of the UK Independence Party, UKIP, and has no problem with Europe. On the contrary, he would be unhappy if the UK was not in the EU. But he is willing to admit that the British social system may be too generous, making the UK a very attractive destination. 'Especially if you are young and Spanish. We have a lot of Spaniards here, and I would have done exactly the same. One of them recently came to my office and asked if I would be one of the references for her passport application. "Of course," I said, "but don't you already have a European passport?" She was afraid that Great Britain would leave the EU, and throw her out. Those fears are out there. It's terrible.'

'UKIP: what can I say,' said the London-based stand-up comedian Omid about the party that makes no bones about its opposition to immigration (and to the EU). He is struck by the perception that the country is full, and that there are too many immigrants. 'Last year, roughly two million Brits were living in the EU, but there are groups who object to the same number of immigrants living here. It is so crazy. The Premier League football teams are full of foreigners; we all eat curry on Sunday, but at the same time we want nothing to do with them.'

'Oh, it is so difficult!' said Coco, the Viennese artist. She expressed what so many artists (and other liberal-minded people) feel: 'We are all equal and refugees should have the same rights as we have, but if you open the borders, too many people will come. And then the system will fail. So I think we should help refugees by creating a great system in their own country, so that they do not have to be depend on us.' And she gives two euro to the two Roma boys I was about to give the brush off to. 'Divide it equally, you hear?'

Markus, a hair artist who works a few hundred metres away in Vienna, has a problem with Turks. Because they always stick together; in some neighbourhoods, all of the shops are Turkish. They only speak German at school, never at home. And that's not good, because people need to integrate, and if you don't speak the language that's not going to happen. Muslim women, for example. It's all right for them to wear the veil, but they need to accept that other women prefer to wear short skirts. If you don't like it, look the other way. 'They are also the only who have a problem with the fact that I'm gay.' He lit a cigarette, and started to go through the list of immigrants. 'The Eastern Europeans are fine. Hungarians are perfect; they learn to speak fluent German very quickly. Slovakians are great too; they're hard workers. And they remember how things used to be, and are really grateful for what they now have.' Take a little, give a little, and make the best of it. That is Markus's motto, and he thinks that the older, more conservative Austrians should try to do the same.

Of course you might expect a world famous chess player and local celebrity in Budapest to have to have an intelligent opinion about the issue, but Judit's views were a bit disappointing. She thinks it is very important to learn from other cultures, and that is why her children go an international pre-school. 'They are already meeting Chinese, Bulgarian and Norwegian children. Accepting and respecting other cultures is important, and it's never too early to start learning that.' It is an opinion you hear a lot among what Eurobarometer categorises as the socially and economically privileged. The slightly gratuitous opinion of people who can afford to be generous.

EVERYONE IS WELCOME IN SWEDEN

Almost no one is unconditionally positive about the arrival of so many newcomers. There are always a few ifs, ands, or buts. Sweden, however, has by far the most positive attitude towards immigration (72 percent pro), something which was borne out by my interviews.

Artist Hedda does not think it is such a crazy idea to open Europe's external borders, because the people who want to come here all have a high energy level and the survival instinct. She thinks they would shake things up a bit (in a good way). 'And from a more philosophical point of view, I find it hard to believe that we refuse to let them in. We have everything here! How can we stand here watching people drown in the Mediterranean Sea? I don't know. Maybe Europe's glory days are over.'

Stand-up comedian David is not joking when he says his country can easily take in ten or twenty million refugees.

One reservation of a medical nature comes from the Swedish general practitioner Ylva. She knows that newcomers, particularly those who are alone, do not speak the language and do not have family here, have a tendency to consume more healthcare because they have more stress, and psychological problems can lead to physical complaints. Nevertheless, the Swedes are willing and able to bear the additional costs.

THE SOLUTION

Frontex, the EU organisation that regulates all of the EU's external borders, is located far away from those external borders, in the centre of Warsaw. They may not have succeeded in making the EU an impenetrable fortress, but they have done a pretty good job with the glass and steel tower that houses their own headquarters. After three thorough checks that would put most airports to shame, I was granted an interview with the intelligent, experienced policewoman Delphine. Accompanied by a communications officer, who zoned out of the conversation after fifteen minutes, possibly assuming that I was an innocuous Dutch journalist who was not going to ask any difficult questions. Which I promptly did, of course, and Delphine answered them.

'Is there a solution? Should we even be trying to stop the refugees from coming?'

'If we do not manage the influx, we cannot guarantee the rights of the newcomers: our EU standards are high: we don't want them to end up on the street.'

'But don't most of the refugees have a fighter's mentality? Aren't they people who don't need to be coddled? They go where the work is. And as result of Europe's ageing population, the amount of work will only increase.'

'There is also a security aspect: we want to be able to refuse entry to those who come with the wrong intentions.'

'Terrorists?'

'For example.'

'Why not stop only those people?'

She thought it was an interesting suggestion, but economically unfeasible, and politically unacceptable.

I found the following recommendations in an article in the Dutch newspaper NRC[7] by Flora Goudappel, professor of European law.
1. Treat the external borders of the Schengen countries as joint borders for which all EU countries are responsible. Help countries like Greece and Italy, make sure that asylum centres there are well equipped, and distribute applicants over all EU countries.
2. Harmonise asylum procedures throughout the EU to prevent refuges from travelling around illegally, shopping for the best conditions.
3. In addition to the asylum procedure, introduce a ruling that would allow economic refugees to do temporary work as needed in Europe.
4. Deport immigrants immediately if they do comply with the procedures.

A EUROPEAN PROBLEM WITH A EUROPEAN SOLUTION

Now that refugees are everywhere, on our own streets, and no longer a television news item about Lesbos or Lampedusa, immigration is suddenly a European problem and not just a Greek or Italian issue. After a series of exhausting negotiations, EU leaders agreed on how many refugees each country should take, but for the most part, the terms of these agreements have not been met.

In the meantime, millions of refugees – economic and political – are seeking a place for themselves in the EU. 'Hundreds of millions in the years to come,' is the fear of Viktor Orbán. Some of them have already scaled the walls of Fort Europe, but have not yet reached their chosen country, while others are still waiting to enter, for example in Macedonia and Serbia.

'*Wir schaffen das*', Mutti Merkel famously said, but public opinion and the ensuing political will had already shifted in most countries: 'we don't want them' is what Europeans were saying (it will be interesting to see how these sentiments are reflected in the new Eurobarometer).

Various European political solutions for the refugee problem have been discussed, starting with what to do about those who are on the move, but have not yet reached the EU. Should we, if possible, hermetically seal the EU's external borders to keep them out? That seems like a bad idea, because what do we expect them to do then? Go back to Syria? Another suggestion involves freezing the movement of refugees and requiring them to stay in whatever country they are in: Croatia, Serbia. Macedonia, Montenegro, Albania. The drawback is that this would cause great disruption in a region that has only recently recovered from a war, while most of these countries are candidates for EU membership anyway.

It is in the interests of the EU to prevent illegal immigration by ensuring that regional reception centres, for example in Turkey, are well equipped and able to guarantee decent living conditions for refugees: enough food, healthcare, and schooling to persuade them to remain there until the situation in Syria improves. And at the same time to prepare refugees for legal immigration, and to help them determine which country is best for them.

ROMA: I DON'T WANT TO GENERALISE, I'M NO RACIST BUT...

It was around half past six in the evening and I was watching a group of gypsy women walk past in single file behind their foreman and enter the Gamla Stan metro station. There were eight or so of them, chattering animatedly, shabby but cheerful, like colleagues who'd just had a good day at work. They are a new phenomenon in Sweden, beggars. They sat on the street, and in doorways, whined that they were *very hungry*, and brandished photos of their offspring while a tear trickled down their cheek.

Gypsies are by definition not bothered about borders, but the open European Union has made things much easier for them. It was to be expected that they would expand their activities to the north: it might be cold there but Swedes are rich, and more importantly they have a world-class social welfare system.

How about the new neighbours?

The arrival of the Roma has sparked a debate. 'Ban begging,' say the Sweden Democrats, the country's most right-wing party. A politically incorrect standpoint there, but not so unusual elsewhere: various Dutch cities, including Amsterdam, have banned begging (although you can ask for money for tuneless caterwauling accompanied by a violin with two strings).

I saw a photo report in a British tabloid a couple of years ago, which included six or so captioned photographs. In the first one, taken from a distance, a man was getting out of an ordinary mid-price car; in the second he took some dirty clothes out of the boot, put them on and went begging. At the end of the day he changed his clothes again and became a respectable citizen again. *They're frauds* screamed the headline in the *Sun* or the *Daily Mail*. That is what the Roma are accused of. What they do is said to be well-organised crime: shadowy syndicates recruit women in Romania for a period of exactly three months. They are assigned begging spots, and given laminated, tear-jerking photos. They work their shift and at the end of the day someone comes along to skim off their earnings.

In civilised Europe, everyone knows that one group of people is fair game: the Roma. They are thieves, everyone knows that. 'You can't call them gypsies,' said policeman Serge in Luxembourg, 'we're supposed to say travellers. We can't send them back because they have EU passports.'

And where would you send them? The Roma are super progressive, and have been proponents of the free movement of people for centuries, they didn't need Schengen for that. To Romania is what most people say, because that's where they come from. 'Gypsies and Romanians have a bad reputation,' 19-year-old Omonia said in Helsinki. 'When I worked in the kiosk I always paid close attention when they came in. You know, they're proud of it; fathers brag about how good their sons can steal.' Madame Paule in Paris also warned me: 'Be careful at Gare du Nord. There are lots of Romanians there, *oh là là,* you have to watch them, they are so fast.'

They are originally from India and Iran, but now most Roma live in the Balkans and, yes, in Romania. When I asked Dragos, an entrepreneur in Bucharest about the Romanian pickpockets in Amsterdam, he interrupted me: 'Hold on, they are gypsies, not Romanians. They are not a Romanian problem, but a European one.' I had read that the Romanian police were working with the Dutch police to address the problem, but Mariana, the charming police officer from Bucharest also confirmed that 'It is mostly Roma who do this, and we can't stop them now that the borders are open.'

'They are seen as Romanian. Does that damage your country's image?'

'We are trying to change that, among other things by participating in an EU-financed project aimed at the reintegration of these people. We are trying to convince them to work instead of steal.' The Bulgarian police officer Anton also denied any connection to the Roma. 'We do not belong to the same ethnic group, and they are not part of historical Bulgaria, which is one of the oldest countries in Europe. And yes, we have problems with them as well. They have the opportunity to lead a normal life, but they don't want to.'

I did not interview any Roma. I'm not crazy: it would have cost me my camera.

13

THE NORTH – SOUTH DIVIDE: ZORBA IS NOT LAZY, HE ENJOYS LIFE

This is Europe

176 The word troika makes me think of a new chocolate ice cream bar, or a martial arts film with Stallone, Schwarzenegger and Van Damme, but in Greece everyone knows it refers to the IMF, the European Bank and European Commission, and that the three of them are out to destroy their country. They drop in every now and then, devils disguised as office clerks, to ask difficult questions and decide whether Greece – the prodigal son – has earned its allowance.

The Troika's torture chambers are located in the Greek Ministry of Finance, which is on Syntagma Square, next to the Nike store and opposite the parliament. But the world has long forgotten that democracy was born two blocks away and that the sport clothing's brand name is derived from the Greek goddess of victory. It is a bit like Brigitte Bardot or Madonna: people say they used to be beautiful.

The Troika was coming and people were ready for them. They did not all come at the same time. There were about twenty of them, and they arrived at ten-minute intervals, which did not seem like a very efficient way of holding a meeting. Police officers cleared a path as they arrived and the car – usually a German make – parked on the pavement in front of the Ministry. Plainclothes police officers, easily recognizable from their earphones, were on high alert, as were the soldiers near the entrance, a little army of ten, while clumps of protestors being held back by the riot squad began to shout even louder into their megaphones. Pretty spectacular you might say, a visit from the Troika. Oh look, another one. A couple of burly suits got out of a grey Mercedes and held the door open for a fresh-faced, impeccably dressed forty-something guy with a stack of files under his arm, and a laptop bag slung over his shoulder. An angry woman – short and thickset – moved to attack him, but was restrained by two of the earphone officers. Calm, almost friendly. Five metres away a few Greeks were waiting at a bus stop, oblivious to what was happening. Spectacle? Not really, the riot squad sees action virtually every day, and every day there are demonstrations somewhere, because people have a lot of time on their hands. That's one advantage of being unemployed.

That was in March 2014, when I visited Athens. The men in their German cars, the Troika, are probably meeting somewhere today too, and there are undoubtedly protestors as well. But for the rest, most of Europe has already put the crisis behind it. In retrospect, the effects were less severe than expected in many countries: relatively few Austrian, Belgian, British, Danish, Dutch, Finnish, German, Luxembourgish or Swedish people were forced to delay the purchase of a new plasma screen or forgo a holiday.

THEY FELT THE EFFECTS

For others, let's say the non-Western European countries, the crisis was sometimes oppressive. And what options do you have, if for example, your clients no longer have any money? The entrepreneurs, the good ones anyway, made adjustments, like Gedas. 'We already had Suit Supply shops in Vilnius and Riga, but plans to open a store in Tallinn were put on the back burner. We are opening there next year.' In Prague, Klara, who is also in the clothing business, but as a designer, had to make a few alterations too. Instead of a big fashion show – a bit impersonal anyway – clients were invited to the store, sometimes for cocktails. Or for a 'Day with Klara' during which clients received personal fashion advice from her. 'A bit like going to see a friend. That feeling.'

Even in hard-hit Cyprus, entrepreneurs found a way of getting around the situation, like George, owner of a hairdressing salon: 'Between 2007 and 2012 our turnover doubled, but last year we lost 12 percent. I can handle it. Fortunately our clients did not desert us for cheaper salons. And we publish a magazine every month.' He proudly showed me a sleek glossy, its red, white and blue cover clearly indebted to Mondriaan, with cartoons he drew himself on pages three and four. George is nothing if not versatile, and the kind of guy you wish well: smart, friendly and hardworking.

Things are tougher for his colleague in Athens, Nikos.

'How's business?' I asked him.

'Bad. Hairdressers who are fired from a salon start working from their home, and they take their clients with them. There's no way we can compete.'

He is a marathon runner whose lean, athletic face shows his unhappiness all the more.

'And they don't pay tax,' he grumbled.

'Do you?'

'Of course.'

The sex workers also felt the crunch, at least Kira on Cyprus did. She saw a drastic fall in prices, and has thirty percent fewer clients, especially during the day. She used to see an average of twelve men a day, who paid her 250 euro each; now four men pay 150 euro.

The police in Cyprus saw a decline in salaries as well as an increase in crime, but Theognossia, the diminutive wannabe-actress, also witnessed the everyday impact of the crisis during house visits in her neighbourhood.

'You have no idea how many people are sitting at home during the day. Sidewalk cafes like these' – she gestured towards them – 'are still full. But people make one cup of coffee last all day. I hope that the crisis will also have a positive effect, and that people will realise what is really important in life, and that it is not money or cars.'

HOW WE GOT INTO THIS MESS

Yes, how did we end up in a financial crisis? I was curious about how Youropeans saw the situation, and whether I asked them this question or not, I got a lot of answers, in Nicosia, Lisbon, Dublin, and above all in Athens. But also in Madrid: 'We were living beyond our means, that much is clear,' Martin said. He is a very experienced and successful entrepreneur for Burger King Restaurants. 'But let's not forget that it was the German banks who loaned money to the Greek, Italian and Spanish real estate sectors. And then made it a European problem and expected the EU to solve it. It was bad for the EU because it has made people more nationalistic.' His walrus-like moustache and deep voice made his arguments sound more convincing. He had made his fortune in the property market, but he diversified just in time – and there's nothing like a Whopper Cheese to ease the pain of a crisis.

But how did we end up here? It is a question that has spawned many a conspiracy theory. Pedro had a few: he sees what others don't see, but maybe that's the artist in him. According to him, Portugal had mortgaged its crown jewels, something they should never have done. He became increasingly angry as he told his story, taking such a furious swig of his beer that Superbock sloshed over the rim of the glass.

'Did they have a choice?' I asked.

'Of course! The big banks blackmailed the government into selling a couple of fantastic companies.' He accidentally brushed his hand against the breast of a passing waitress, as his voice grew louder and his gestures wilder. 'People are becoming more politically aware. They are protesting, just like in the seventies. The system needs to change, become more democratic. Right now we are at the mercy of all kinds of invisible powers.'

The Cypriot cardiologist Anistassiades was angry too, and justifiably so. He had already told me how he had lost his family home as a result of the Turkish occupation in 1974, because it happened to be on the wrong side of the new border. He found himself on the wrong side again, in 2013, after the haircut. Dr. Anistassiades found this hard to swallow. 'We built an enormous banking industry out of nothing, and we made a good living out it, along with tourism. But instead of telling us to place some restrictions on the industry, gradually over a period of three or four years, using the argument that Luxembourg should have the banks, they just left us dangling.' His piercing eyes looked even more fierce, and his voice climbed an octave, as the little man behind an impressively big desk spit out his question: 'Do they want us on our knees so that they can force us to admit Turkey and give them half of our country?' Think about your heart, doctor!

The medicine men have an astute understanding of pretty much everything. When I asked the young doctor Maria in Lisbon about the situation in her country, a grey-haired colleague who was having lunch at another table jumped into the conversation. In fairly basic English he advised us that Brussels — or to be precise monetary union — had created this crisis. The euro fuelled inflation and weakened Portugal's influence in Europe. His words, not mine.

What do they think in Dublin? A few decades ago Ireland was experiencing such strong economic growth that it was known as the Celtic Tiger. 'We made fools of ourselves,' Sean the hairdresser said. 'We wanted to be the best little country in the world, yeah... We shouldn't be complaining about the EU now, on the contrary, we should be glad they're still willing to help us. Look at all the money they have pumped into Ireland over the years!' As in Portugal, that financial support is all too visible here: witness the many bridges bearing that blue and yellow starred insignia.

STAYING POSITIVE

Entrepreneurs are by nature optimistic: they see challenges instead of problems, and opportunities everywhere. According to the businessman Antonio in Lisbon you can fill an entire newspaper with good news. He saw the crisis give rise to a whole new crop of companies: sustainable, creative companies geared to new markets outside Europe, such as Angola, Mozambique and Brazil. Hairdressers also never allow their clients to leave the salon in a bad mood. Like Fred in Brussels, they are always upbeat. 'Something good is bound to come out of it; we've seen that after previous crises and wars. 'When one thing disappears, that creates new space for something else. For new ideas.'

'People only change when there is a crisis,' said George, who can be counted on to say something sensible. 'And how it happened? I don't know. I am not an economist. Nor do I know if the politicians have been honest with us. Maybe there were clear signals all along, and warnings from the EU. We don't know.'

EUROPE IS A GREEK WORD, AS ARE PATHOS AND ETHOS

Yes, how can we tell how open and honest politicians are, whether they're European, Dutch, Cypriot or Greek? And how reliable is media reporting? The Greek tragedy had dominated the news for months when this book was written, in June 2015, and the Troika and the Greek Prime Minister Tsipras and his Finance Minister Varoufakis were negotiating a solution for the Greek debt crisis. The negotiations seemed to be on the verge of H-Hour many times: was this the meeting that would decide the fate of the Greeks? Was it sink or swim? I attended a European conference in Brussels in May of that year and from my hotel window, just eighty metres away from the office of the European Commission, I could see a row of TV vans, where reporters were probably waiting patiently until the meeting had finished and they could collar a harried minister for a quote. The meeting was still underway when I went to bed, and the next morning I saw a weary Dutch news reporter commenting on events. He had had to wait until four in the morning. And had the die been cast? Not really. But I was struck most by the fact that it was never really clear from the reports what was being proposed on either side. Maybe these proposals had not been revealed, or were too complex for the six o'clock news. In the Western European media, the gist of the reporting was this: 'We have submitted a good proposal to the Greeks, but they continue to make unacceptable demands.' The underlying narrative was that the EU had already lent them 240 billion, but that Greece was a bottomless pit, a nation of lazy tax dodgers who could not be trusted to keep up their side of a bargain. It was all their own fault and it was now time to pay the piper.

That was not the story the Greeks were hearing from their own politicians or reading in their own newspapers. I heard the other side of the story from Youropeans in Athens. Like Nikos, the hairdresser: 'The Troika is forcing the government to act as it does. They are the ones governing our country, and they could not care less about Greece. They shove loans down our throat that we have to pay back with 15 percent interest. The worst mistake was when we switched from the drachma to the euro. Everything suddenly became much more expensive.'

He thought for a minute. 'Europe is a Greek word, right?'

'Yes.'

'Like democracy. And marathon.' This is Nikos's field of expertise: he runs a few every year. 'Do you know how much money Greece earns on the marathon?'

'Nothing?'

'Nothing. But every day, there's a marathon being run somewhere in the world. I think they should all pay us for the use of the name. The same goes for the Olympic Games. It would be logical for the organising country to pay us, say, ten million.'

The Gynaecologist Kostas is a little more nuanced, but he also lays the blame elsewhere. We should be one big family, helping one another. He brought WWII into the discussion. 'After the war Germany had a lot debts, also to us, but we didn't force them to pay them back. We wanted them to rebuild their country.'

ZORBA IS NOT LAZY, HE ENJOYS LIFE

'Yes, the image of the work-shy Greek...' Yiannis, himself an extremely hardworking and ambitious entrepreneur with a high-tech start-up, has to laugh a little. 'They spend a lot of time at sidewalk cafes, maybe that's where it comes from. But there simply isn't any work for very many people. There are so many highly educated Greeks, but they are all leaving the country. Already four of my friends have left, and they were successful here.'

And in view of the never-ending stream of criticism, the Greeks are hungry for some positive news about themselves. That 'they', Europe, are really at fault. They are so hungry for goods news that a YouTube pep talk by a well-known marketing strategist has been viewed four million times. In the film, Peter Economides (his real name, I'm not making this up) talks about rebranding Greece, and it is such a hit with the viewers that he is now a local celebrity (and Youropean).

'Look around outside, do you see a crisis?' he asked me. From his austere designer apartment just outside of Athens, which is subtly dotted with expensive modern art, I can see the blue Mediterranean Sea, and in the distance the vague outline of some islands. 'The country is not a crisis, the people are. It is an identity crisis. The Greeks are under enormous pressure to become more Northern European. A Greek will never make a good German, but he can be a superb Greek.'

'Our definition of a European is determined by Northern Europe?'

'Yes, and by the Protestant work ethic,' Peter said lighting a Davidoff, 'while the essence of this country is to appreciate life. Greeks live hard. And so we have the image of Zorba, lying around on an island, drinking ouzo and doing a little philosophizing. But the essence of Zorba is not laziness, it is knowing what life is all about.' The fact that Peter, the advertising strategist, could just as easily have pitched the same story about Ukrainians or Mongolians doesn't matter to the average Greek. They were as receptive to this message as the ancient Greeks were to the word of Zeus.

BUT WHAT DOES EUROPE THINK?

So much for the Greek point of view. But what does Europe say? The response is mixed. Pierre Bokma, Dutch actor, is dismissive of Peter's argument: 'Get real. The point is that the whole Southern clan – the Greeks, the Spaniards and the Italians – do not pay their taxes. That is thirty percent of the problem. And I think it is just as absurd that they refuse to admit it.'

Various people, including Serge, police officer in Luxembourg, and the Berlin-based dentist Matthias, told me that Greece had falsified its financial figures (with the help of Goldman Sachs, often referred to as the world's biggest criminal organisation) in order to join the EU. And that we are now paying the price for that, with money that would have been better spent on road maintenance or to build schools. Scandalous!

Martin, a lanky junior doctor/model in Vienna, said what many people were thinking: 'I don't want to judge, but everybody knows that the work ethic is not good in Greece, Spain, and Italy. They think their siesta is more important. I don't think we should pay to help them. It's not fair.'

Everyone knows, is a common rhetorical device. And although there are those who would support Martin's statement, like the Italian actress Sara ('Yes,' she giggled, 'Southern Italians are a lot like the Greeks, the same sense of humour, work-shy), it is not true. According to the Organisation for Economic Co-operation and Development (OECD), the Greeks work longer hours than anyone else.

The Finnish government was more strongly opposed to further EU support for the Greeks than any other EU member state. The surgeon Pippa agreed with her government. 'It is very simple,' she said in a deceptively sweet voice: 'If you spend more than you earn, you're in trouble. Giving the Greeks money will not help the country. It's like a dog. If you always lead it to the couch, it will never learn that he's not allowed to sit there.'

Estonian entrepreneur Karoli, is also clear: 'We also had a recession, but our government dealt with it by introducing strict austerity measures and lowering salaries – for everybody. And they were re-elected by an even greater margin than in the previous elections. I like that mentality, that everyone knows where the money comes from. Unlike Southern Europe, where everyone is stealing a little from everyone else. People here realise how value is created. More Europeans need to understand that.'

But right or wrong, not all Finns (or reserve-Finns like the Estonians) are equally hard-nosed. Of course the Greeks should be more careful with their money according to hairdresser Joni (just turned 19) and super market owner Aarre, 'but we are all Europeans and we should help one another.' Solidarity! 'You know,' police officer Joanna said, 'it's only money.'

Madame Paule in Paris also offered a few words of wisdom on the subject of solidarity: 'You know, today things are going well for me, but tomorrow I may go hungry, and then I need to count on the others to help. You have to show solidarity. United we stand. The crisis is affecting the whole world, people need to have some patience. But it's hard for them because they are so used to their luxury. But you know, in life you have to take the good with the bad. But people now refuse to accept the bad.'

Xavier, the current prime minister of Luxembourg and local Youropean celebrity, agrees wholeheartedly. 'In the past we were the ones who needed help, now others do. *Ça tourne, la caroussel.*'

One more note to the story we hear in the West about the Greeks. The reality is slightly different, according to Ewald Engelen, renowned professor of financial geography.[8] The greater share of the 240 billion Greece received was used to pay off loans from banks, mainly Dutch, French and German banks, so that those (private) parties would not suffer if Greece went bankrupt. According to figures published by The OECD and the International Labour Organisation (ILO), the Greeks are among the hardest-working EU citizens, and their retirement age has been raised from 62 to 67. Zorba is not lazy! Moreover, the Greek government has introduced such draconian spending cuts that it has converted an enormous budget deficit into a small surplus in the span of just five years, and as a result their economy has collapsed. Did the Greeks make a mess of things? It was not ordinary men and women, but construction companies, bankers and politicians who profited from the cash that flowed into the country in recent decades to finance infrastructure projects. And much of that money also flowed right back out of the country. To London, for example. In 2009-2010, at the height of the crisis, the Greeks were at the top of the list of those buying properties worth more than a million. Zorba is living it up, Zorba enjoys life!

14

EAST – WEST: THE RUSSIANS ARE COMING

This is Europe

188 I know Europe — it's where I'm from. These days it is not unusual for children to go on holiday with their parents to Vietnam, the US or Ecuador, but my family mostly vacationed in Europe. We drove to Austria for spring break, occasionally went to London or Paris for our autumn break, and spent two weeks in Switzerland during the summer holiday. We usually also spent two weeks of the summer sailing in Friesland, in the northern part of the Netherlands, where because it always rained my brothers and I sat in the cabin squabbling while our father stood on deck swearing and trying not to ground the boat. My classmates returned from holidays in Spain or Italy with a tan; I came back with a cold. For me, Europe meant Western Europe.

On 9 November 1989 the Wall came down. I was a third-year law student with all the time in the world and could (just about) afford a train ticket to Berlin, but I felt absolutely no urge to experience this historic moment first hand. I watched the news, of course, and was otherwise socially involved, but for some reason, this event did not spark much interest. 600 kilometres seemed too far away. How different things were a year later when the First

Gulf War broke out. My housemates and I stayed home for that, turning on the TV late at night to watch Peter Arnett reporting live from the roof of some hotel in Baghdad as bombs and grenades exploded in the background. Iraq was much farther away, but somehow closer too. It was a war in which the Americans, our friends, were fighting the Arab bad guys. And the Eastern European countries behind the wall belonged to our enemy, Russia, and while they might not have been evil themselves, everything behind the Iron Curtain was grey and impoverished. Slavish people, the Slavs. Was the fall of the Berlin Wall such a good thing for the West?

Now, twenty five years later, I live in Berlin and I am older and wiser. One of the main reasons for moving to this city was its remarkable history, which is still visible and tangible everywhere. I live in Prenzlauer Berg, a neighbourhood in East Berlin, about three hundred metres away from Mauerpark, named for the infamous part of the wall that once stood there (and where every Sunday shabby hipsters visit a popular flea market, correction, *vintage market,* that is so in character with today's Berlin). Oliver, a 45-year-old Berlin entrepreneur and Youropean, told me that for years after the Wall fell, he continued to take unnecessary detours. 'If I had an appointment in Prenzlauer Berg, I drove though Bornholmer Strasse to Checkpoint Charlie. "Why are you taking the long way around?" a passenger asked me. That was when I realised that I was automatically taking the old route from west to east.'

One of the best parts of my Youropeans Project was the opportunity to see all of Europe, including the 'new' part, that mysterious area that had been sick for so long, suffering from the disease of communism. That's how it felt. Of course I had read and seen a lot about Eastern Europe in recent years, and knew they now had McDonalds and Starbucks and were 'cured' of communism. But I was curious about the scars, and the influence of Russia, which was up to some of its old tricks again.

YOU WERE HAPPY TO HAVE A BANANA

There was nothing in the shops: I heard this again and again when I asked about daily life in the communist era. 'They were basically empty. There was just one style of shoes, for example, and so everybody wore them,' hairdresser Vytas said in Vilnius. Or worse: 'One style of trousers,' said Lenny, a TV presenter in Prague, which must have been a nightmare for a style icon in the making. 'Yes, bananas were exotic. Sometimes a shipload of them arrived in the harbour, and if you were lucky you knew someone on board who could swipe one for you,' Ivo, Vytas's colleague in Riga told me as I lay back in the hairdresser's chair. 'No questions now, I have to shave your throat.'

I shut my mouth.

People used old newspapers because there was no toilet paper according to Julia, a Polish sex worker who now lives in Stockholm. 'Everything was so grey then, but now there are colours.' Even I had noticed the difference, for example, between Bratislava just after the end of the communist era in '94 and now. Then, during my very first visit to the area formerly divided by the Iron Curtain, the big barrack-like apartment buildings on the wrong side of the Danube were grey and depressing. Now the walls – maybe sixty metres high – were freshly painted in primary colours. Public spaces are one of the focal points of the work of Juraj, Slovakian architect and entrepreneur (and as a singer a local celebrity). No one cared about them during the communist period. 'Everybody owned everything, or nothing belonged to everybody. If you wanted to make something your own, you had to steal it. There is a Slovakian saying "He who hasn't stolen anything for an hour, is stealing from his family".'

They can all remember their first encounter with the West. 'It is difficult for someone who didn't live in Eastern Europe to imagine how big the difference was,' TV anchor Maciej said. 'In '77, when I was 17, I visited Brussels and Paris for the first time. And I was in shock.'

'What was different?'

'Everything. The shops, of course, but also the people. They dressed differently, moved differently, they didn't walk with heads bowed.'

Everyone has their own first Western experience: Ivo still remembers drinking his first Coca Cola, that quintessential Western beverage, and Pavlina, a Czech hairdresser, once visited a West German hotel as part of her training at a hotel school and simply couldn't believe the luxury. It was a four-star hotel, not even five.

BUT THERE WERE GOOD THINGS AS WELL!

Scrooge may have been in charge of Eastern Europe's kitchens, but many Youropeans still had fond memories of those days. Especially in former Yugoslavia, where it is remembered as a time when there were no drugs, and very little crime. 'The health system was so good that even the Scandinavian countries copied it from us,' said sex worker Nika. I'm not sure whether that's true, just as I have my doubts about her age. According to her site she is 30-something, but the following story makes that impossible. 'There was a sense of solidarity. Sometimes we worked together for weeks, building bridges and highways.'

'You were forced to, I assume.'

'No,' she said somewhat indignantly, 'it was voluntary. I went three times before I was twenty one. We worked hard, but you made friends and it was fun. People practically fought to be part of it!' If she went for the last time in 1990, when Yugoslavia still existed, that means she is now at least..... Well, you can do the math.

And don't that think education there was sub-standard. Janis, a plastic surgeon in Riga, later studied in Toronto and Hannover, but he got a thorough education in his own country. 'I know medical Latin, which is something no American doctor can say.' The Russian textbooks were more specific, I heard in Estonia; the school system was good, I heard in Romania (the fact that doctors in Eastern Europe live primarily on tips from patients is discussed in a previous chapter). Not everyone agreed that the level of education was high. Dr. Anistassiades on Cyprus laughed derisively when he talked about Cypriot colleagues who had been trained in the Soviet Union in the sixties. They had attended the university for African students, he said: 'It was developed for work in the tropics, and it was really little more than a glorified First Aid course.'

Nor was it all bad for artists, as is evident from the stories of Ieva and Kiwa in earlier chapters. The government kept a close watch on subversive elements, and made them dependent: they had to join a union but they got a reasonably well-paid job in return – and of course their work couldn't be too weird. In Sofia, rock guitarist Nikolo has fond memories of the Soviet era. He is glad they didn't enjoy unrestrained freedom, because the Bulgarians are disciplined now. They were better off financially too. His elderly mother now has to live off 130 leva, a pension of about 70 euro a month. It is not even enough to pay her electricity bill. It was not like that in the past, according to the rocker, who by the way bears a passing resemblance to Queen's Brian May. Everyone worked then, everyone had a salary, food was cheap and rent affordable.

But no, those were not good times for everyone. Not for the vassal states, and especially not for the Baltic States, which were actually part of the Soviet Union, and where the populations were terrified of Moscow's iron fist. In Tallinn, Riga, and probably also in Vilnius, people still curse the local KGB headquarters, which are now museums where everyone can see with their own eyes what gruelling tactics the Soviet Union used to subdue the Baltic States: in Riga I saw that the walls of the torture chambers are still blood-caked. 'In the 1930s the Soviets murdered the intelligentsia. If they hadn't done that, their grandchildren would be government this country today,' Ieva said. 'But they aren't there. And we are also suffering from a significant brain drain.' The few remaining smart people are fleeing the country. 'More tea?'

THE BALKAN WAR

She still doesn't understand how it happened. The war began in 1991, when the different parts of the Yugoslavian federation began to declare their independence, one by one. 'Why couldn't we just agree to a peaceful dissolution and accept that this period of coexistence was over?' Mara, the 72-year-old Croatian doctor lit a cigarette and waved to an acquaintance walking past the sidewalk café. 'But what happened, happened; it was an experience.' One she wished she hadn't had, because now she knew how people can change, what they are really like. And it wasn't a pretty picture.

Every Youropean I spoke to in Zagreb had a war story. Local celebrity Lydia, the opera singer, had almost been hit twice by snipers. And of course she knew people whose house had been burned, or who had been raped. Ana, now 32, remembers sitting in a shelter while the bombs fell. Ivan, who is even younger, recalls that his father brought him and his mother and sisters to safe place in Slovenia, and that he came back from the front with such a long beard that he was unrecognisable. The front was just 45 kilometres from Zagreb. X, the artist, was working in the National Theatre when it was hit by a bomb. He pointed to the other side of the square, 'There,' at the beautifully restored building on Tito Square, and for the first time during our conversation he was not laughing, as he told me about the sirens, the burning cars, the broken glass.

Every now and then I saw men of my own age in Zagreb – those were eighteen or older between 1991 and 1995 – and I realised that they had fought in a real war. A war that had an enemy, a front, weapons, and in which people died or were wounded at a time when I was leading the carefree life of a student. They are fathers now, working and watching the same football games as I do, our lives are ordinary lives, but I wondered how war had affected them.

The priest Anton suffered the most: the communists imprisoned him in a work camp in Slovakia for years. He could talk about it for hours, and he did. I spoke to the 85 year old in the tiny kitchen of his small apartment on the first floor of one of a Bratislavan apartment blocks that had just been given a fresh coat of cheerful red or blue paint on the outside walls. 'They stole our dream of freedom,' he said in his deep bass voice, and he poured me another glass from a Coca Cola bottle filled with red wine. 'And since then things have not got much better. In the Soviet days we dreamed of democracy, of values such as love of one's fellow man, a frugal life, but it has all come to nothing. Most people act like dogs that have just been let off the leash. We see so much egoism, arrogance and it's all about money now. Where was this need hiding all those years?' He suddenly looked very sad, a man old yet still so strong.

Tina Maze, Olympic ski champion and Slovenia Youropean, agrees with Anton: she too thinks that materialism has taken the place of communism. 'Now every family has three cars, whereas it used to be hard to have one. People keep buying; it seems to make them happy.'

'Not you?'

'No,' said the fastest woman in the world, who is also the most famous woman in her country. She arrived for the interview on a beat-up old Piaggio, her hair still wet under her helmet.

Jaruslav, a well-known Czech writer, confirms this. 'I was 17 when the Wall came down. Before then, nothing had been possible, and now everything was, and we took full advantage of it: travel, but also parties and drugs. And then the party was over. At the time people were convinced that capitalism was good, and we all behaved like nouveaux riches. It took a while for us to understand that capitalism and democracy were not the same thing.'

THERE ARE FIRST AND SECOND CLASS COUNTRIES IN THE EU

It took Eastern European countries about ten years to recover enough to join the EU, starting in 2004. Croatia was the last to join, for the time being, in 2013. They were overjoyed to be finally rid of Russians, finally part of one big European family.* But were people in the West equally happy? Or did they look down on their poor Eastern European relatives the way I had once done?

The answer is the latter. Here in the West we see them as second-rate and underdeveloped, according to Mara, the plucky, 72-year-old Croatian doctor. She thinks we are mistaken, mostly because the Croatians who came to the West were uneducated, and not representative. She sees it in her own profession: Croatians are not asked to sit on important committees, and do not have their articles published in *The Lancet*. She has attended many medial conferences in Western Europe, where she was never addressed as Dr. Dominis, but as Dr. Dominis from Croatia. She was judged on her address.

Dr. Romana in Bratislava agreed wholeheartedly. 'There is a lot of prejudice against Eastern Europe. You think we still live in the past. Why? There is simply too little communication, maybe too little interest on your part,' she said tactfully. That inferiority complex and the suffering are also part of the Polish mentality according to Małgorzata, a Polish film director. It surely hasn't affected her, but she is internationally renowned and celebrated, she has worked with Juliette Binoche. 'Look, salaries are low here. You can earn more from scrubbing floors in London than here. Lots of Poles choose that; they do the heavy work everywhere in Europe, and come home with lots of money but no pride.' I can confirm this: Marta, my cleaner in Berlin is Polish. She also worked in England as a cleaner for a long time.

'Are they ashamed?' I asked Małgorzata.

'Yes. And they compensate for it by showing off in a fancy car or with other things they have been able to buy.'

Stevo, hairdresser to the stars in Ljubljana, summed it up nicely: 'In Yugoslavia, we were the star pupils. Slovenia was relatively

---

* The cheering has now tapered off considerably in many countries: the EU has a favourable image in the eyes of only 37% in Slovenia and Slovakia compared with 62% in Romania. According to Eurobarometer, the average is 41%.

rich and was doing well. In Europe, we're at the bottom of the class.'

This is simply a matter of perception, since all EU countries are created equal. You would think so, at least. But they aren't. When I talked to Pejic in his hairdressing salon, and he told me that for him (and for many hairdressers) London is the promised land, I said: 'Then go there, go work in London! That is the great thing about the EU, the free movement of labour.'

It doesn't work that way, according to the Croat. His country's membership is still restricted; he cannot work in most countries for the first two years after admittance, and in some countries for the first five years. I didn't believe him at first, so I looked it up, and he is right. The five-year ban applies in Austria, the United Kingdom, Slovenia and the Netherlands. Croatians need a permit to work in the Netherlands, which is a complicated procedure requiring an employer to demonstrate that they cannot find qualified candidates in another EU country.

Romania and Bulgaria did not fully pass their EU entrance exam in 2007, and were assigned a few do-overs and some extra homework. Both countries were requested to improve their legal systems and step up the fight against corruption; Bulgaria has also been instructed to tackle organised crime. Every year the EU checks whether sufficient progress has been made, under threat of suspension. Such punishment has never been imposed – threats are more the EU's style – but after seven years, in 2014, the European Commission issued a diplomatically worded statement saying that Bulgaria still had a lot of work to do.

Petr Petrov, the public relations officer of the European Commission's agency in Bulgaria explained while we were having a sandwich across the street from his office, a hyper-modern building in a fairly rundown street in the centre of Sofia. 'The first few times that the Commission published its report, people were nervous here: were we in or out? Now the government just shrugs it off. We are used to being monitored: by Istanbul and Moscow in the past, and now by the EU.'

Sofia. Rickety trams rattle past severe Soviet-era buildings, an old church, dilapidated houses and a few modern offices, through shopping streets where you can buy things for nothing, but there is almost nothing to buy. No Louis Vuitton here, not even a Zara; this is Lidl territory. The walls are papered with posters, sometimes for events that took place two years ago, and there are holes in the pavement, only some of which are cordoned off.

So it's true that there are first and second class countries in the EU; it is in fact official policy. There are core countries and peripheral countries (Ireland, Portugal, Spain, Greece and the former Eastern Europe). This term is used not only by the financial media, for example, also by EU officials. Little wonder that they feel like second-class citizens in Eastern Europe.

'AT LEAST WE HAVE NATO'

After the Second World War, when Estonia, Latvia and Lithuania (listed from north to south, but you knew that) were part of the Soviet Union, Moscow transported workers from all corners of its immense empire to the Baltic States as part of its general policy of mixing populations, but also because they needed people to work in newly-built factories there. When the Soviet Union collapsed, most of those new residents stayed on, and Russians now constitute a quarter of the total population in Estonia and Latvia, and in the cities an even greater portion. Almost half of the population of Riga is of Russian origin. Even my unaccustomed eye was able to recognise them fairly soon: women wearing jeans bleached a slightly lighter colour, and slightly more make-up. Men who drove just a little faster and talked a little louder. And even though they have lived there for generations, Latvian Russians are second-class citizens. Their language is not recognised, and they are systematically excluded from government, although they have recently been elected mayor: there was no stopping that.

For some things are even worse: one sixth of the country's residents are stateless. They had Soviet passports, but when Latvia became independent in 1991, they were declared invalid. They are called 'non-citizens', or 'aliens', and they cannot vote. It was virtually impossible to become a Latvian, even if they could sing the national anthem while standing on their heads. EU membership has made it slightly easier.

The Russians really are different, nearly everyone assured me in Estonia and Latvia. I would have liked to speak to one, or better yet, two out of eight per city, just to keep things strictly proportional. It didn't happen, although I almost caught one in Riga, where I located a Russian hairdresser. But when I asked for an interview, she looked at me like I had just propositioned her. Her colleague, 22-year-old Merje, an 'Estonian' Estonian who was only too happy to be a Youropean, explained later that this was typically Russian.

'They are not quick to trust someone. I get along with her fine now, because if they like you, they are really open.'

The majority, however, keep to themselves, in their own Russian community. 'They do not speak a word of Estonian and only watch Russian TV, listen only to propaganda and regard Putin as their president,' entrepreneur Eva-Maria said.

The hostilities in Ukraine have brought matters to a head. The growing fear of Moscow was palpable everywhere in the Eastern Bloc countries, but it was most noticeable in the Baltic States: Moscow had simply annexed the Crimea, which had also been part of the Soviet Union. 'We are afraid,' said Piret, former pop star and now a TV journalist. 'We are just so close to the danger, to Russia.' Eva-Maria said that she had almost started to think of Russia as an ordinary country. Not now. Things have changed so quickly. She is not afraid that Russian tanks will roll into the country, but for the first time in twenty years, she is worried.

At least they had Barack Obama. He came, he saw, he spoke. When I arrived, a week later, people were still talking about it. 'You have to watch his speech on YouTube,' Karoli,entrepreneur, and the former head of MTV Baltics,demanded. I did, and this is what he said: 'The defence of Tallinn, Riga and Vilnius is just as important as that of Berlin, Paris and London.' Followed by his most important statement: 'Nato's Article 5 is crystal clear: an attack on one of us is an attack on all of us.' The message was that Nato, but primarily the US, would help, and it was a great relief.

A few days after the American president's speech, an Estonian intelligence agent was kidnapped near the border. On Estonian territory, according to the Estonians. Russian territory, the Russians said. 'It was a statement,' Karoli said, 'something like: do whatever you want, go ahead and invite the American president, we know who's the boss.'

THEY ARE ALREADY HERE

In the meantime, the Russians are already coming, and in some respects they are welcome, at least their money is. My somewhat flashy hotel in Jurmula, a seaside resort near Riga, featured not only a nail bar but also an oyster bar, a casino, and a legal support centre. Not to deal with possible disputes involving minibars, but because of the Russians. This is where they can find information about the easiest way of buying a house in Latvia, thereby becoming a resident of that country and therefore also of the EU. The house has to cost at least 150,000 euro — no more than any self-respecting Russian would drop at the casino in a single night — and a small price for the opportunity to travel freely in Europe and spend their money in Europe's chique shops.

Just below my hotel window a Russian spent an hour shouting drunkenly in the middle of the night. At breakfast, fat Putin look-alikes ordered champagne for their blonde bimbos, perhaps before stopping to chat with the girl at the legal support centre about buying a house. They are welcomed with open arms: not all Russians are the same, apparently.

A PROJECT AIMED AT RESCUING MISTREATED LABRADORS WOULD HAVE RAISED MORE MONEY

Youropeans is my personal initiative. My expenses for travel, hotels, websites, telephone calls, trainees, fund raising and living expenses came to approximately 140,000 euro. I financed this in three different ways, starting with the proceeds of the columns I wrote for two Dutch companies from every Youropean city. I also started a crowd funding campaign*, which is how things are done these days. While it helped boost the project's name recognition, the campaign raised only 6,000 euro, most of which basically advance payments to this book. The columns and the crowdfunding together covered roughly 20 percent of the budget. The fact that financing was such a stumbling block was my first indication of the Dutch level of interest in Europe. By the end of 2013 I had 'done' the first seven cities,** and the Youropeans website went online, in English, to be added to with every new city I visited. Now I had something to show potential sponsors, whom I confidently began to approach. I started by contacting a large number of funds and foundations I found in a book that lists all funds and charities in the Netherlands: one had been set up to promote good journalism, another to promote peace, others to foster democracy and even a sense of community: a perfect match for my project, with a little bit of freedom of interpretation. They saw things differently. Regrettably. Actually, the entire official Dutch Book of Funds, of at least two kilos, did not contain a single organisation that had anything at all to do with Europe. Such organisations exist in Germany and France, but the applicant has be German or French.

*The crowdfunding campaign took place on a Dutch and international platform (CrowdAboutNow and Indiegogo), and payment was possible via iDeal, PayPal and credit card.
I couldn't have made it any easier. The majority by far chose to participate in funding by paying for their book in advance, the price of which included their choice of either a friendly word of thanks or a personal insult (the latter cost five euro more and was the preferred choice). Other perks included the possibility of accompanying me to a city (one person chose this option: a friend went with me to Malta), financing a flight, buying a question to put to a Youropean, or even buying your position as a Youropean p provided you lived in an EU capital and qualified for one of the eight categories.
** Lisbon, Berlin, Helsinki, Dublin, Luxembourg, Madrid and Nicosia.

And Europe itself, didn't Brussels have some spare cash? No. I explored all avenues, but it all boiled down to the fact that the EU only supports projects that foster cultural co-operation between member states. If I had set up the project with a Finnish photographer and a Croatian documentary maker, I might have stood a chance of mining some Brussels gold. I briefly considered transforming my one-man band into a pan-European army, but it seemed too complicated: it would only hamper my manoeuvrability, and even then the long and winding road to a subsidy was unsure.

What about companies, the multinationals which are active in Europe, perhaps one them would be willing to be associated with a positive European project, set up and carried out in a professional manner? No. Heineken, AKZO, Shell, KLM, LinkedIn, Carlsberg, Allianz, and many, many others all thought it was incredibly interesting, but no, it really wasn't a good fit, wasn't part of their strategy. Anyone who has ever been in sales will be familiar with the spiel (and the frustrations).

Of course, the problem may have been the quality of my project. Or with the way in which I had submitted my requests. Had I simply showed up at the wrong counter? It's possible. But it gradually began to dawn on me that the subject itself was the problem. Europe is not pitiful enough. It would have been much easier to find financial support for a project aimed at rescuing sick Labradors. Europe, or at least the EU, has a reputation for being expensive, even profligate. A book or project aimed at fostering European cohesion is as likely to garner support as a door-to-door collection for Apple or Nike.

I was forced to conclude that there is simply not much interest in the EU. Ordinary people are not interested, and that is probably why companies are not interested: because their clients could care less.

But the fact the Youropeans project was so difficult to finance indicates just how badly it is needed: the Dutch do not find Europe a compelling subject, even though the EU has long had a much bigger influence on my country than many realize. It is, as my publisher said after gauging the interest of the bookstores before the book launch, an uphill battle. Always the best kind of battle — at least least if you win them.

15

THE EU IS A CATHEDRAL. BUT HOW BIG SHOULD IT BE?

It was warm, too warm, and sweat was dripping down his back. Two weeks before, at the end of April, it had been snowing in Paris, but now, for more than a week, the temperature had climbed to over 30 degrees. He had no hope of being able to undo the top button of his shirt, or open a window in Salon de l'Horloge, the state room of the ministry of Foreign Affairs on the Quai d'Orsay. Robert Schuman looked around and saw the waiting journalists, their notebooks open, pens at the ready. They were about to witness the speech that marked the birth of the European Union, a speech they would be hearing for the first time, but which had already been read 500 kilometres away by Chancellor Konrad Adenaur, after a special emissary had delivered it to Bonn in person. The German response was prompt and enthusiastic: Adenauer had given the message his full support.

Schuman sought eye contact with diplomat Jean Monnet before standing, clearing his throat and beginning to speak – his German accent seeming more pronounced than normal. 'World peace cannot be safeguarded without the making of creative efforts proportionate to the dangers which threaten it. The contribution which

The EU is a cathedral. But how big should it be?

an organized and living Europe can bring to civilization is indispensable to the maintenance of peaceful relations.'

Monnet knew the speech by heart, having written most of it, after he and Schuman had spent hours working on it in his garden in Bazoches-sur-Guyonne. A little surreptitiously, without the knowledge of other diplomats and civil servants, whom they regarded as competent, but too conservative, and incapable of looking ahead with vision. He had asked his driver and his wife to read it, as was his habit: if they liked it, parliament might also approve.

Schuman was already halfway through – it was not a long speech. That was something else the two, who were at first glance entirely dissimilar, agreed upon. Schuman (64) was a German born in Luxembourg who became a Frenchman when Alsace Lorraine reverted to the French after the First World War. A member of the resistance who had been captured by the Germans and had later escaped from Dachau. By contrast, Monnet (61) had remained outside of France during the war, first in London, and then in the US as an advisor to Roosevelt. The cognac trade, the family business, had made him a man of the world: he was married in Moscow, to an Italian woman. He almost succeeded in uniting France and England at the beginning of the Second World War, an idea that Churchill thought would help in the fight against the Germans. The plan was never implemented because president Lebrun resigned and his successor, Marshall Pétain, preferred doing business with the Nazis.

'...and the obligations of all kinds imposed on Germany'. Schuman looked up when he had finished his speech, and again sought eye contact with his friend Monnet. It was 9 May 1950, the day that would go down in history as the birth date of the European Union.

THE EU IS A CATHEDRAL

It would take a while before this union was called the EU: it started out as the European Coal and Steel Community, became the

European Economic Community (EEC) in 1958, then the 'economic' was scrapped and it became the European Community (EC), and in 2009, with the signing of Lisbon Treaty, the European Union (EU).

The first community was small – only six countries – and a bit makeshift. I read somewhere that at its first meeting in a Belgian castle, the first chairman, the German Hallstein, had to ask a servant to go out and buy some notebooks, pencils and erasers. The EU now has 28 members, a budget of 141 billion (euro: the currency in 17 of those countries). Peace prevails, as does prosperity, and all European countries are democracies (which was definitely not the case in 1950). Long live a united Europe!

The peace, prosperity and democracy are there *in spite* of the EU, according to the union's opponents. The union squanders money, is undemocratic and the euro should be abandoned as soon as possible. The common army once envisaged has not materialized, nor is there a common foreign policy. But, proponents argue, the EU is a cathedral, not a shed, and it may take centuries to build. We are only 65 years into the project. Save your breath, say the opponents, who are increasingly vocal: we should cut our losses now. Schuman and Monnet are long gone, so we don't know how they would have responded. The former died in 19963, and Jean Monnet in 1979, at the age of 90.

MY SPEECH HIT HOME TOO

I also once gave an important speech to a room full of European ministers, assistant secretaries and their partners, among them the Dutch Ministers of Defence and of Foreign Affairs and the then Prime Minister Lubbers. It was a winter evening in '92 and parked on the square in front of my student house in Leiden – which was usually auto-free – several large, gleaming cars were parked, with a gaggle of shivering drivers standing by. They were waiting for their bosses to finish dinner, one of them told me. Who? That bunch of ministers. They were to have a dinner in the hall of the National Museum of Antiquities, a hundred metres away.

Interesting, I thought and went back inside. Two of my housemates agreed and we decided to do what we always did when something interesting was going on: join the party. The year before we had sneaked into the neighbouring Pieterskerk where the then President Bush was paying a visit.

Just as we were putting on our good suits we looked out the window and saw the procession of dignitaries making their way across the square in the direction of the museum, surrounded by security guards. Ten minutes later we rushed after them, and seeing that the back entrance was open, we put on serious faces, marched confidently past the security guards, and ended up in the kitchen. 'Hurry up people,' we urged, trying to blend in with the catering staff who were running back and forth with trays of drinks and hors d'oeuvres, as we cautiously hastened towards the hall where the guests were chatting near the tables where they would be having dinner.

A bell rang, someone, possibly even the Prime Minister, gave the sign to be seated, starting a game of musical chairs with a probable unhappy ending: of course no places had been set for us.

Just in time I saw a lectern among the tables, and a microphone. I turned it on, tested it with a little tap, and immediately all eyes turned to me and my two housemates, who were standing next to me.

Clearly, a speech was in order. 'Welcome to Leiden, on behalf of the Leiden Student Board,' I began in English, and the room was quiet. 'What a privilege it is to see so many important people from all over Europe,' I continued. As a student, I was trained in the art of the impromptu party speech. The audience listened politely and attentively, while in the background staff were consulting with one another, anxiously leafing through the script for the evening. I managed to keep it up for six minutes. Every now and then I stopped so that my housemate could translate into Spanish, which was only polite, we thought. Six minutes before security intervened and dragged us away from our baffled audience. Some of them applauded, but most of them looked confused, perhaps a little worried.

A police van drove us at full speed to police headquarters, where we were interrogated in separate cells by the special police officers who were apparently responsible for the security of the event. I could hear the laughter of the local police in the background, who knew us and had already brought us coffee in our cell; they knew it was a joke, but they were enjoying the fact that the national police, their arrogant colleagues, were the butt of this particular joke. An hour later, we were back on the street, and soon after that back in the bar. It was my most important European speech, Schalekamp instead of Schuman, just this once.

It wasn't until a year later, in March 1993, that I really encountered the EU. My girlfriend at the time and I had dinner reservations at Château Neercanne, just outside of Maastricht, fifty metres from the Belgian border. It is beautifully situated on a little hill – we could have been in France – and there is even a vineyard at the foot of the castle, the first in the Netherlands. Château Neercanne is an expensive, Michelin-starred restaurant, and I was still a student but we were celebrating and I had saved up. Actually that's not true – I had won 1500 guilders at a casino the week before.

It was the restaurant's custom to offer guests a welcome drink – not in the dining room, but in a marl cave on its property. There we were, champagne glass in hand, in a cave lit by torches and decorated with expensive bottles of wine. The names of visitors had been scratched into the marl, some willy nilly and indecipherable, but other more distinguished guests had their own marked off area. Part of the wall had been used for Very Distinguished Guests, whose signatures were protected by plexiglass, among them Jacques Delors, Wilfried Martens, Ruud Lubbers, Helmut Kohl, and Queen Beatrix. They had apparently celebrated the signing of the Maastricht Treaty with a dinner at Neercanne, one year before. There was something exciting about those important

The EU is a cathedral. But how big should it be?

names scratched on the wall, like a secret society I knew little about at the time.

I understood that the treaty was important, and had read about it in the newspapers, but there were so many treaties and co-operative agreements, none of which seemed to affect me personally. I was born after the war, and therefore peace was a given. It would not have occurred to me to thank the Union for it. I sometimes had to show my passport when I was travelling in France or Spain, and I paid there in francs or pesetas, because it would be another ten years after Maastricht before the introduction of the euro. And sometimes I still convert prices to guilders, just to demonstrate how absurdly expensive something is. As a student I had the opportunity to study abroad via an Erasmus programme, but even though it had existed since 1987, it was still relatively unknown, and nobody I knew had ever taken part.

To a large extent, age determines attitudes about the EU. Luise, an environmental activist in Berlin and a local celebrity: 'For me, it feels like it has always been there – I'm not that old, you see.' She is 28. The Luxembourgish entrepreneur Mike is 43, my gen-

In the marl cave of Château Neercanne

eration. According to him, we are of the generation when Europe was a dream and a project. Although Europe had played little role in my life in the Netherlands, he told me that he got European funds when he was eighteen: the equivalent of 12,000 euro to start his first European magazine. There were all kinds of resources and projects he said, because he was in that first target group who needed to be encouraged to become pro- European.

'Did it work?' I asked him.

Definitely, and the same is true of his whole country. 'But there is the European dream, which is great, and the European reality, which is complex. The EU is poorly managed: too many countries, too many bosses.'

THE EU IS MUCH TOO BIG

Belgium, France, Germany, Italy, Luxembourg, and the Netherlands were the founding members in 1958. The first new additions were the United Kingdom, Ireland and Denmark, 25 years later. Greece followed in 1981, Portugal and Spain in 1986, Austria, Finland and Sweden in 1995 for a total of 15.

In 2004, ten new countries joined all at once: Cyprus, the Czech Republic, Estonia, Hungary, Latvia, Lithuania, Malta, Poland, Slovakia and Slovenia. Bulgaria and Romania were admitted in 2007, and Croatia was the last in 2013.

Then there are the candidate member states: Albania, Macedonia, Montenegro, Serbia and Turkey are still negotiating their membership. Becoming a candidate member requires the unanimous approval of the European Council, and the country must meet what are known as the Copenhagen criteria, which relate to matters such as having a well-functioning rule of law and a market economy.

Bosnia-Herzegovina and Kosovo are one step further removed from membership; their status is that of potential candidate member state, which is what Ukraine would like to become. The EU entered into an association agreement with Ukraine in 2014, which

The EU is a cathedral. But how big should it be?

is the first step in the relationship. Although it has been ratified by the European Parliament, and all national parliaments, the people of the Netherlands will soon vote on the advisability of this, after political activists demanded an advisory referendum on the agreement.*

Morocco also once applied for membership, but the application was rejected in 1987. Since then, it is a requirement that an EU country must lie in Europe, although Cyprus is an exception. Not to be deterred by this criterion, the prime minister of the Cape Verdi Islands has announced that his country would like to become a member. Switzerland and Norway have considered membership, but the populations of these two countries voted against it in a referendum.

Too many countries, was a common complaint. 28 at last count. Only 28, you might say, because it means that only half of all European countries are members of this union. In that respect, it seems almost pretentious to refer to this co-operative union as the European Union. Are you familiar with Visegrad? That is the name of the union between the Czech Republic, Hungary, Poland, and Slovakia, and its headquarters are in Bratislava. Romania is expected to join them. The Benelux unites three countries, the Scandinavian countries work closely together, as do the Baltic states. They are also European unions, albeit with less far-reaching consequences.

Too many countries. 'The EU should not expand further. Where will it end? For me, Turkey is Asia!' police officer Serge said in Luxembourg. That's correct, one might say: only three percent of Turkey is on European ground. Negotiations were opened with Turkey in 2005, but Europe does not appear to be very enthusiastic about welcoming Turkey into the club. Serge's prime minister, Xavier, confirmed this. He thinks that the union has expanded too

---

* In March 2016 a majority voted against the association agreement, although only 33% bothered to go to the voting booth at all.

quickly in recent years, and it is more difficult to accept new people if too many of them come too fast. He thinks it would be better to help those countries develop and modernize their industrial and agricultural sectors, in order to eliminate major differences before they are admitted to the EU.

Too many new neighbours too fast is not helpful, and it makes the EU virtually unmanageable: important plans can be carried out only if every member state agrees. 'It is easier to run a company,' entrepreneur András said in Budapest, 'because it is not a democracy. I determine my company's values. I make the decisions, and if you don't agree with me, you need to look for another job. Politics are different: you have to convince people to co-operate, and the problem is that it is not always possible. The bad thing about the EU is that it doesn't have an effective way of dealing with this kind of problem.'

Or: 'Right now we are trying to please too many people and there are too many people at the table,' police officer Patrick said in Vienna.

Or: 'The EU is a very bad thing,' hand surgeon Serge said in his consulting room in Paris. '28 member states, most citizens of which do not have our French level of education or standard of work. But we have to drag them along with us, people from Romania, Bulgaria and Lithuania. A few countries are pulling the EU train, and the others are following, acting as ballast and slowing us down. We are simply not the same. In '54, the six founding countries wanted to form a United States of Europe, but that is impossible. It's impossible!' Every now and then he repeats a sentence, something I've heard French politicians do. 'The Soviet Union was strong because it was a tyranny, and the United States, in contrast, are ruled and united by their only god, the dollar. Europe, in the middle, is democratic and has an awareness of things like human rights, etc. Values that do not help to create a united Europe.' He stopped a few seconds to take a sip of water, but raised his finger to indicate that I shouldn't even think about interrupting him. 'More and more people are talking about leaving the euro or the EU, something which was unthinkable not so long ago. It was a good idea at the beginning, but now it isn't.'

'Is there a solution?'

'No.'

So now you know.

Too many countries, unmanageable. And that is why some Youropeans think that the EU's days are numbered. 'There is so much disagreement,' said Irene, an immigrant who makes it her business to foster harmony and happiness in the hotel breakfast room she manages in Dublin. According to her, things were better when the union consisted only of Germany and the Netherlands, and other countries at the same level. 'Not Romania, Poland and Bulgaria. In those countries, electricity used to be cheap, in line with wages, but not anymore; life has become too expensive.'

Margaret, an Irish doctor — a medical microbiologist to be precise — agrees with that. She thinks that the whole thing may fall apart soon. 'You know, all those different currencies are nonsense. That should be the same. The only way to make progress is as a big group. But we doctors do not need the EU.' She told me how she and her colleagues from all over Europe meet every year in the mondaine Swiss ski resort Wengen. 'It's a hard life,' she laughed. 'We discuss difficult cases in the morning, and then we're off to ski.'

A KIND OF UNITED STATES OF EUROPE

His speech was neatly typed out, but towards the end, at the bottom of the fourth page, was a note Churchill had handwritten: 'We must build a kind of United States of Europe'. In much the same way that an early sketch of, say, Rembrandt's Night Watch, might make an art lover drool, these words, spoken on 19 September 1946 at the University of Zurich, are the holy grail of true Europhilia, the first public announcement of What The Future Holds.

The initial plans for a united Europe were first set out two year earlier, when the continent was still on fire. In June 1944, just a few weeks after the hard-fought allied landing in Normandy, members of the French resistance who had joined forces as the French Committee for the Federation of Europe, drew up a resolution.[9] It was concise and clear (so very un-French) and consisted of six points stating that only a federation could create a prosperous and peaceful Europe. Nation states could continue to exist provided that they were progressive, and their laws and decisions did not contravene federal laws. The federation would have its own army, its own foreign affairs policy, and a European passport in addition to national passports.

It was not to be, and 71 years later, when the French president Hollande argued in favour of a similar construction in a letter to the editor of the *Journal du Dimanche*, i.e. a parliament and government for the euro zone, he received little support. It is surprising that he proposed it at all. In general, it is not government leaders who propose such far-reaching measures, since a stronger European government comes at the expense of a country's own say in its affairs. Nevertheless, Hollande would like to see *more*, not *less* Europe, because the Greek crisis – and the banking crisis and now the immigration issue – demonstrated once again that a strong central government would have been much more capable of tackling the problem.

MORE, LESS OR NO EUROPE AT ALL

Both friend and foe agree that given the present form of government and the size of the European Union it is insufficiently capable of decisive action. There is less agreement on the solution. In simple terms, there is a choice of three flavours: more, less or no Europe.

No Europe. Those who do not think that government reforms or fewer members would work either, and want their country to extricate itself from the mess as soon as possible. They already have representatives in the European Parliament. Nigel Farage, of Britain's UKIP is the most famous Trojan horse, but unfortunately it is a voice that is underrepresented in this book. No shortage of Youropeans who have a low opinion of the EU, but none quite so eloquently capable of expressing their disgust as Farage. And yes, underrepresented: those who agreed to be interviewed apparently thought it was more socially acceptable to share mostly positive views about the EU.

Less Europe. The second group is moderate, simply less pro-Brussels. No, we really shouldn't have a federal government, they say, and at present they are in the majority. It would be a disaster according to Guy, a London-based entrepreneur, expressing a widely-held fear. 'It is impossible for someone in Brussels to determine what is good for Notting Hill or the West coast of Scotland, or Slovakia. Locals know best, right?' And he, half-Scot, cites the example of the recent referendum on Scottish independence 'in one of the oldest, most successful unions in the world, the United Kingdom'. The Scots too wanted more autonomy to determine what they think is important for themselves.

'What can Europe learn from the UK model?'

'That we are better together. Better Together was the title of the campaign to preserve the union. But also that a certain amount of autonomy is necessary.' He is convinced that decisions regarding education and culture should be made at the national level, and that decisions about defence, climate change or foreign affairs should be coordinated at the European level. Most people agree.

The third group wants to proceed full speed ahead; they want a much stronger union. In Brussels, Guy Verhofstadt, the head of the liberal party, is the leading proponent of this viewpoint, and as result he frequently clashes with Nigel Farage in the European Parliament. His kindred spirits among the Youropeans can be divided into several sub-categories.

> The Eurobarometer, available online at www.ec.europa.eu, conducts a survey twice a year. They ask people in every country a range of questions: what they think about economic prospects, unemployment, immigration, climate change, fear of terrorism, political engagement, and political trust. Anomalies are listed separately, as in: 'In Bulgaria, 33 percent is concerned about price levels (+14 percentage points high than the average).' The Eurobarometer clearly indicates that 48 percent is opposed to further expansion. A notable difference is that in the nine non-euro countries, a small majority is in favour of it. The countries that have the most favourable opinion about admitting more countries are Romania (72%), Lithuania (65%), Poland (64%) and Malta (63%). Clearly opposed are Germany (68%), Austria (67%), Luxembourg (67%) and France (65%).

There are those from small countries, like Malta and Luxembourg, who for centuries have been used to having their fate decided by someone else, and who know there is safety in numbers. The EU is a good thing, according to Frank, a doctor in Luxembourg, but if we want to be competitive, we will have to become the United States of Europe; there is no other choice. More Europe, although the devil is in the detail, according to Mike, a publisher in Luxembourg. 'Now some things are done well, and others are not. That is OK. What you don't want are compromises. They are a nightmare because they make everything mediocre.'

Then there are the idealists. Most of whom live in a rich country like Sweden, which can afford solidarity. David Batra, for example, is comedian with outspoken political ideas, and he is also married to a politician. 'I am not in favour of the nation state. I much prefer the idea of a European community, or of the United Nations. My ideal world would be a world without countries, ruled by a UN-like government. Different people, different languages and different cultures, and no borders, so that we could travel, live and work where we want,' he said in his agent's office in Stockholm's hip Södermalm district. 'It is human nature to be free, to want to try new things. And there are political constructions that make this possible. The EU is certainly a step in the right direction, but if it were up to me, there would be many more measures aimed at eliminating borders.'

'So the next step is the United States of Europe?'

'I certainly think we should federalize. A lot will depend on technical progress, for example on innovations in the area of communication and public transport. Politicians can pass all the laws they want, but we can't stop innovation, and in the final analysis, technical infrastructure shapes the world. If we can provide cheap internet and public transport, we will see this happening.'

Mark, Lithuania's favourite immigrant, compares the EU to the British Empire. A fellowship, a commonwealth, in which you foster one another's development. He thinks that the borders should be even weaker so that there is more freedom of movement. And that diplomas should be valid everywhere, so that you can work anywhere and pay taxes in the county where you work. 'I believe that most people are well intentioned, and try to work hard and make something of their lives. If they don't, punish them: I am not talking about unlimited freedom to do whatever you like,' he said, just in case I thought I was dealing with some kind of hippie.

Those in the third category hope that a stronger union will take care of the mess in their own country, like the Bulgarian doctor and entrepreneur (and former member of the Foreign Legion) Georgi. He was categorically in favour of a European federation, and he wanted Bulgaria to be run by a governor from Brussels: then European laws would be implemented correctly. In between swigs of whisky he regaled me with tales of how Bulgarian politicians ignore the rules and pocket EU funds themselves. 'Two billion just recently.'

The fourth and final category thinks a federation is no more than logical. 'If we hadn't got cold feet we would have had a central government long ago,' said Pierre Bokma, an actor in Amsterdam. 'But I don't think the majority in the Netherlands would support that. Have you ever seen Freddy Heineken's map of Europe?' Beer was not the only thing on his mind, apparently. Pierre drew a vaguely Europe-shaped map on a napkin, with circles and squares. 'He divided Europe up into cantons, a sort of tribal areas.'

'So he put areas like the Ruhr Valley and Limburg together, possibly with Liege?'

'Yes, something like that. South Limburg was detached from the northern part, and the area around Achen was added. He envisaged different combinations everywhere.'

The map of Europe has changed so many times. Scandinavia and Iceland were united for centuries, as were the Low Countries, and Poland and Lithuania once formed a mighty kingdom (that included Ukraine and Belarus. That arrangement lasted two centuries and ended in 1795, but they are still mourning the breakup in Vilnius: those were the days). Czecho-Slovakia existed until very recently, as did Yugoslavia. In the past Europe was often more or less united, as during the Roman Empire or under Napoleon.

Europe (like the world) is not the same as it was in 1950, when Schuman gave his speech. Nation states are less important, borders have become blurred. Big companies and big cities have become more powerful, and all kinds of European networks are on the rise. The memory of a horrific war was still fresh then, which made countries considerably more willing to co-operate with one another. That willingness is now is short supply and co-operation is harder to achieve when there are so many parties at the table. Only in the case of an emergency, such as the need to address the financial crisis, are national governments prepared to set aside their aversion and create joint structures. The process has speeded up a little, but it is still too slow and too makeshift to avert a new crisis. This has made the case for the 'neuro' stronger: a euro limited to only some Northern European countries. 28 member states today, possibly more tomorrow, all labouring away on the construction of what some call a cathedral and others a monstrosity.

16

EVEN THE FORMER CHAIRMAN CANNOT SAY WHAT A EUROPEAN IS

'No, l am not a fan,' Stefan Lindfors said as he took a swig of Aura, a Finnish beer. 'You know, during the elections in 1995, when we voted on EU-membership, I was asked to give my opinion on television.' Lindfors, designer, entrepreneur, famous Finn, and above all, professional *enfant terrible*, was willing to oblige. 'I placed a big signboard in the studio with a map of Europe on it. Then I painted each country a different colour: red, green, yellow – it was beautiful.' He took another drink, and waved to woman on a bicycle; he waved at a lot of people during our interview. 'The paint was still wet when the show began. I took my brush, and drew it across the painting, and mixed until all of Europe was brown. One colour, and not even a very nice one. And unfortunately, this is what has happened. We are becoming a one-size-fits-all place.'

He was expressing a common complaint: we are losing the diversity that makes Europe so attractive, because of open borders and Brussels legislation, or to be more precise, petty regulations.

'We are no longer allowed to make our world-famous marmalade,' said the Czech celebrity Lenny disdainfully. Salvatore, an Amsterdam-based hairdresser of Italian origin was indignant:

'They want to teach an Italian how to make pasta.' According to Azadeh in Copenhagen: 'They want to decide how much cinnamon we put on our cakes.' And: 'Our peppermint has been banned because it is classified as medicine,' Piret Järvis said in Tallinn. 'But I don't really know if that story is true. The way I see is that it gives us something to laugh about.' Every country had its own variation of this same complaint, which was always followed by the same standard phrase: 'And as far as I know, it hasn't killed anybody yet.'

Other complaints? Yes, Lionel is enraged because the EU is forcing Luxembourg to drop its bank secrecy rules. 'It will cost us 40,000 jobs, and decimate the entire financial sector.' Luca, a Roman, is no fan of the EU, and certainly not of the euro; according to him everything has become more expensive, and the EU serves only the elite.

I would guess that the EU complaints department probably receives the most letters from Greece, since the majority of the Greek Youropeans I spoke to had nothing good to say about the EU, and were also susceptible to wild mini-conspiracy theories, like the following: 'They forced Croatia to become a member.'

'How?'

'Economically, via debt. That's how they occupy countries these days.'

'They' means the Germans, whom the Greeks accuse of waging financial war.

United in diversity is the official motto of the EU. Europe, with all its different languages, landscapes and cultures. It is all old and all different. We want to preserve that diversity, because it is what makes Europe attractive, according to so many people – particularly tourists from outside Europe. Abroad should be different, but home should feel like it belongs to us. There is resistance to the fact that Brussels wants to change things that are typical and local; what can *they* possibly know about us? Mind your own business. Brussels should not interfere with culture or with people put in their shopping carts, according to Hilde, a doctor in Amsterdam. Her Romanian colleague Maria thinks there should be some room for local interpretation of the rules.

The question, however, is whether or not the EU is responsible for reducing diversity. Europe is globalizing: English (or rather TV-American) was spoken almost everywhere I went on my tour of the capital cities — everywhere except Paris of course. In Bucharest and Vilnius I met my interviewees at a McDonalds, every shopping street had an H&M and Zara, and little boys everywhere wore Barcelona or Manchester United shirts.

According to the Eurobarometer, the EU gets pretty good reviews. But why, what is it we like about the EU, and why? People were most enthusiastic about the fact it is so easy to travel without passports or visas in the Schengen countries.

Yes, it does make it easy to travel... I have admit to that I was a bit irritated when I had to dig through my bag at Schiphol Airport because I needed to show my passport for travel to Bulgaria or Cyprus. But is that such a bad thing? Is it so terrible to have a customs officer board your train, or to have to wave your passport out of our car window at a man in sitting in a booth, dozing above a sudoku puzzle. It takes time at the airport, but the airlines are doing their best to spoil the fun anyway by forcing passengers to sit in cramped seats with their legs practically around their neck, and pay extra for a soggy sandwich and a bottle of lukewarm water. Travel, travel, travel. We are supposed to enjoy it, but for years I was terrified of travel — a bit more about that later. Daniela, a sex worker in Riga had refreshing if socially unacceptable response. 'I don't like to travel,' she said. 'I don't like to change anything. Not my telephone, apartment, perfume, food or friends. So I don't want to go to an unknown country full of strangers speaking a foreign language.'

According to the Eurobarometer, European peace ranks third on the list of the EU's merits. Too low, according to Xavier, the prime minister of Luxembourg, who thinks that peace is priceless, the most valuable possession of all. Peace makes the EU the best thing man ever devised, said the Portuguese entrepreneur Antonio, never one to shy away from the superlative. Owen, the giant Irishman, is a fan because of his grandfather, who fought in two world wars and told his grandson a lot about them. From that perspective, he thinks that what has happened over the past few decades is nothing short of miraculous.

Others hesitated to give the EU all the credit for this, saying that it was the US and the substantial number of troops stationed here that kept the Soviet Union at bay.

While some see EU regulations as a hindrance, others think they are a blessing. For Christina, a Filipina working in Cyprus, they mean that her employer has to give her time off for holidays, and more importantly, that Sandra, my Ugandan cleaner was allowed to stay in the Netherlands even though on the basis of Dutch law she could have been forced to pack her bags. Not every country observes the rules as strictly as they should: the extreme right wing government in Hungary ignores a number of rules, but at least they have Brussels breathing down their neck. 'Without the EU, Hungary would have become a dictatorship long ago,' Péter, hairdresser in Budapest said.

Have you ever seen a little blue sign with yellow stars posted somewhere along a sleek new highway or a shiny new bridge? You are most likely to see one in Greece, Hungary, Poland, Portugal and Romania. They are biggest net recipients of EU funds. Only eight countries pay more than they receive: Austria, Denmark, Finland, Germany, Italy, the Netherlands*, Sweden and the United Kingdom.

Not surprising then that hairdresser Michael and doctor Filip say that their Poland has developed so much thanks to the EU.

---

* The Netherlands contributed 6 billion in 2012, and received 2.1 billion. At the same time, the Dutch Central Planning Bureau (CPB) calculated that the country earns between 20 and 30 billion euro on EU trade, and benefit greatly from the huge internal market.

The same is true of hairdresser Vytas in Vilnius, his colleague Merje in Tallinn, and doctor Maria in Bucharest, although Maria understands why some people object. She senses that the big countries do not like Romania, 'because we cost them money'. She understands, but they should not take this as far as 'that Englishman, Nigel Farage, who says he would not like to have Romanian neighbours.'

> The 2015 Eurobarometer reported that 41% of the Europeans have a positive view on the EU, while 38% is neutral and 18% have a negative opinion. Managers and students are more positive (46%) than stay-at-home mothers/fathers (25%), people looking for work (30%) and pensioners (31%).
>
> When asked what the EU stands for, the most common answers were: freedom to travel, study and work anywhere in the EU, followed (at some distance) by the euro, and peace. Cultural diversity was in fourth place, and bureaucracy in fifth, followed by wasting money. Then: increasing our voice in the world, too few border controls. Unemployment, more crime, prosperity, loss of cultural identity and social protection were mentioned fewer than 20 percent of the time. The trend is upwards: increasingly, positive things are being mentioned first.
>
> Those who see themselves as middle class or upper middle class are more inclined to associate the EU with freedom than people from the lower class (people who describe themselves as working class and those who often have trouble paying their bills). As are young people.

Every country had its own reason for becoming a member. France wanted to make Europe like France, Germany wanted to be loved again after the wars, the UK and the Netherlands wanted easy access to the markets, Belgium hoped it would keep the country together, Greece and Spain that EU Membership would draw a line under the dictatorships of the past, and for Eastern Europe it marks the end of the communist era.

That era is still fresh in people's minds, which explains the relative popularity of the EU in those regions. 'We are well aware of what it used to be like and we don't take our newly acquired freedom and prosperity for granted,' was something I heard often. Or: if you're born without air, being able to breath makes you happy. 'We were in prison for fifty years, behind the Iron Curtain!' Karoli said in Estonia. 'And that is why we have such enormous respect for the EU, and yes, we are always the first one to implement new rules. Our national character combines the German love of *Ordnung* with a certain Soviet-style obedience.' Estonia, the EU's star pupil.

ENTREPRENEURS ARE PRO-EU, SEX WORKERS ARE NOT

As a group, almost all entrepreneurs have a favourable opinion of the EU, especially those who operate internationally. Fewer rules would be even better, although the Parisian Alexis is not quite sure whether the rules hampering him (for example those governing the right to fire employees) are French or European. Even the euro is popular with entrepreneurs, who say 'only the banks were better off when we had all those different currencies'. The euro is also strikingly popular in countries that don't (yet) have it, such as Denmark, a country that cannot possibly become more expensive if it switches from the kroon to the euro. In my new country, people still refer to it as the *teuro* (a reference to the German word *teuer*, which means expensive). If it had been up to the Germans, they would have kept the mark, but they were the only country that was not allowed to choose.

One category of Youropeans was relentlessly negative about Europe: the sex workers.

'Bad idea, that EU,' said Anabela, who is from Slovakia, but is a sex worker in Luxembourg. According to her, prices in her own country had risen dramatically: petrol, for example. And Slovakia was now forced to import many products because the politicians had sold the factories to the French and the Germans. She fully expected the EU to disintegrate because things couldn't go on like this. Daniela in Riga agreed with this: 'Everything has become much too expensive, although they promised that prices would stay the same.'

'But has nothing been done with European money?' I ventured.

'Yes, a few really expensive projects. Like the bridge. The most expensive in the world. Why!? And the library.' She went there sometimes to read scary stories by Stephen King or Edgar Allen Poe. 'Something was wrong with it. A construction flaw or something, and it has been closed for two years. And we didn't *get* any money from the EU, you know,' she said staring angrily at me, 'it all has to be paid back.'

'Do you vote?'

'No, it's useless. The elections are not honest. No one was in favour of joining the EU, but suddenly 86 percent had voted YES. The vote was manipulated.'

Her colleague Nicola said thoughtfully: 'Yes, when we were poor it was a good idea to be a member of the EU, because we received a lot. But now the situation in Slovakia is relatively good, so no, we don't need them anymore.'

Diana did not want Bulgaria to join the EU. Her motivation is unusual: now that the Bulgarians are free to travel, they are everywhere in Europe, and she doesn't like it one bit. When she goes abroad, she doesn't want to meet her compatriots.

Jojette has a low opinion of Brussels in general. 'Why do we need another government? The Austrian government is good enough, and it doesn't need a boss.'

When I interviewed her, Slovenian Nika resembled a librarian, so I wasn't surprised to hear her say she had read a few books about the EU. 'The EU is good for big countries, but not for small ones. And Brussels is very undemocratic – they change the rule in every country to suit themselves.'

She looked triumphant.

'What about the European Parliament? The members are elected, aren't they?'

'Yes.'

'By you and me, right?'

'Ach, what can a county do with only four EP members?'

'*Only* four?' I asked. 'That's way too many. Did you know that Slovenia is the country with the most members per inhabitant? Yes, you're right, Brussels is unfair.'*

It seems to me the fact that so many sex workers are anti-EU is not so much related to their profession as to their position in society: they are usually somewhere between the lowest and middle level, with a poor-to-average education, and a low-to-average income. They do not enjoy many of the much-touted benefits of the EU: no Erasmus scholarships for them. Most (except for Bulgarian and Romanian women) work in their own country; sex workers do not tend to be city hoppers either, and they have been left behind by their countries' march to prosperity. As the Eurobarometer indicates, the biggest fans of the EU are the highly educated and the successful.

Take the highly-educated sex worker Eva, who lives in Amsterdam. She studied in Paris for six months on an Erasmus scholarship and she is pro-EU.

'Why?'

'Because things are pretty much the same everywhere. You know you can trust the police, that the water is safe to drink, that you can take people at their word.'

That is precisely how Dutch journalist Rob Wijnberg once explained it in a great column[10]: the story of Europe is a story about the disappearance of problems, the disappearance of enemies. 'What Europe does for us mostly has to do with things you don't notice until they've gone: peace, freedom, prosperity and security'.

---

* Big countries have more members of parliament than small countries, but as this is not entirely proportional, small countries actually have an advantage. All 28 Euro Commissioners have one vote, and the ministers in the Council of the European Union all have one and the same right of veto.

'How else does the EU affect you?'

'Not much in my day-to-day life,' Eva said. Sitting on the edge of her bed in massage salon. 'Yes, it's easy to travel if I want to. But I think it's probably a good thing we don't notice it much. You shouldn't notice the government that much. It's sort of like a football referee. When he's good you don't see him.'

'Oh?'

'Yeah, my boyfriend explained it during the World Cup.'

DO YOU FEEL EUROPEAN?

You live in a house, on your street, in your neighbourhood, your city, your region, your country, and, yes, you live in Europe. Or you're from there. Geographically, that makes you a European. But what does that mean? Do you feel connected to that part of the world? Do you feel European?

It is easier for Africans. 'In Amsterdam or Sweden, wherever, if I see a black person, I greet them with "hey brother",' said Rido, who is Nigerian and lives in Zagreb. For many Africans, the words *brothers* and *sisters* refer not only to those who share a father and a mother. Africans share more, starting with the colour of their skin – because by Africans in general those who live south of the Sahara are meant, with the exception of white South Africans, even though, ironically, this group includes the only people who call themselves Afrikaners, and speak Afrikaans. Anyway, families are bigger in Africa.

Max, the Slovenian Zimbabwean, explained that there is something called Africanness. Co-operation is part of it, and solidarity and cohesion. 'We call it *Ubuntu:* I am because we are, a person is a person through other people.' Apparently I looked sceptical at this point because he said: 'This is not just a lot of bla bla bla – it's true. You are successful as an individual because the community is successful. This encourages you to contribute to the community. That is why families or villages send their best men to Europe in the hope that they will earn money for them.'

Even the former chairman cannot say what a European is

It all just looks more alike, according to Thierry, who is from Cameroon. 'Europeans want to travel to see what it is like in other European countries. I didn't feel the need in Africa: whether you're in Guinea or Kenya you see the same black men, talking too loudly and dancing in the street.'

There is an African Union, founded in 2001, and it has 54 members; all African countries are members, with the exception of Morocco. The Brussels of Africa is Addis Ababa in Ethiopia. I was there a few years ago, and saw its headquarters, a steel and glass colossus towering over the rest of the city's low-rise buildings. According to my Youropeans, the union does not function.*

But do you feel European? No, not really, the Greeks said. Hairdresser Nikos is only Greek, because if he was European he would not have to feel constant fear of the Turks. As it stands, his government spends a fortune on military defence because they cannot trust the EU. The relationship between a Greek and some random nationality, say a Chilean, is the same to him as the relationship between a Greek and a German, despite the fact that Germany is also a member of the EU. The crisis exposed the absence of a European identity: public opinion in Western Europe was stacked against the Greeks from the beginning according to gynaecologist Kostas. 'We are family, but apparently we don't like each other very much.' In his opinion, a shared identity also implies solidarity.

Nor could I find an Irishman who could identify with Europe. 'I am 100 percent Irish,' the surly police officer Dennis said.

'Do you feel more connected to Spaniard than, say, a Vietnamese?'

'No. They're all alike, all foreigners,' was also hairdresser Sean's opinion. 'I am Irish. Europe is over there,' he said, pointing out the window. England is far away, across the sea, and Europe is even further away, across another sea. As Margaret Thatcher once

---

* Often heard complaints: it doesn't have any influence, it only costs money.

said: 'We visit the continent, they live there.'

Countries on the edge of the continent, tucked away in a corner like the Baltic States, also feel less connected. Ieva feels Latvian. Lithuanian Romas feels Eastern European. 'Especially when I was living and studying in Paris. I was seen as an Eastern European and while it didn't feel like discrimination, it wasn't positive either. Later, in New York, I felt European.' Joni, a hairdresser in Helsinki, feels Scandinavian. Not European, because Europeans are darker, with brown eyes and a darker skin. 'And I like that type, that's why I think Tel Aviv is so awesome. It's full of handsome, dark men.' In contrast, Madame Paule, who is dark-skinned, thinks of her white clients as Europeans.

The average Italian is also unlikely to feel European. Restaurant business owner Luca summed it up nicely, 'I am a Roman. Period.' For an Italian, it's the region that counts. Claudio, who has lived in Riga for years, feels most connected to Piemonte. 'I miss the mountains, the skiing,' he sighed dramatically, as only an Italian can. If you ask an Italian where he's from, the policeman Stefano explained, he will tell you the region, because Italians are not nationalistic. Except when the Azurri, the national football team, plays. Maybe Italy is too young for that: the country has only existed since 1861. It's already a stretch for the actress Sara to feel Italian; feeling European is one step too far. 'The differences between the countries are too big,' she thinks. 'People in northern Europe have a strong sense of justice that is lacking here. I happen to be a decent person with a decent profession, but on every street corner I see dishonesty, corruption and people using tricks to get ahead of the game.'

Sex workers leave no room for doubt when I ask them if they feel European.

'What do you mean?' Vikki said in Budapest, sounding almost angry. 'No, not at all.'

'Do you feel Hungarian?'

'No. I don't belong to anyone. I am free.'

Claudia in Copenhagen, Nikola in Bratislava, Kim in Vilnius,

Maria in Madrid: the list goes on. They all said 'no'.

Angie in Paris, who at forty is considerably older than most of her colleagues, was a little more nuanced: 'I am French, not European. I never voted for all that European nonsense. The president never asked me.' Maybe he didn't have her phone number.

'What would you have said if he had asked?'

'No, I would not have wanted the EU. Because I don't know all those people, especially not the Eastern Europeans. They should never have been allowed to become members; things were already complicated enough. It is not good for us or for them: they sleep on the street, their children do not go to school.'

Also included in the group of people who do not recognise a European identity are those who reject it on principle. Ferenc, for example, says that European identity means nothing to him because the concept of 'we' is uninteresting and has no added value. But then he is the founder of the Anarchist Theatre in Budapest.

> According to the 2014 Eurobarometer, 74% of the Dutch feel an attachment to their village or city, 86% to the Netherlands, only 55% to Europe, and a meagre 31% feels an attachment to the European Union. The average European feels more attached to their village or city (89%), but also more attached to the EU (45%).

EUROPE IS A HOUSE WITH MANY ROOMS

There were however Youropeans who did feel European, including those who work with other Europeans, like Olympic ski champion Tine Maze. She has a whole team of people around her. Andrea, her coach and friend, is Italian, as is the man who prepares her skis. Her manager and physio are Swiss. She explained that everyone brought something different to the team, and told me that the mix had changed her totally, and made her more open.

Another sporting hero, the Danish former football star Henrik Larsen, played for Pisa, Aston Villa in Birmingham as well as Waldhof Mannheim. 'That is how I came to feel European. I do not feel like a foreigner in countries I have lived.'

Maša, Slovenian artist, is an active European. Her mother was a member of the European Association of Hospital Pharmacists, and she is the coordinator of European Cultural Parliament. It exists, I'm sure, because I looked it up. Founded in 2001, its objective is to strengthen the role of culture and art in Europe. It meets once a year somewhere in Europe (but the last time was in 2011).

Kestutis, the Lithuanian police chief, is on the board of Europol: he too feels like a fully-fledged European.

A common, but slightly clichéd answer, was that people only feel European when they are or have been outside of Europe. As Umberto Eco said: when I am in Rome I feel Milanese, when I am in Paris, I feel Italian. Luise, a well-known environmental activist in Berlin, spent some time in Central America with a group of students and young scientists from all over the world, and there she noticed that Europeans think and work alike. Phil, who has seen every podium (and every pub) in Europe as the singer for The Pretty Things, put it nicely: 'I feel at home in Europe. It feels like a house with different rooms.'

Coming from a small country also makes you feel European. 'When your own country is so small, there is a lot of "abroad", a lot of Europe,' Maltese artist Celia said. Italy is close (although still too far for some boat refugees) and they get Italian radio and TV stations without needing a special antenna; every Maltese child grew up with Rai Uno.

A country so small that almost everyone is a foreigner. 'Over half,' said Xavier Bettel, who was the mayor at the time but is now the prime minister of Luxembourg. 'As a result I am very European. You will find all European languages spoken here, all ideas,' he said in praise of his city – no wonder: in his capacity as mayor, he is of course also head of the national tourist office.

For some, it is self-evident.

'I see that you are a member of the European Association of

Cardiologists,' I said to doctor Anistassiades. I had seen it on one of the many certificates on the wall of his consultation room.

'Yes, I was one of the first,' the old doctor said a little too nonchalantly.

'Do you feel European?' A dumb question, not my first that afternoon.

'Look, we Cypriots grow up with the idea that we are Europeans. Not Asian, like the Turks,' and he launched into a tirade, the upshot of which was that he was not on friendly terms with the Turks. 'European is something you are, not something you become. It is culture, Christianity, values such as freedom of expression, democracy – a Greek invention you know; it is ours.'

The Hungarian hairdresser Péter and the Austrian police officer did not hesitate to say they feel European. 'And privileged!' Brigitte, an entrepreneur in Copenhagen added.

What would your answer be? It is a difficult question, of course, one you could spend a whole evening debating, and carry on discussing the next day, probably with a whole different outcome. This evening I thought the following: I am first and foremost Dutch. They are my people, and when I'm abroad I recognise them from a distance: their faces, their body language and their clothes (and usually I can also hear them from a distance as generally speaking, the Dutch are not shy and retiring). I I understand people; I get where they're coming from, I support the Dutch football team, and I like the Dutch sense of humour: direct, blunt even, and self-deprecating. Moreover, Dutch is the language I write in.

I am certainly also a Rotterdammer, although I have now lived in Amsterdam for ages. When I visit the city where I was born, I automatically revert to the fairly ugly local accent and I am cheered by the warm-hearted, no-nonsense mentality of its residents with their even blunter sense of humour.

And I am a European. I feel at home in this part of the world, particularly in Western Europe. This is where I spent my vacations, and still do. At school I learned almost exclusively about

Europe, its wars, its understanding of the world, and the map of the world in my geography class had Europe at its centre, not Asia or America.

I learned European languages, although English, French and Spanish are also spoken outside Europe. Every year my favourite football club tries to qualify for the European competitions, not for a world cup. I feel at home in Europe, Europe is my neighbourhood.

Those who had thought about this from time to time produced answers such as 'Ach, European or Estonian/Swedish/Croatian, I am a man/woman/citizen of the world.' This was not a typical answer in any specific country, but it was typical of well-educated frequent flyers. Like JC de Castelbajac, for whom Europe is much too small. The world is his playground: Monday in Seoul, Dubai on Thursday and Stockholm next week. I was lucky to catch him is his studio in Paris.

The answer I got from Maciej, TV journalist in Poland, was also one I had heard before: 'I am aware of the fact that I am a European citizen. And I am proud of that, because in my view, Europe's history makes it a special place. I think that as a European I am part of the world's elite.'

The Lithuanian Gedas replied thoughtfully that European identity implied not only a shared cultural history but also shared social concepts, and said he had become aware of this when he visited Japan the year before. The Japanese have a totally different sense of humour, but there is less difference between his own humour and that of the Dutch or the Portuguese. 'What we also have in common is a sense of aesthetics or fashion,' the owner of several Suit Supply stores is Lithuania and Latvia said. 'In our case, fashion refers to the suit business, which is heavily influenced by the Italians. And the way we furnish our houses by the Swedes, for example. These things make me feel European.'

Even the former chairman cannot say what a European is

IT'S POSSIBLE TO HAVE SEVERAL IDENTITIES WITHOUT BEING SCHIZOPHRENIC

The question of identity is less clear-cut for immigrants. Omid Djalili, now 50, became a refugee when he was 12. It happened all of a sudden, but he didn't have to flee, because he was born in London, although his parents were Iranian and they had always intended to return there. But they are Baha'i, a persecuted minority, and when the revolution broke out in 1980, they were no longer allowed to return, and from being an ordinary schoolboy, Omid became a refugee overnight. Suddenly things were different, and he was an outsider. 'At the same time, my British identity was my anchor; it grew. I speak like an Englishman, my feelings and thoughts are strongly influenced by England. But I retain my Iranian side, and it is slightly crazier. So I like to dance on stage, do strange things.' The British public think it's hilarious, and so do I.

And apparently your need to find your roots can become stronger, according to doctor Azadeh in Copenhagen. 'The older I get, the more Iranian I become, so weird,' she said in an accent that revealed her years in the US She has an American passport, but she now feels at home in Denmark; most of her friends are Danish but she enjoys being more involved with her own origin.

Doctor Jeanette works in London, also has a US passport, but she comes from Sweden. 'When I am there I realise how un-Swedish I have become. Oddly enough, home for me was Japan, where I spent my childhood. But although I speak fluent Japanese, I never really fit in. And that is why I have always held on to my Swedish identity.'

For Mohammed, his identity is a huge issue, as is evident from the anger he felt when I wanted to include him in the Youropean immigrants category as well as that of police officer. He finds it frustrating that a Swedish police officer, who of course speaks fluent Swedish, is seen as an immigrant by the majority of his compatriots.

'I have been to Eritrea, the country of my birth, and there I am seen as the Swede, or the European. Here as the immigrant.' He had to search for an identity, and he found it in his religion: Mohammed is a devout Muslim. 'Many young European immigrants do the same.'

Hairdressing salon owner Abi is also a Muslim. His identity is constantly in flux. In Bratislava he is a European, but twice a month he goes to Morocco and there he is African and Muslim. He adapts to his environment.

'Identity is a slow-cooked dish,' museum director Ferran said. That has a nice, philosophical ring to it. 'I moved from Argentina to Spain when I was eight; I live in Madrid now, but I lived in Barcelona longer, so you tell me!'

SPOT THE DUTCHMAN

When Queen Máxima was still a princess, in October 2007, she was called out for saying in a speech that there was no such thing as a Dutchman. How dare she! There was no such thing as an Argentinean, either.* She simply meant to say that being Dutch was too diverse to be described in clichéd terms, and she quoted her father-in-law, Prince Claus, who said that he also has divided loyalties: Dutch, European, citizen of the world. That is possible, of course, because identity does not have to be exclusive, and you can have more than one without being accused of being schizophrenic. I once heard F.W. de Klerk speak at a symposium in Leiden[11], during which he said that as president of South Africa he and his successor Nelson Mandela had discussed how their deeply divided country could be united. Zulus, Boeren and coloured had to take on another identity on top of their old ones, namely the South African, in order to create a new Rainbow Nation. Whether it has been successful remains to be seen, but Europe can learn from the idea. In any case, the motto of post-apartheid South Africa is the same as that of the EU: *Xam* means 'united in diversity'.

---

* Queen Máxima was born and raised in Buenos Aires.

MADE IN EUROPE

Identity, group identity, is defined as a person's awareness of belonging to a certain group, and being treated as such by others. The group projects an image of itself, and is seen by others as unique.

All well and good, but what exactly is this thing we call European identity? What is unique about it, and distinguishes us from others. Do we have something in common despite all that diversity? In short, what makes a European a European. That was the million-euro question, and it turned to be too difficult, the question that the Youropean would rather skip or answer incompletely or only semi-coherently.

The most frequently cited example of the typically European was, as Gedas said, our long, shared history. Europe is a grand old dame and her years have left tangible, visible marks that you do not need to visit a museum to see. A visit to almost any historical city centre will do (many tourists see the old European city centres as one big open air museum, or worse, as theme parks, which is the fate of my own city, Amsterdam). Klara thinks that our tangible history is what makes us different from Asia. 'You don't feel the deep-rooted history there. I was recently in Shanghai for the World Expo, and I was looking forward to seeing something of the old China, but everything is new, with the exception of a tiny bit where a few colonial villas from the British era have escaped the bulldozers.'

Another grand dame, Elisabeth, queen of Vienna, also mentioned China: 'When I went to a Van Gogh exhibition there I felt proud, because like me, he was a European. As for fashion, I always wear European designers, mostly French. I don't think I would ever wear Chinese fashion.' She is the owner of Sacher Hotel, and the entire image, from the mint-green banquette she was sitting on to her Italian heels and her coiffure said old Europe. 'But you know, we have our common values and are proud of our brands, So I drive a BMW or a Mercedes, not a Dodge.'

'We make the best stuff?'

'I think we value quality more in Europe. And I have a feeling that Asian and American companies are more interested in short-term success.'

Delphine, Frontex employee in Warsaw, also takes clothing as an example: 'Maybe the European spirit will come in time. I recently saw a few stores in Cannes that had a European flag on their labels. *Made in Europe* they said, not in Poland or France. Being proud that something was made in Europe is a good sign, don't you think?'

'And "Europe" stands for quality and good design?'

'Yes, and I pay attention to such things, and I buy European products because I want to be able to wear my clothes for more than a few days.'

'You are wearing a Tommy Hilfiger polo shirt.'

She glanced a little distractedly at the brand name on her shirt.

WE ARE NOT AMERICANS, NOT ASIANS AND NOT AFRICANS

'I really don't know,' Petr said, a police office in Prague, as he nervously glanced at the communications officer next to him. It was not the first awkward answer he had given. 'For me, Europeans are relaxed and easy-going.' Pierre Bokma's definition is straightforward and based on race: Europeans are Caucasian. According to psychiatrist Nicolò, Europe is more cosmopolitan than other parts of the world. He has an extremely high opinion of his fellow Europeans: they have a strongly developed sense of justice, a very well-defined value system, and in general a fairly high level of intellectual knowledge. It is all down to prosperity, he thinks, because if you have to fight to survive, you have no time for intellectual development.

'And if Europe was a person, and one or your patients, what would it look like?'

'A baby, not an old lady.'

Even the former chairman cannot say what a European is

When I was halfway through my project, and had heard a lot of criticism of Brussels from my Youropeans, I decided to add a ninth category: people who work for Europe. More about them in chapter 19.

Euro parliamentarian Marietje Schaake, for example, is 36, Dutch and a member of the ALDE party, the liberal alliance. For her, being a European is about having a huge amount of security in your daily life, which most people are unaware of. 'For instance, the fact have we have five weeks of paid vacation. Maternity leave. No capital punishment. In theory, you can lead your life as you choose.'

'Isn't that simply the result of prosperity, and not of a specific value system?'

'The two are inter-connected, in my view: if a society is focused on survival, there is no room for it, and education often suffers as well. I sometimes get the impression that you're not allowed to use these arguments anymore because it seen as beating your own drum. But I think they are incredibly valuable.'

In spite of being a professor, Andrea also had trouble with the question: 'A positive description of Europe, explaining what it is and not what it isn't, that is a tough job. I think that it is about an awareness of being part of a community that nevertheless respects our differences. And I enjoy it immensely, especially here in London, with all those different cultures in such close proximity.'

Of course I also put the question to Herman van Rompuy. 'Ach, here in Belgium we have always had different identities. I am Belgian, I am Flemish, and from a particular region and town. We have a strong sense of those complementary identities. European identity is an important part of the whole. But what it feels like?' He examined the question, repeated it himself, looked away briefly. 'If we make a negative comparison, then we are not Americans. Not Russians. Not Asians.' *Amai*, as the Flemish say: *what now* if even the newly retired chairman of the Council cannot come up with a better answer.

Worse yet, at a symposium in Amsterdam, where a number

of our leading lights had gathered to talk about Europe, I heard a former Euro Commissioner, a Cypriot woman, say that she is European 'because she values culture, and culture is typically European.' Ouch. At the time it had been difficult to get culture included in the European negotiations, even though, as she said somewhat grandly 'the people place so much value on culture and cultural diversity.' Indeed.

17

THE VALUES TRAP

Sometime around 2002 a site was created where the people of the Netherlands were invited to discuss their norms and values. It was called sixteenmillionpeople.nl, and was presumably inspired by a song written for a Postbank commercial in the nineties, which became a hit, partly because it seemed to describe the state of the nation at the time, and its changing values (it referenced children who call their parents by their first name, and the Dutch disregard for those in uniform). The website was the initiative of the Balkenende government, whose pet project it was; this Prime Minister even wanted to set up a commission on norms and values. For several years it was high on the agenda, suddenly everyone was talking about norms and values. I noticed at the time, in 2002, that the discussion centred around having values, but said little about what constituted Dutch norms and values. They are probably not the same as they were in the fifties: Dutch society has undergone a drastic change since then, as has our understanding of how we should interact with one another and what we think is important. It was always a tacit understanding, and maybe that is how we wanted it to stay, because the commission never materialized, and the site faded away and has not been heard from since.

If the people of the Netherlands found it difficult to pin down their values, how much harder must it be for Europe? Nevertheless, the *two-million-euro* question often came up, because asking people what it means to be European is just one step away from asking them what we Europeans think is important, and which values we share.

And according to many Youropeans, we think alike about a number of essential matters. Above all about freedom. 'I still remember talking about homosexuality with a number of scientists during lunch at an international conference. It was striking how the Europeans shared the same liberal viewpoint,' said Luise, a well-known environmental activist in Berlin. I talked to Guy, a London-based entrepreneur, the day after the Charlie Hebdo attacks in Paris. He told me that the shocking events had made him realise how European he is, because he felt such a connection to the victims, and felt that our freedoms were being attacked, particularly our freedom of expression. One of Europe's key values, according to former Dutch politician Felix Rottenberg. 'The old European civilization, the one which came into being around 1800, stands for freedom. Thinkers such Erasmus and Spinoza played an important role in its development.'

Other values? Older people are not taken seriously in Europe, Ieva, teacher and artist in Latvia said. 'Less than in Asia, for example. Teachers there are listened to, not doubted, while my students here just think: what is that old woman on about?' On the other hand, for her, Europe means openness and transparency.

'Social security,' Nicky in London, also an artist, looked pensive. 'I would like to work in New York, but the prospect of having no social safety net at all is off putting. The security here gives me breathing space, and I think that is something typically European.' And it's true: even the most conservative government in Europe provides a reasonable level of social benefits to prevent the gap between rich and poor from becoming too marked. Every employee in Europe gets a paid vacation, many more days than the measly two weeks that the Americans are forced to accept.

In Europe, or a large part of it, one job per family is supposed to be enough. There is equality, relatively speaking, which is characteristic of Europe according to a speech given in 2014 by Paul Scheffer[12], a Dutch publicist and professor of European Studies. Other distinguishing features include a low level of corruption, a reasonably robust rule of law, a liveable urban environment in comparison with the mega-cities that have sprung up or are about to spring up in other parts of the world, a university culture and pacifism.

OUR VALUES ARE GOOD VALUES AND THAT IS WHY THEY HAVE BECOME UNIVERSAL

The Hungarian entrepreneur András sees no European values, let alone common values, but he agrees that the EU should have them: 'It should determine a set of values.' Like he has probably set for his own company. 'We are not clear anymore, unlike in the past when we were informed and bound by Christian values.' We still are according to the Swedish entrepreneur Håkan, who designs hip ties. Today's European values are deeply rooted in Christianity even though a large percentage of Europeans no longer attends church. Anton still does: he is a priest (and Slovak local celebrity). 'Values do not just fall from the sky,' the 85-year-old said at his kitchen table. 'They are in our body; we know the difference between good and bad. Christian values are human values, and the world was here before Christ was.'

Spanish businessman Martin, the old walrus, sees how values are becoming more global as the world shrinks and international contacts increase. 'Take my children: they have studied abroad, and seen how things work in other countries.'

'What are European values?' Cayetana Álvarez took a sip of her tea and looked at me as if to say 'how much time do you have?'. She is a member of the parliament for Partido Popular, and probably one of its brightest: she is also active in the think tank that advises Prime Minister Rajoy. 'Basic, essential values are democracy, open markets, political pluralism, freedom of expression and religion. And they have become universal values. They are not good because they are ours, they are good because they are good.' Amen.

Luuk van Middelaar does not entirely agree. He too is a political thinker, just turned forty, but he has worked in Brussels for years, first for Euro Commissioner Bolkestein, and later for four years as a speech writer and advisor to Herman van Rompuy. He is now a columnist for the Dutch newspaper NRC.

'So our values are not universal?' I asked. 'Not even if they play a worldwide role as the basic ingredients of, for example, the United Nations charter?'

'Even then it may be a product of Western domination, imposed and forced onto others. I refuse to debate the issue of universal values, because if you do not agree, there is no philosophical zero-point position that can be used to determine who is right. Except that, of course, our values are the best! We have no trouble agreeing on that!' Van Middelaar laughed.

'Do European values coincide with Western values?'

'There are differences. Take capital punishment. In Europe we abolished it in the last century, but the United States did not. That does not mean that we are more civilized than the Americans, but it does say something about the relationship between the state and the individual. The American state believes that it has the right to make life and death decisions about its citizens. The US is seen as being more individualistic, but in this respect it is not: the collective has more power over the individual, the ultimate power of capital punishment. Another example has to do with the welfare state. Obama was called a euro communist because he wanted to introduce universal healthcare coverage, at about the same level as that of, for example, Spain. That level of solidarity indicates that the European societies are slightly less individualistic than the United States.'

EUROPE DAY

My boyfriend went to Europe and all I got was this lousy T-shirt. I didn't ever want my girlfriend to say that about me, so I brought her something special from every city I visited. Something every woman wants, something that would really make her happy: she now has 28 city magnets on her refrigerator. You've seen them in the souvenir shops (often run by Indians or Pakistanis) on sale for a euro. The Eiffel Tower, the Acropolis, Big Ben, Ceaușescu's palace, and Europe's many other landmarks now adorn her refrigerator. The collection also includes a dancing Bulgarian couple, and a Sisi from Vienna. A city, and sometimes a whole country reduced to one eye-catching symbol.

Every country has idiosyncrasies, national heroes, and languages, which have developed organically. Every country also has a flag, and a national anthem, which have been invented. Flags contain the national colour*, or an animal that typifies the country, or a reference to some historical event. Preferably an extremely ancient event, while the anthem provides a narrative of the things the country is/should be proud of (it is, by the way, striking how many foreign countries are mentioned in national anthems: Germany and Spain in the Dutch anthem, Sweden and France in that of Poland, to mention but a few). Organic or invented, these symbols help to create national cohesion.

But what about Europe? The EU has a number of official symbols: a flag, the European hymn, based on the 'Ode an der Freude' from Ludwig von Beethoven's ninth symphony, the euro (although not every member state has adopted it) and Europe Day. I wonder how many people even know when it is.**

Both were included in the 2004 European Constitution, or rather the Treaty establishing a Constitution for Europe, but the

---

* The Dutch flag has an orange pennant.
** 9 May, the day on which Schuman, the French foreign minister, gave the 1950 speech that is regarded as the starting point of the EU.

constitution was rejected following a no vote in France and the Netherlands. And in the successor to the constitution, the Lisbon Treaty, the flag was scrapped because some countries, including the Netherlands, objected to its being named explicitly in the agreement. Instead, the sixteen member states confirmed the symbols in a separate statement.

'The flag had to go,' Luuk van Middelaar said, 'because we wanted to keep our own flags. That was the feeling, which is based on the common misunderstanding that being part of Europe means ceasing to exist as a country or nation. I still like to see leaders standing in front of two flags. The European and the French flag, for example: double identity.'

But isn't that European identity still an empty identity? I put this question to Herman van Rompuy. There is of course a blue flag with twelve yellow stars in the corner of his office.

'Don't we have to fill in that identity?' Fill in? He frowned and I rephrased the question, this time without the marketing jargon. 'I mean furnish it, like a house.'

'People aren't fools,' Van Rompuy said. 'It's no use waving flags until certain things have been been stabilised, such as the euro zone, the whole set of problems related to freedom of movement and immigration. We have to let the economy grow first, so that people realise that the measures taken in recent years have served some purpose. You have to give people some substance before you start waving flags.'

'Maybe not flag waving – I just meant to say that it might help us to create a European identity if there were more things to remind us that we are European. For example, I am a football fan'

'So am I, I'm a supporter of Anderlecht,' he interrupted me, but his tone was suddenly different, lighter.

'Feyenoord is my club. In 2020, the European championships which are usually held in one country will be spread over thirteen cities throughout Europe, from Baku and Lisbon to Amsterdam, and the finals will be held in Wembley Stadium in London. I think that is a great plan.' Of course Van Rompuy knew all about this. 'A brilliant idea from UEFA's Michel Platini. I also recently read an article that raised the subject of a joint European Olympic Team. It would have been by far the biggest medal winner in the last games.'

UNITED IN RYANAIR

Sport can play an important role in bringing people together, even though you're supporting your own country in the tournament and are therefore opposed to the others. It might be worth trying to select a European team for some sports, and having it compete with other continents, along the lines of the Ryder Cup, the prestigious annual golf tournament between the US and Europe.

The first European Games were held in Baku, the capital of Azerbaijan in 2015. The European Olympic Committee decided to award the second edition, in 2019, to the Netherlands, but they were forced to retract their offer when the Dutch minister of sport refused financial support, to the chagrin of the combined Dutch sport federations, who did not agree with the minister's decision. They argued that the level of competition of these games was in fact high, and the cost involved relatively low. I suspect that the unpopularity of the EU was the reason behind the Dutch government's refusal: although the event has nothing to do with Brussels, they did not want to reinforce the public perception that 'Europe' always costs us money.

There is one event that produces a winning country, but virtually no sour grapes, and never any brawls. A hundred million people watch the Eurovision Song Contest every year, which I discuss later in this chapter.

The Erasmus project also binds people together, melts them together you might say: the method of measurement is unclear, but it has been said that there are already a million Erasmus babies, the result of three million students taking part in the exchange programme. And to involve those without a university education a compulsory social service programme could help by requiring every 18 year old to perform social work in an EU country of their choice.*

Ylva, general practitioner in Stockholm, had a surprising take on the subject of things that bind us together. According to her, Ryanair, and not the EU, has contributed most to the unification of Europe. The budget airlines, which also include EasyJet, Air-Berlin, Vueling and Transavia, have made it possible for everyone to travel and get to know one another's countries. 'In the past, everyone had been to London, Paris and Copenhagen. Now people, especially young people, go to Belfast, Cracow or Prague for a weekend – cities you would never have gone to in the past. Simply because it is almost free.'

A EUROPEAN MAN ON THE MOON

I suggested to Herman van Rompuy that what would really strengthen the European connection is a compelling common objective, something that we Europeans could achieve if we just put our minds to it. The way president Kennedy held up the prospect of a man on the moon to the Americans in the sixties; we need what the business world calls a Big Hairy Audacious Goal – though I didn't use this term in my interview with van Rompuy. Business newspeak is not really his style: he is more of a haiku kind of guy.

'The union was created to prevent war, which it has been doing for seventy years. Do we need another objective?' I ask.

'That has actually also happened in the history of the EU. In addition to the peace objective, the second objective for the founding members, plus Great Britain, was to anchor democracy. That is why Greece, Portugal and Spain joined the EEC when the fas-

---

* The figure of one million persists, but it seems high to me for a total of three million students. If every couple has an average of two children, then there are 500,000 Erasmus couples, or a million ex-students, meaning that one in three is reproducing with another Erasmus student...

cist regimes had been overthrown. And now the former communist countries have joined. The reasoning was that they belong here because they are part of the European Union's democratic project. Of course, it also opened up a market. When it joined, Poland, with its 38 million inhabitants, had a per capita GNP that was the same as ours in the early nineties. Poland is now three times richer than it was then.'

'During my cities trips I noticed that the new countries are more positive about the EU. Here in the West we take peace and prosperity for granted. We see freedom of travel, and students the Erasmus scholarships, as the main advantages of EU membership. Isn't that a pity?'

He shrugged his shoulders. 'But also human. Peace has become almost a part of the furniture.' And a little more sharply, 'People should think twice, given all that is happening all around us. A war in Ukraine. While good old Europe, that used to be in war for ages, is completely stable. And on our southern border, from Afghanistan to Nigeria, the whole zone is at war or is unstable. You could ask yourself why that is.'

'But people do not do that.'

Irritated he said: 'I accept human nature as it is. As soon as people become accustomed to one thing, they start looking around at other things.' He nodded towards the portrait on the wall of Jean-Luc Dehaene, former Prime Minister of Belgium. 'My political mentors taught me that life, society, is a mixture of own interest (usually economic), ideas and ideals. The weaker the latter are, the stronger the influence of own interest. Enter the calculating citizen, with his "what is the added value", – a terrible expression. People forget that the calculation is sometimes to your advantage, and sometimes to your disadvantage. It's about the whole picture and not just about added value.'

INTELLECTUAL AND ARTISTIC THINK-TANKS

Fine words, but at the same time a bit disappointing that a former EU chairman dismissing the idea of a European dream as irrelevant — no time for that, the economy comes first. It sounded almost bitter, and I can imagine that Van Rompuy, who grew up with strong European ideals, is himself disappointed. As his former right-hand man Van Middelaar said: 'If you are painting a picture of the future, but run into an insurmountable object halfway there, you have to abandon that particular view of the future.'

The European Union's website lists the five overarching priorities mentioned in the European Council's 2014 strategic agenda:
- A Union of jobs, growth and competitiveness
- A Union that empowers and protects all citizens
- An Energy Union with a forward-looking climate policy
- A Union of freedom, security and justice
- A Union that is a strong global actor

All worthy, but not a man on the moon. And yet, cautiously, and so far under the radar that it hasn't registered yet on its website, the EU is answering the call for an overarching, appealing vision. Andy Klom, the brusque head of the EU agency in the Netherlands, told me that every member state has been asked to set up a think tank to encourage intellectuals and artists to discuss the future of the EU. In 2013, José Barroso, then chairman of the European Commission announced that he was seeking the co-operation of European intellectuals, artists and politicians to lead a discussion of what he called the New European Narrative. Its objective is to clarify Europe's overarching philosophies and ambitions, and to rediscover the European identity.

Van Middelaar: 'And because every country has its own reason for joining, and therefore projects its own hopes and fears onto the EU, it is always going to be difficult to write a European story that suits everyone. That leaves only peace.'

WE NEED A EUROPEAN OBAMA

Just by coincidence I happen to have spoken to a lot of European artists, intellectuals and politicians, in addition to so many 'ordinary' people, with a view to asking them how Europe should proceed. Peter Economides, for example, the man whose speech about rebranding Greece has been seen by millions of Greeks. According to him, Europe is a great brand too. 'But do you know what the problem is with the EU? They have lost touch with a large part of the electorate, especially young people, who do not consume politics in the way their parents did. Politics used to be conducted by means of public speeches or by literally connecting with people. Today's youth are all on social media, and I don't know any politicians, except Obama, who have the knack of using social media. Instead of investing in TV, which no one watches, why not create an interactive pan-European platform for real democracy?'

'A digital agora?' I said, wanting to give the impression I had some knowledge of the Greek classics.

'Precisely, a return to the agora. But they are afraid, so the EU will not do it. What we now have in Brussels are bureaucrats, but we need visionaries.'

We need a face was an opinion shared by many. 'A charismatic figure,' David Batra, Swedish comedian, said. 'One who can speak as eloquently as Obama, in at least a few of the major European languages.' Based on those criteria, the current chairman Tusk is not our man. His English was so poor when he took office that he had to sign up for a quick refresher course. Nor is Juncker a particularly talented speaker. Twice I saw him in person, reading, or rather mumbling, his soporific speech. Twice I saw the audience nodding off.

Cayetana Álvarez, the Spanish politician, agrees. She thinks we should re-examine the question of why the EU is worth the effort. According to her, there are several good answers. We would not be able to survive on the highly competitive world stage without the EU. At the same time, she thought that some major reforms were needed: more transparency, more responsibility, less bureaucracy, more unity in our markets, and a better economic union. 'People should feel more responsible. Naturally this also raises the question of European leadership, because these matters go hand in hand.' Maybe it would be a good idea for Cayetana to succeed Juncker: I for one enjoyed looking at her, and thought her audience was unlikely to nod off, even after a heavy lunch.

Felix Rottenberg is an ex-politician, which is perhaps why he is so much more outspoken than his former colleagues – or conversely, perhaps he was always outspoken and that is why he is now an ex-politician. 'Historically, there has always been a cultural undercurrent in Europe, made up of the artists – painters and composers – who travelled around Europe and worked in the royal courts. We should do more to develop that culture, on one the hand to combat poverty and class barriers in all corners of Europe, and on the other hand to ensure that Europe becomes a viable third power and a binding force in the world. It will take a lot of practice.'

Rottenberg enjoys talking about Europe; he instructs and postulates like he's performing on Dutch television. 'Then we should have a European peacekeeping force, because that is the new way of thinking about the military. The army could play an important role in helping to extinguish those enormous, dramatic conflagrations around the world. And we should have European diplomacy that specializes in the Middle East. The question is whether each individual country should send an ambassador or whether we set up European embassies in those countries. Take Africa, where a modern, unprecedented form of colonialism is developing. The Chinese are taking over economic power and it is extremely important that Europe forges a strong, modern form of co-operation that is informed by its own democratic insights.'

Another Spaniard, museum director Ferran, would like to see Europe involve its citizens more closely in order to give them a sense of being truly represented. 'Europe now has a somewhat fatalistic approach: we feel we have to do this or that, as if our fate were not in our own hands, as if it were not our own choice. Europe is now a place that seems to limit our rights, instead of protecting them. I want Europe to plant a flag of security, culture, and democracy, maybe the rights of the French Revolution. The money is elsewhere, in China or Asia, but the values should be European, no discussion.'

The Estonian Kiwa, avant-garde artist, is hoping for an unattainable combination of anarchistic freedom, a socialist welfare state, and a well-functioning economy.'

And in the free state of Christiania Finn, once an avant-garde artist too, has no doubt: 'Our way of doing things is the future of Europe. In twenty years' time everyone will be growing their own food,' he said, taking another drag on his joint. 'Look at the way we take decisions here: by consensus. That is real democracy. It only takes two intelligent people who are capable of convincing all the others. That is how it works here. Does the drainage system need renewing? Convince everybody else that it is necessary.' In that respect, Christiania and Brussels have more in common than he thinks: in Brussels too everyone has to agree on a decision. And it doesn't work there either.

THE SONG CONTEST HELPS TO CREATE A SENSE OF EUROPEANNESS — AS LONG AS IT'S BAD

Many of Youropeans had some kind of connection to the Eurovision Song Contest: Ira Losco placed second for Malta, the Croatian opera singer Lidija Horvat-Dunjko tried her hand at pop music in 1995 and placed sixth, TV presenter Maciej Orłoś was for many years the person who called in the Polish jury's *douze points*, and Piret Järvis' Estonian band Vanilla Ninja competed on behalf of Switzerland, finishing fifth. And no, it is not unusual for singers to cheat on their country: Celine Dion won in 1988 on behalf of Switzerland, and the Greek-German singer Vicky Leandros won the contest for Luxembourg in 1972.

'Our official standpoint was that it is a pretty lame event,' Piret said, 'but it was enormous fun to participate, mainly because you meet so unbelievably many different people. Precisely what Europe means to me, all those differences.'

I remember a barefooted Nicole singing *Ein bisschen Frieden*, Sandra Kim with *J'aime la vie* and Milk and Honey's *Hallelujah*. When I was in primary school we spent every Friday afternoon for months play backing *Making Your Mind Up* by Buck's Fizz, including the dance steps, and I still have a weakness for *Waterloo* and *Ding-a-Dong*, the winning Dutch song in 1975. That was in the seventies and the eighties; things went a bit downhill after that. The Song Contest was no longer the place for serious artists, but for bizarre performances. We saw a lot of those in the nineties: background choirs made up of mentally handicapped singers, drum sets suspended from the ceiling, acts that were more like an SM session than a musical performance, the low point being the Finish group Lordi – hard rockers dressed up as monsters. They won in 2006. Initially, Ira's second place was a disadvantage and not a single record company was interested in her. 'Maybe next year, when people have forgotten that you participated,' they told her.

'It was seen as a blot on your record,' I said.

'Yes, as kitsch.'

And as a gay event. Andy, the hairdresser in Copenhagen was still wildly enthusiastic: two months before he had witnessed Conchita Wurst's triumph. Conchita is a good friend of Markus, the Youropean hairdresser I interviewed in Vienna. He is a fairly butch sort of guy, but the subject of the Song Contest makes him emotional. 'Of course I knew she was good, but I never expected this. It was fantastic.'

The Song Contest began in 1956, and it is organised by the European Broadcasting Union (EBU), which sounds like it is part of the EU, but it is in fact older and even bigger than the EU, with members in 56 countries, including Israel, Lebanon, and Morocco (which competed in 1980). Although it is routinely dismissed as camp, the contest has often been the subject of serious discussion over the years. The University of Surrey, for example, examined the Song Contest's role in and contribution to the creation of a European identity.[13] The conclusion of the study was a very cautious 'yes, it contributes to a sense of Europeanness', but I read somewhere else that the Song Contest unites only insofar as the quality of the competing songs remains as low as they are now. The explanation may be that it doesn't matter who wins because it's good for a laugh and there's no need to be jealous of the winning country.

> ### AND TWELVES POINTS GO TO.....
>
> Same story, every year: the agitation about the scores. All those countries that give points to a friendly ally instead of the best song. Scandalous! Greece and Cyprus give each other top marks almost every year (11 points on average), and the Scandinavians divide up the points equally amongst themselves, but Eastern Europe is worst. The Dutch EP member Toine Manders seriously (!) proposed a return to the good old days when these countries were still hidden behind the Curtain. In the past, points were allocated by a professional jury, but since 1997, the public is also allowed to vote via telephone, and that has only made the nepotism worse. It is all very logical: people tend to vote for a song in a language they recognise (even though most songs are now in English — who knows, someday even France may give up the ghost) but above all for a song from a country they have historical and cultural ties to. Those ties often transcend national borders, particularly in view of the composition of the populations of some countries. Take the ethnic ties between Romania and Macedonia (an average 11.3 points go to Chisinau), Russia and Belarus (10.9 points to Minsk), Greece and Albania (9.9 points for Tirana). In Estonia, which has a large Russian population, Moscow receives an average of 8.2 points, but they give only 2.5 points to Tallinn. There are not many Estonians living in Russia.

I think the Song Contest is more important than we realise in Western Europe. For all those countries who gained or regained their independence in the past few decades, the evening provides an opportunity to present themselves to millions of TV viewers, and is tangible proof that they exist and they belong. It was the Song Contest that gave us our first glimpse of someone from Azerbaijan, or the Belarus flag, the first encounter with Croatian music. It is fundamentally different from that other big European event, the UEFA European Championship, in which only the strongest countries are allowed to compete in the finals: at the Song Contest little countries frequently reach the finals, while the Netherlands is usually eliminated early on and hasn't won since 1975.

Music says a lot about a country. The English, Irish and Swedes are frequent winners because they have the best understanding of pop music. France tends to submit difficult, pretentious pieces, and the Balkans excel in turbo folk. Some countries are just more musical than others, judging from the music that assaulted my ears in hotel breakfast rooms in Bulgaria, Slovakia, Latvia and Greece.

18

THE URBAN LEGENDS OF BRUSSELS

The European Parliament looms up directly behind the charming Place du Luxembourg, the heart of the stately, 19th century Leopold district. It was already enormous when it was built in 1989, on a site formerly occupied by a brewery and a shunting yard, but it has since become even bigger as the growing number of member states necessitated the addition of a new wing here or an extension there.

There are names emblazoned across the top of these steel and glass monstrosities: Paul-Henri Spaak, Jozsef Antall and Alturro Spinelli. European heroes, I assume, but they might just as well have been the names of Manchester City's defence. The square in front of the main entrance is a one-hundred-metre expanse of smooth stone, built on a slight decline and therefore an ideal place for skateboarding. But that won't happen here: this is Brussels.

At the security check near the main entrance, a new shift was taking over, and one guard greeted another, both male, with a kiss. That does happen here: this is Bruxelles.

Once inside I wandered down corridors, climbed a staircase, and then another, and ambled into a conference room and the only person I met was an employee with a cup of coffee-to-go. Where were all the Euro parliamentarians? Finally someone enlightened me: they were in Strasbourg. That's where the whole circus decamps to for a few days, twelve times a year.

I bicycled another kilometre or so to Schumanplein. This is where the office of European Commission is located. Here too, gleaming glass giants tower over an old and otherwise unremarkable neighbourhood. I noticed quite a few beggars on the square. Lobbyists do their begging wearing a suit and carrying a sleek briefcase, others do it dressed in rags, clutching an empty coffee cup. But they all know that Brussels is where the money is. On the square, more of a roundabout, there is an entrance to the underground, a coffee place, and a flower stall.

'Bonjour Monsieur,' I said.

'Just speak Dutch,' he said, while he trimmed a few bunches of flowers (diagonally of course). The florist has been here for years, it seemed, watching the Euro-folk pass by, and therefore a good vox populi.

'What kind of people come to your stall?'

'As you can see, I'm in the flower business. Neelie Kroes comes here often, your Dutch Commisioner. I don't talk to her about politics, but about football. I don't ask about her work, not because I am not interested, but because she is a client. Here we talk about other things.'

'I assume she is a Feyenoord fan, since she's from Rotterdam.' Inside his stall, there were two football photos hanging above the cash register, so I hoped this approach would give me leg up.

'*Amai*, I don't know about that. But when Holland loses, I ask her if she is not too upset.'

'Are they normal people?'

He gave me a meaningful look. 'Well, normal... I have been here twenty years, and I have seen them all. Yes, the Swedes are normal, the German, the Dutch, the British, the French are normal, but then it starts: Spain, pffff; Italian men are normal, but the women, oh my, and then there is Eastern Europe. They think

I'm a hawker and they look down on me. You can tell, you can feel it.'

Brussels, the unofficial capital of Europe, the seat of power (or is that Berlin?). Brussels, *Petit Paris*, chosen as the EU capital expressly because of its limited political clout, has evolved into a real metropolis in recent decades, and countless nationalities can be seen and heard on its streets. The main language is no longer French (and it has not been Dutch for a long time), but English, as a result of the European Union. Half of all office space in the city is taken up by European institutions (and a good chunk of the other half is rented to suppliers and other interested parties).

This is where the money-wasters hang out, unless they're meeting in Strasbourg. An army of faceless technocrats spend their time holed up in this undemocratic stronghold, thinking up petty rules. They declare that cheese cannot be made in the traditional manner, that restaurants cannot keep olive oil in open containers, and that bananas should be straight. These and other more damning complaints are what I repeatedly heard about civil servants and politicians in Brussels. They can also be applied to Luxembourg, where the seat of the European Court of Justice is, to Warsaw, where Frontex has its headquarters, to The Hague, where Europol is located, or even to Athens, home of the European Agency for Network and Information Security (ENISA). Brussels does not have a great reputation. Nor do most national administrative centres, but Brussels gets the worst press, because it has added a new layer to existing layers of hated bureaucracy, but primarily because it does not defend itself, and is perhaps incapable of doing so.

So, when I was halfway through my European tour, somewhere between Tallinn and Zagreb, I decided that if I was writing a book about Europe, I should get a better picture of its capital. Of course I had already visited the Belgian capital, interviewed Fred the hairdresser there, along with poet Els, police officer Nancy, doctor Benoît, entrepreneur Patrick, sex worker Monique and immigrant

Rachid. But that Brussels was not quite the same as the capital of Europe, and that is why I spoke to the man in the flower stall, member of the European Parliament Marietje Schaake, Christian, the receptionist at the European Council, Frontex spokesperson Delphine (in Warsaw), strategist Luuk van Middelaar, the EU press officer Petr (in Sofia), EU ambassador Jimmy and Herman van Rompuy, who had just retired as President of the European Council. Eight people, from eight different walks of life.

THE DECOLLETÉS OF EUROPEAN WAITRESSES

First, receptionist Christian, whose friendly face contrasted sharply with the line of defence that had been erected in front him: in the week after the Charlie Hebdo attacks the city was on maximum security alert, a job that was right up the street of an army of security guards who didn't look the kind of men you'd want to mess with. Some of them were in uniform, emblazoned with a capital S (for stupid), others in civilian clothes but easily recognisable because of their headsets and the face of someone who had served in Korea, Vietnam, and all of the Gulf Wars. I had noticed during visits to other institutions that the EU takes security seriously: I couldn't enter the Frontex office in Warsaw without a passport, or the Dutch EU Representation — the equivalent of an embassy — which is situated in a nondescript office on the *Hofvijver* in The Hague. The European Parliament does a more thorough bag check than El Al, and I was almost refused entry to the Justus Lipsius building, which houses the European Council, because according to the security officers I hadn't obeyed orders quickly enough (they wanted to have me arrested; it was a scandal in the making, but the chief press officer defused the situation just in time). There does not seem to be any parallel between the level of security and the EU's standing in society, but maybe this display is part of an effort to beef up that image. It reminded me of a friend of modest means who once hired two huge bodyguards to accompany him on a night out in Ibiza; he was able to bypass the long queues outside every club and was given VIP treatment everywhere.

Back to Christian. You have to cross the hall of the Justus Lipsius building, about half the length of a football pitch to reach where he sits between the lifts on one side, and a newspaper stand and a travel counter on the other side. A courteous man in his late fifties who offers friendly assistance in any number of languages. 'In the past, 90% of the questions were in French,' he said, but now they are almost all in English. Not surprising as initially the French-speaking countries were in the majority: France, Luxembourg, and Belgium, and Italy, where French was also often spoken.'

I commented that he knew a lot about it.

'Yes, I make it my business to know. I sometimes listen to a press conference while I sit here, sometimes I see it on intranet. A lot of it is beyond me, too technical.'

'When you're at a party, do people ask you about the EU?'

'Yes, frequently. Many of them, even in my own family, have a pretty hazy view of how it works. Often people are either for or against, all black and white. While if people knew more about what they were voting for, like recently, the constitution, it is almost impossible to be against it.'

'Do you explain that to them?'

'I used to. I told them that national governments are often forced to speak in two tongues, one for the voters at home, their clients, and another for here because they have to co-operate.'

Lack of familiarity is an issue. Delphine also admitted that her friends know next to nothing about Frontex. 'I think that they should learn about Europe at school.' The Dutch have a saying: unknown is unloved. Ignorance about the EU is a breeding ground for misconceptions and urban legends. 'Oh, all those rules...' Delphine said. 'They are there to make things safer, so that you can sell food products abroad via the internal market. We can no longer export our French cheese because it is made from unpasteurised milk.'

'Has anybody ever died from eating it?'

'No, but you have to reduce risk to a minimum if you want to sell internationally. It is inconvenient for us, but fortunately we can still eat the cheese ourselves,' she laughed.

Marietje Schaake, Euro parliamentarian for the liberal party was somewhat irritated when I raised one of the anti-EU camp's favourite subjects: cucumbers.

'Yes, and window washers' ladders, hairdressers' shoe soles, and the protection of waitresses' cleavage from UV rays. It's not always about EU rules, not by a long shot, even though people think it is. That business about the ladders came from the unions, who wanted fair competition and a level playing field in the internal market.' There are plenty of countries which use targeted legislation to favour their own national companies. An example of this is the sugar content of muesli, which one country set so low that only their own local products met the requirement. Foreign producers retaliated by complaining to the European Commission. 'The harmonisation of the wattage of vacuum cleaners, another notorious example, was the result of a sustainability agenda, which is something that has to be done on a European level, not by individual countries.'

The portfolio of Euro Commissioner Frans Timmerman is one indication that Brussels has taken these complaints — justified or not — to heart; it includes Better Regulation, which for him means above all 'less European regulation'.

Marietje was elected to the European Parliament on a preferential vote following a strong social media campaign. She learned how to do this when she was working on Obama's election campaign. She works in Brussels during the week, and returns to Amsterdam on the weekend, where I spoke to her.

'So you live and work in two different places?'

'At least two,' she laughed, 'because I am also in Strasbourg once a month. But I don't live there — I usually stay in a hotel. You have to arrange that yourself, and pay for it from your allowance, so some people stay in a five-star hotel, others in a B&B. I stay in a quiet but modest place since I only need it for sleeping.'

Once a month the entire circus decamps from Brussels to Strasbourg. The annual travel and hotel expenses (and the cost of transporting lorry loads of dossiers) come to approximately 200 million euros. The buildings in Strasbourg are empty the rest of the time.

'Yes, it is very inconvenient,' she admitted.

'Can't it be stopped?'

'The point is that it is a matter for the Council to decide, the ministers. And it cannot be changed unless they are unanimously agreed.'

'Let me guess. There is always one dissenting voice: the French?'

'Yes, and the French are unaware of how incredibly annoyed the Dutch are by this. Many other countries are less bothered by it.'

'Why is that?'

'I think we tend to keep a tighter hand on our purses, and we see this as a symbol of waste. The meeting schedule is also inconvenient; there is one on Tuesday, nothing on Wednesday and another on Thursday, so that you have to spend an extra day there doing nothing because it is not worth going home again.'

'Is Brussels home for most of them?'

'No, everyone is expected to live in their own member state. In some countries, it would be a scandal if their parliamentarians lived in Brussels; people in the district they come from actually want to be able to see them.'

'My impression is that the Dutch mostly expect you to be on the job in Brussels.'

'That's right, but they want you to be in both places: there and here. Or even abroad, like Iraq, where I was a few weeks ago.'

They are out there, these preconceived ideas. In addition to accusing Brussels of focusing on petty rules, or of interfering in things they have no right to interfere in, many think that Brussels is is unnecessarily expensive, populated by incompetent politicians, and that decision making is undemocratic, to mention but a few of what are seen as its major shortcomings.

THEY'RE ALL CROOKS!

Dutch news site Nu.nl, July 20 2015:

> *The diplomatic service of the European Union wants its own tableware for banquettes and dinners. The possible price ticket: 1.5 to 3 million euro. The tender process starts on Tuesday according to media reports from Brussels on Monday.*
> *The silverware for the European Service for External Action is budgeted at approximately 2 million euro. That is the biggest item of expenditure. But a set of top quality china (500,000 euro) is also required: it must be dishwasher safe and stain resistant. The European logo of twelve gold stars will be on every piece.*

Here is a sample of the online responses to this article, and the number of pluses and minuses they got:

'SCANDALOUS!!' 76 pluses, 2 minuses.
'Does it taste better with the logo, what a bunch of idiots. I'm not saying anything, just give them standard coffee cups and instant soup like the rest of us get. Elite madness.' (49+, 1-)
'Another bizarre decision by the new aristocracy, while people go hungry and the food banks have waiting lists, and not enough supply. People are in terrible pain because they can't afford to see a dentist. It's a bloody shame.' (54+, 2-)
'Oh no you don't. Let them buy their plates and silverware somewhere like IKEA. They're stark raving mad there.' (43+, 0-)

This is a random sample, but whenever an article about the EU has anything to do with money, this is the general drift of the public response. These particular responses from news site Nu.nl can be regarded as fairly neutral in political terms, and its readers as average Dutch citizens. On more conservative sites such as Telegraaf.nl and GeenStijl.nl, the responses are even more rabid. The general impression is that the whole operation in Brussels is expensive, and that it is staffed by too many overpaid civil servants and politicians.

> ## SALARIES IN BRUSSELS
>
> - The gross earnings of European civil servants are between 4,350 and 18,000 euro a month.
> - A Euro Commissioner earns approximately 22,000 euro.
> - A European parliamentarian? My neighbour, not in Germany, but in the Netherlands, is a member of the EP. Coincidentally, I also read that he is the person who argued in favour of cutting salaries by three to five percent as a gesture of solidarity with EU civil servants who had their salaries cut. Easy for him, you might say: a Euro parliamentarian's gross monthly salary is 7,956 euro, and his net earnings 6,200 (European taxes are lower). Add to that a daily allowance of 304 euro if parliament is meeting in Brussels (or Strasbourg) and he has signed the attendance list, as well as an expense allowance for office space, telephone costs and staff. Travel expenses are reimbursed separately, as are two thirds of all medical expenses. Before 2009 the allowances of Euro parliamentarians were linked to salary levels in their own country. But that is no longer the case, and they now all earn the same. That is a highly favourable situation for politicians from Bulgaria and Lithuania, but not for Danes or Swedes.

The reality is more nuanced. The EU's budget is made up of less than one percent of the respective national budgets (and it has been further reduced for the next seven years, to 908 billion). The EU spends only six percent of the total budget on itself, for offices and salaries. The European Commission, headed by a Euro Commissioner, is responsible for the ministries, and it employs 32,000 civil servants (in The Hague, by comparison, there are 120,000 of them). Their salaries are high by Dutch standards, but not by Scandinavian or Italian standards. The reasoning behind this was that salaries should not be so low as to discourage people from taking themselves off to Brussels (in 2004, when the new Eastern European countries joined, salary were adjusted, and civil servants from those countries earn a third less than their Western colleagues).

The intended consequence of those salaries that many would consider generous is to ensure that the quality of Brussels-based civil servants is high. So high that the Dutch rarely qualify, even for internships: the Dutch speak Dutch and (sloppy) English, while Luxembourgers speak four languages effortlessly, and Romanians, Lithuanians and Poles are better educated, more ambitious job applicants. The Dutch occupy a shrinking number of important positions in the EU. In the eighties, Piet Dankert was the chairman of the European Parliament, and of course somewhere back in the Middle Ages Sicco Mansholt was the Agricultural Commissioner — a crucial position at the time — and he was also the President of the European Commission for seven months.

Translators are another major expenditure: one billion a year, or 'two euro per person per year,' which is how the EU prefers to calculate the cost. There are 24 official languages for the 28 countries, including some very strange ones, as I noticed when I was making the promotional film for my crowd funding campaign. I wanted it to be funny, but also the kind of film that would mobilize support and subsequently go viral, so I decided to speak one sentence of my text in each of the EU languages. In the preceding days various embassies had helped me, and I had learned the minute-and-a-half long text by heart. In Latvia I said something like 'the Youropeans project is incredibly important', and in Finnish 'please give me money' (in retrospect, the text could have better; maybe that is why it raised such a miserly sum). The most unusual was Maltese, which has Arabic origins.

Should that also be translated in Brussels? Chris, Maltese

entrepreneur, does not think so. 'Look, I am extremely proud of my language, but English should be the official language.' That may be asking too much, but surely it is possible to let everyone speak their own language but to translate only into English. That is unlikely to happen. The UK and Ireland would agree, and Germany and the Scandinavian countries would probably not object. France, however, would protest, as would the smaller countries, because they already have the impression that they have too little say, and have made too many concessions.

THE ELEPHANTS' GRAVEYARD

Over the past two years I sometimes came across formal portraits of the European Commission: in the corridor of the EU Representation in Bratislava, in the House of Europe in The Hague, in the hall of European Commission's office in Brussels. Such photographs are always interesting, and who is standing next to whom, and who has been banished to the back row, say something about the relevant hierarchies.

This photo was primarily a collection of double chins, crepe-soled shoes and bad haircuts. Clearly, salaries were not being spent in Brussels' clothing stores or hairdressers. It was a photo of the previous commission, and Neelie Kroes was the only elegantly dressed person among them. But if we don't send our prettiest people to Brussels, maybe we do send our best and the brightest? Civil servants apply for their jobs and are thoroughly screened, but politicians are sent, and there is a lot of variance per country and per party. 'For some of them it is form of pre-pension, for others a jumping-off point,' Marietje Schaake said. 'Take Nick Clegg, the leader of the British Liberal Democrats, Jeanine Hennis, the Dutch Minister of Defense and Alexander Stubb, Finland's current minister of finance; they all began in the EP.'

EUROSIGNS

Italians honk their horns, speak loudly, play their music just a little too loudly, and on squares where tourists congregate there is always a street artist. Not a man with lute or a flute, but with an amplified guitar playing at a volume more suited to Wembley Stadium. The one in front of the Pantheon was playing Pink Floyd, while the guy on the Piazza del Popolo thought he was Guns N' Roses.

So if you are unfortunate enough to be deaf, Italy might be the best place for you. It's quieter and Italians use sign language all day anyway. That is not an opinion shared by the ENS, Italy's national association of the deaf. They had set up a tent in front of the gates of parliament and were protesting. There was another tent where two handicapped brothers had been living for the past year, a RAI TV car, and a clutch of reporters: in a few days parliament was due to choose a successor to its 90-year old president Napolitano.

'We are the black sheep of Europe,' said a thin man in a jeans jacket. 'Italy is the only country in Europe that doesn't officially recognise sign language. Well, neither do Malta and Luxembourg.' He can hear, his colleague can't. They tried to coax a passing politician into their tent, a vain man who spent his minute with the deaf man scanning the crowd for a more interesting person to talk to, and hoping that the TV cameras would not capture their good-bye hug.

My dentist Marten is deaf. He is very active in the deaf world, and was, for example, closely involved with the *Deaflympics*, the Olympics for deaf people. He told me that sign language is not international, as I had assumed. I was under the impression that a Chinese, a Surinamese and a Finn would all be able to express anger, sadness, the sun and a bird in the same manner. That was a misconception. Sign language is not *Pictionary*: it's different in every language, and there are even local dialects, and every language has its own grammatical structure. There have been attempts to develop a kind of deaf Esperanto, Gestuno. It was not a success, but there is hope. The increasing level of contact among deaf communities in Europe has given rise to a new language: Eurosigns. Wouldn't it be great if street artists could be taught to use this language to perform Nirvana's *Smells Like Teen Spirit*?

This is Europe

This is what Youropeans thought about the politicians in Brussels, on a sliding scale from bad to worse: they sit around in their ivory towers, they have no connection with ordinary people, they are lazy, possibly corrupt. Even Donald Tusk, the new president of the Council, came in for criticism from his own compatriots. 'It's good, isn't it, that Tusk landed such an important job?' I asked a few of his compatriots, who replied, 'Ach, maybe it is good for the country, but I think he should have stayed home and taken care of his own party. It's a mess.'

Italian Euro politicians are mercilessly satirised in TV programmes. 'Because apparently they do nothing,' said Helvia, who is a Dutch immigrant, but just as fiery as the Italians. 'All they do is sit in the European parliament for an hour week. People think it's scandalous.'

Estonia is the only country that is enthusiastic about its politicians. 'The country is so small that we all know one another, and we know who we are voting for,' doctor Toomas said. 'I know Andrus Ansip, who has just been appointed Euro Commissioner, from our time at the university. He studied chemistry and was a very good athlete.'

'Of course we send our good people too,' said Cayetana, Spanish politician and Youropean, 'but traditionally it is a elephants' graveyard, for people at the end of their career, presidents and provincial governors, people who were once important in the party. And this must change of course.'

The Croatian Euro Commissioner whom I met, Nevem Mimica, an otherwise remarkably colourless man, cleverly manipulated a press conference by managing to use every journalist's question as an excuse to tell his own story, and doing this so successfully that he answered only three or four questions from journalists during a forty minute session. 'No, we don't send our top people,' Vedrana, a member of the Zagreb municipal council, had assured me several months before. 'They are political appointees, and that is a pity, because I would rather see a capable German as a European Commissioner than a Croat who is not up to the job. I am convinced that, for example, a Swede would pay just as much attention to Croatia's interests.'

I agree with her, and thought it was strange that I was only allowed to vote on a strictly national ticket during the European elections: let the best man or woman win, regardless of whether they're from my country, because as far as I am concerned they do not necessarily have to serve Dutch interests. However, a transnational list of candidates would require a treaty amendment. 'For many people, that would be a step too far down the road to European unification, and it is not likely happen any time soon,' Marietje said.

UNDEMOCRATIC?

A common complaint is the accusation that the European Union has a democratic deficit. Important decisions, most recently those regarding a possible Grexit, are taken behind closed doors. Or by the European Commission, an unelected body that is appointed and prepped by technocratic EU servants.

While that may be true, it does not necessarily constitute a democratic deficit, since even though the decisions are taken in backrooms, they originate with the national ministers who sit on the European Commission's Council of Ministers, and they are often armed with strict instructions from their national parliaments. The ministers are appointed, but via elected representatives of the people. And it is government leaders who appoint the European Commission via the European Council.

It is therefore indirect democracy. Nothing new there: the Upper House of the Dutch parliament works in the same way, like many other European houses of parliament. Moreover, the 2007 Lisbon Treaty considerably strengthened the position of the European Parliament. Before that its role was strictly advisory, but now many decisions require the approval of parliament, whose members are democratically elected.

The complaint that the EU is not very democratic is partly

due to the low turnout at European elections. In every country it is lower than for national elections, with Slovakia producing the lowest score to date: 13 percent in 2014. Moreover, election issues are often national issues that serve as a measure of the popularity of the national government. The EU can do nothing about this; it is a matter for national government.

Thierry Baudet, a Dutch Eurosceptic, has argued that democracy cannot function without a *demos,* a people.[14] And that is the problem, according to him, because a *demos* implies a shared language and culture, and therefore the EU is not democratic. I don't think this arguments holds water: there most certainly is a European culture, and it is the result of centuries of trade, war, emigration, cultural exchanges and travel on the part of writers, composers and painters, all of which are rooted in the Judeo-Christian tradition. There is also a shared language, and it is English.

> **THE DIFFERENCES**
>
> The European Council determines the general policy of the EU; its members are the 28 heads of state and of government, and the current president is the Pole Donald Tusk. The composition of the Council of the European Union is variable, and the ministers who sit on it are dependent on the policy areas under consideration, while the chairman is the minister of the country that currently holds the presidency of the EU.
>
> The Council of Europe is not an EU Institution; it is an older body set up in 1949 to foster European democracy. It has 47 members, its headquarters are in Strasbourg and the chairman is the Norwegian Thorbjørn Jagland.
> The Council of Europe does however have the same official song as the EU, Beethoven's ninth.

'It's nonsense to say that the EU is not democratic,' Xavier Bettel said, who was at the time the mayor, but is now the prime minister of Luxembourg, which is due to chair the EU during the second half of 2015, and therefore possibly not the most unbiased person. 'We are the EU, all 28 countries, we are all represented.'

Undemocratic? In my opinion the EU is *too* democratic and its structure, size and decision-making process make it virtually unmanageable. There is one area which you might justifiably say is undemocratic, and that is the infamous 'gap between the people and politics.' Because we know almost nothing about the EU. According to the Eurobarometer, most people (97%) have heard of the European parliament. Of all professional categories, students are the least familiar with the European Commission (73%), the self-employed the most familiar (100%), which to me says a lot about the academic level of European students. These outcomes are not too disappointing. But then, the European Central Bank rings a bell, but no questions were asked about the European Council or the Council of the European Union, which were probably considered too obscure. Do you know what the exact relationship is between the European Commission and European Council? Or, even more complex, the difference between the European Council and the Council of Europe? And the Council of the European Union? Brussels is unnecessarily complicated,* and all those poorly chosen names do not exactly help to foster a better understanding.

So, to summarise, the preconceptions are largely false. Most of the stories about crazy EU rules can be relegated to the realm of the urban legend. They are not the result of over-zealousness, but a response to protesting companies or the initiative of a particular industry. The administrative machinery is relatively slim-line, but reasonably well paid. The quality of the civil servants is high,

---

* To prepare for the Netherlands' presidency of the EU, I joined a group of Dutch journalists who had been invited to Brussels for a two-day crash course that included tours, meetings with civil servants and politicians, but above all classes explaining how laws were made in Brussels. The answer was: via countless lawyers, labyrinthian systems and consultation processes. I couldn't make heads or tails of it, and I have a law degree…

which cannot be said of all politicians. Nor would I say that Brussels is particularly undemocratic. Which brings us to question of why the European Union has such a bad reputation.

19

IT'S THE COMMUNICATION, STUPID!

It is the *Davos* of development work, so consider it an honour to be present. That was the subtle message I got from the organisation which, acting on behalf of the EU, had invited me to attend as a journalist. The European Development Days (EDD) had gathered five thousand participants for a two-day conference in Brussels: EU people, representatives of NGOs, Africans, and Asians. Speaking from the main stage, Jean-Claude Juncker opened the event, droning on, broadcasting clichés ('there is too much poverty, too many people who have to subsist on a dollar a day'). We journalists were sitting in the dark in the back row; my Lithuanian colleague to my left was checking her Facebook page, and the cheerful Greek to my right was nodding off.

The next person up was Martin Schulz, the chairman of the European Parliament, who as a speaker is no Obama either. When the prime minister of Latvia, which at the time still chaired the EU, began addressing the conference in her own language and everyone scrabbled to find their interpretation headsets, the president and the chairman apparently decided they had more important things to do; they moved towards the exit, close to where I was sitting, chatting in fairly loud voices, as Juncker put his arm around the shoulders of his German buddy.

My little group of journalists was well taken care of, having been flown in from all corners of the union and put up in a four star hotel next to the European Commission building. The objective being to encourage us to write about the EDD, and in order to ensure that we did so in a relatively well-informed fashion, we had attended a series of mini-master classes in the hotel conference room the day before.

'It is the European Year for Development,' an EU department head, an Italian, said.

Oh.

'And do we know what last year was?' he quizzed us.

Fifteen journalists stared at the thick information packet they had just received, fiddled with their pens, and hoped they would not be called on to answer. A brave Slovenian ventured a guess: 'The Year of Equal Rights'?

'No, the Year of the European Citizen.' An effort to encourage involvement.

We subsequently learned that the EU spends over 70 billion annually on foreign aid, 8 to 10 percent of its total budget, making it the world's third largest donor, after the US and the United Kingdom. 'And if all the individual countries are included, Europe is the largest,' the Italian explained. Because of course individual countries also engage in development work. It sounds like duplication, and somewhat illogical, and the EU head admitted that there is some overlap, and encroachment on one another's territory. But according to the Eurobarometer, 80 percent of Europeans approve, and I read in my information pack that 60 percent would like to spend more money on foreign aid. And, believe it or not, 50 percent of the population would like to know what happens to the money. Why is it all so unclear?

'Well,' said the Croatian Euro Commissioner at a press conference the next day, which had been organised specially for our group. 'Much of the work is contracted out to other organisations, who plant their flag and claim the successes as their own.' Who knew that the EU supported operations in Mali and was also active in Somalia, or that the EU was feeding the soldiers who were fighting the terrorist group Al Shabaab. I didn't. Why does no one know?

There are several reasons, another EU departmental head explained, the first being journalists themselves. 'In general, you are less interested in European affairs than in national politics, where you know all the players. And as result, you are also poorly informed.' In addition, the lack of interest means that journalists find it hard to get their articles published.

'The second is that the EU has a limited communications budget.'

'Why don't you increase it? It's what the people want, according to the Eurobarometer.'

'The member states do not want it.'

Hence, the citizens of Europe do not know very much about what goes on in Brussels, have indicated that they would like to know more, but the European Union cannot respond. Because the member states refuse to co-operate.

A crazy-making situation, you might say, but Brussels reserves judgement. The EU people I spoke to over the past two years, including communications officers from various European Representations — embassies, in effect — were clear: their work is difficult, and they don't receive much help. They do not complain openly, are perhaps discouraged from doing so by some form of agreement with the member states. But Juncker had harsh words to say about this in an interview with *de Volkskrant* immediately after he took up office as the president of the European Commission; 'The traditional Dutch parties are as quiet as mice on the subject of European integration. I remember the 2005 referendum on the European Constitution. The PvdA, CDA, VVD (respectively the Dutch Labour Party, the Christian Democrats and the Liberal Party) all refused to campaign on behalf of the Constitution, for fear of being associated with the EU. And then things went wrong. The 'no' vote against the Constitution was not the success of the populists, but the fault of the traditional parties.'[15] The Netherlands responded with outrage to this article, which found its way into many news broadcasts. Politicians were given plenty of scope to explain that things were not as he had presented them, and anyway, who did that funny little man from Luxembourg think he was!

I put this to Van Rompuy; 'It seems as if the national governments do not do much to promote the European Union.'

'Yes, and that is putting it mildly. The opposite is true. What one often sees is that government leaders meet in Brussels, take unpopular decisions, and when they get home, or worse, even before they leave Brussels, they give a press conference in which they distance themselves from those decisions. As if they have not been part of that decision-making process! How can you expect to galvanize public opinion, which is already full of doubt about government in general, if your own leaders distance themselves from their own decisions?' he said sharply.

It is an unusual phenomenon, one that it also certainly newsworthy: the press conferences following European deliberations take place simultaneously: the Italian minister in a room next to the German minister, who is next to Czech minster, and judging from their statements, you would not think that they had just been seated around the same table.

'It must be frustrating.'

'Yes. [Political leaders] move in a certain direction because they know that public opinion is sceptical. They take advantage of this by suggesting "we are not such Europhiles ourselves".'

Janus-faced, two-faced, hypocritical: that is what national politicians are guilty of where Brussels is concerned. 'National governments are often forced to speak in two tongues, one for the voters at home, their clients, and another for here because they have to co-operate,' receptionist Christian said in the preceding chapter. The result is that national politicians present any good news from Brussels as something they have managed to rescue from the flames, or they claim successes as their own, and ignore the fact that the outcome had long been decided on a European level. Unpopular measures are Brussels' fault: we were outvoted, shouted down, there was nothing we could do.

Mateja, the old communist firebrand in Slovenia, nicknamed Khmer Rouge, doesn't believe it. 'They blame the EU when they have to take unpopular measures. So we checked up on them, got the documents and reports from Brussels.'

'And?'

'Politicians will say anything, it wasn't true.'

The same probably applies to many other EU countries. They would not get away with it in national politics: the press, the fourth estate, would be all over them. But not in Brussels, for the reasons mentioned above. There is little interest in Brussels, and it is telling that RTL News, the Netherlands' second most popular news show, does not even have a correspondent there. When in my country there is a TV-programme about the EU, its few viewers are generally already well-informed (and pro-European).

'You notice that journalists are overwhelmed and simply copy press releases or pass them on,' Marietje said. 'And that is also down to the Dutch focus of the media. I don't think it promotes healthy debate, and it is does not provide a good check on power.'

'Politicians do not want to relinquish power to European institutions,' I read in an interview with Guy Verhofstadt, the leader of the liberal party in the European Parliament.

'Nor are the citizens in favour of that,' was the Dutch journalist's response.

'Is it not the politicians' job to point out a better way?' the Belgian replied.

It is the kind of remark you might find on an anti-EU poster, but true again: that is what politicians are for. They are supposed to understand the subject matter, and to have thought about a proper course of action. If the voters do not agree, or if it turns out to be a bad choice, they can vote for someone else the next time around.

Politicians are opposed to giving Brussels more power. Because more Brussels means less power in The Hague. Or in Paris, Zagreb, Copenhagen, or Warsaw. It is not in the interests of national politicians to give up power, but it is in the interests of the voters.

The fact that people do not know much about Brussels, its unpopularity, may be just what the Dutch government ordered, as suggested by its refusal to lift a finger during the referendum on the Constitution. Over the past two years, I sometimes heard the following comment: the Dutch government is not prepared to do anything except brief its citizens about the Europe. Inform them. Not make them enthusiastic and certainly not sell them on the idea. That sounds more logical than it is, because surely the agreements that Dutch representatives reach in Brussels are for the most part favourable for the Netherlands. Maybe not right away, but in the long run. The father who buys his son a new bicycle and says, 'Yes, it works but don't expect too much of it', shouldn't be too surprised if his son does not take very good care of his bike.

I don't know whether or not we should have a 'neuro' – a euro only for the financially strong North European countries, or hold out for a United States of Europe. I do think that the EU is not as good as it could and should be. The EU should be given a fair chance, but that would require having national politicians who are not afraid of making themselves superfluous, or of losing elections, if that is in the best interests of their voters and their part of the world. And there are not many of those around.

EPILOGUE
MARK DOES A FEW CITY TRIPS

It is one o'clock. One more round then. I bicycle past the ferry that will leave for Estonia tomorrow morning, up through Kaivopuisto Park, and down again, bouncing faster and faster over the cobblestones, in the direction of the harbour, a route of at least two kilometres. On my way I see a man and his dog, a couple making out on a park bench, and two taxi drivers leaning against their Mercedes'. That's all. Helsinki is a quiet place; the streets are deserted.

On summer nights when I was a boy my mother used to call me to come in when it got dark. She called me in to brush my teeth and go to bed, no more fun. The best thing about mid-June was that it didn't get dark until almost ten o'clock.

It is half past one in the morning, the sky is blue-grey, orange in the far west. A Tuesday night at the end of June in Helsinki. I tear across Senate Square, earlier that day the domain of pigeons, tourists and ice cream carts, turn onto the Esplanadi, the Finnish Champs-Élysées, and turn up the volume on my earphones. The shuffle throws up *Flamenco Blues,* but I refuse to believe the procedure is random; it has to be mood-adjusted since it always plays exactly what I want to hear at that moment. Have you ever noticed that? The city is empty, and it's an uncanny feeling, a bit like a party where everyone has gone home but the last one to leave has forgotten to turn out the lights.

It's not even twilight. Paul Weller, *Wild Wood*. One more round? Through Eira, the high-rent district, where the embassies are and the self-proclaimed Finnish elite – the Swedish speakers – live, something I had learned that afternoon.* My iPhone has had enough, and has gone to sleep, like the city. Two o'clock. It feels like night; it is quiet, the birds have stopped singing, the wind has died down, and all I can hear is a tram creaking and rattling a few blocks away. But it is still light, the day is not over yet, and I can stay outside and play.

That was Helsinki, possibly my favourite destination. But Bucharest was also impressive, Zagreb a pleasant surprise, Vienna beautiful, Lisbon never a disappointment, and I liked Berlin so much that I decided to move there. Travelling cheered me up, made me happy. First of all on account of the weather, which was usually better than it was at home, because I followed the sun, visiting Northern Europe in the summer, and countries with a continental climate in the spring and autumn, and saving Malta, Athens and Nicosia for the winter. It was an adventure to arrive in strange city I had never visited before, to feast my eyes and do my best to take in as many impressions of the place as possible, to get the feel of the city and pinpoint its landmarks: the train station there, the river here and over there the famous square. That's a bad neighbourhood, these are the local mores, this is how the subway works, and that's where I can rent a bike.

I set off each day armed with a camera, notebooks, pens, a phone battery and the phone itself. My iPhone was my lifeline. I need-

---

* Finland was for a long time part of Sweden, and Swedish had long been the language of the aristocracy. The Finnish Swedes lived mostly in the southern, more prosperous part of the country, which includes Helsinki.

ed it not only to make calls, but also to navigate the city, record conversations, make films and do online research – I don't think I could have done Youropeans ten years ago. (My biggest fear was of course losing my telephone. Every now and then I had a moment of panic and could be seen rooting frantically through my bag in the metro or on a park bench, and every night I did back-ups in two places.)

'I am so jealous of your project, I would switch places with you any time.' How many times did I hear that? 'Yes, you fly to all those cities, talk to interesting people, and you get to write about it.' What can I say? The travel itself was often an ordeal: the stress of catching a flight and then finding out that my seat was more suitable for someone without legs, or that the woman in front of me was determined to place her seat in the full reclining position, or the man seated next to me was the fattest passenger on board, the wailing baby was just one row behind me, and the two businessmen across the aisle were discussing their boring commercial affairs in very loud voices. Fortunately, the longest flight from Amsterdam to anywhere in Europe is four hours and ten minutes (to Cyprus). But it wasn't all fun and games: a lonely stay in a strange city is not exactly what somebody with a suppressed fear of travel dreams of.

My fear of travel began about ten years ago when I got sick in the middle of the Serengeti, a National Park in Tanzania. It wasn't even very serious, just a run-of-the-mill stomach infection, but I longed for coolness, yoghurt, and the close proximity of a doctor, preferably one wearing a white coat, and in possession of a spotless consulting room instead of a ramshackle clinic where a few days earlier I had sat amongst the lepers and other people afflicted with terrifying diseases while I waited for my antibiotics. I panicked, cut my holiday short, and that was the start of my little phobia. When I had to flee New York in fear six months later, my world suddenly shrank and in the end I hardly dared to leave Amsterdam. I tried, though. Once I made it as far as Schiphol because I had booked a trial trip to Mallorca. I lingered at the check-in counter but wimped-out at the last minute and returned home with my tail between my legs. But things gradually improved and over the last five or so years I had begun to enjoy travelling again, although I was always afraid of relapsing. Now that I have travelled virtually fear-free to 27 foreign capitals, some of which were far away and fairly strange, I think I can say that I have slain that particular dragon.

But OK, you want to trade places with me. Are you sure? The interviews were often fun to do, because the people I talked to were interesting, funny or kind, but that was only the start. I then had to produce a transcript of the conversations I had recorded. Have you ever done that? It is every journalist's nightmare: if someone can come up with reliable speech recognition software he deserves a Nobel Prize. One minute of conversation equates to approximately three minutes of listening, and listening again to the tape, because a waitress was talking at the same time, or someone was revving up a motorcycle. A thirty-minute interview with a police officer in a meeting room is manageable, but sometimes the conversation lasted an hour and twenty minutes. The longest conversation I had was with the oldest Youropean: Anton, the priest, spoke for almost three hours in a mishmash of rusty English and German; what he said was often moving, wise and interesting, but not always relevant. And I didn't feel comfortable interrupting an 85-year old man. In all, I did 240 interviews with an average length of 50 minutes.

Step two involved transforming the interview into a readable story, with a beginning, a middle and an end. In English, even though not all of the interviews were conducted in English. When that version was ready, I emailed it to the interviewee, so that they could check for factual inaccuracies. This is standard practice for journalists, at least in the Netherlands. However, my Youropeans usually baulked at my version of the interview: they frequently sent it back, full of what they referred to as 'minor changes' and comments to the effect that they had been misunderstood, and that in retrospect it would better not to include certain remarks. My response was to take a deep breath and do a little compromising. Doctors were the worst, and the worst of all was Dr Anastassiades, who had spoken very freely and expressed outspoken views. He rewrote three quarters of the interview, and in the version he returned to me, his anger at the Turks had been toned down considerably, and the conversational tone of the interview replaced by 'official language more befitting of a doctor'. His version did not make the cut; it was mine that was posted on the site. Usually, six of the eight interviewees responded. Fewer in Brussels and Dublin, where the response was 25 percent. Tallinn had the highest response rate, once again confirming its reputation as Europe's star pupil. Doctors and entrepreneurs responded to my worked-up version of the interview almost all of the time, and hairdresser and sex workers almost never. Perhaps doctors think it is more important for their words to be recorded as precisely as possible, and they may also be more authoritarian than hairdressers. One of the reasons why the sex workers did not respond was because the email addresses they gave me were wrong. Never let a journalist get too close.

What did I do the rest of the day? I worked up the interviews, looked for people to interview, did a little photo shopping, tidied up my films, looked for sponsors, shouted at interns, managed my crowdfunding campaign, tried to drum up publicity, planned my trips, fed the Facebook page. I had a lot to do. In fact I had way, way too much to do. The busiest days were the city trips during which I had to complete at least eight interviews in four days, about half of which I had yet to arrange as I navigated unfamiliar streets and neighbourhoods. I usually also had two or three other appointments with journalists or embassy people.

Youropeans was incredibly educational. I now know how to keep a straight face and continue asking serious questions with a shemale on my lap*, who has just discarded the top half of her bikini. I can stay in character when the mayor of Luxembourg

---

* Yes, it takes all kinds to make a world.

tries to do a headstand on a couch.* I have developed the skills you need to gain the trust of a police officer so that he will stop feeding you only the official line. Not always, but most of the time. And I learned a lot about Europe, a beautiful continent, rich in every respect. Where I know my way around, and feel at home. Where the wonderful, beautiful people I met far outnumbered the horrible, ugly ones.

There is a reason for this, or so the story goes. A man comes to a village and asks to meet the local wise man. 'I'm thinking about moving here; can you tell me what kind of people live here?'

The wise man thinks about for a minute and then asks the stranger: 'What kind of people live in the place you come from?'

The visitor said, 'Nothing but riff-raff. They're all crooks and liars.'

'You know,' the old wise man said, 'the same kind of people live here too.'

The stranger disappeared in a flash.

The next day another visitor strolled into the village, and he too came to the wise man, and asked him the same question. The wise man asked the stranger what kind of people lived in the place he was from. 'Well, they were the nicest people ever: hospitable, hard-working, cheerful people, and I will miss them enormously.'

The village wise man said: 'Exactly the kind of people who live here too.'

---

* Yes, it takes all kinds to make a world.

TIPS FOR CITY TRIPS

This is Europe

I can imagine that after reading this book you might be thinking of taking a trip to Helsinki, Bucharest or Lisbon yourself, and you're wondering if I could give you a few tips. I'm happy to oblige, and I'll throw in my eight local friends for good measure: say hi to the police, the hairdresser and the sex worker for me.

I can also recommend a hotel in most of the cities; sometimes I stayed in more than one in each place, after thorough online research (I preferred four-star boutique hotels to the more formal five-star hotels, which were often too expensive anyway). You may not be able to get such a good deal as I got, since I never travelled in the high season, and was sometimes able to negotiate a journalists' discount. (I initially planned to post a travel blog in addition to my serious Youropeans site, and call it CapitalMark. I hoped to enlist KLM, TripAdvisor, and possibly a hotel chain as sponsors, but after three cities I abandoned the idea because it is too much work, and the sponsors were not biting.)

So here are my tips:

Tips for city trips

1. **Amsterdam**. I lived there, so obviously didn't need a hotel. But I can recommend the Lloyd Hotel, which is a good, attractive hotel that offers discounts for arty types. And the Ysbreeker on the Amstel has been my favourite café for at least fifteen years.

2. **Athens**. Although it is full of tourists, especially at the foot of the Acropolis, Athens is not an open air museum, but a real city where people live and work. A bit rough around the edges, with holes in the pavement, dodgy neighbourhoods, and at least three protest marches every day.

    HOTEL: the New Hotel, number 5 in my Hotel Top 10. Located in the city centre, beautifully designed, gorgeous roof terrace, very friendly personnel and a good breakfast.

3 **Berlin**. I read somewhere that it is one of the only major cities where fewer people live now than before the outbreak of the Second World War, and it's true, the city feels spacious. Especially in Tempelhofer Freiheit, the former airfield that has become a park, but without trees. It has a horizon, which gives it a sense of freedom.

    HOTEL: I live here now, but before that I stayed in Airbnb apartments in Prenzlauer Berg and Kreuzberg, and once in a hotel: Honigmond in Mitte. It was OK, although the antique wooden bed collapsed when I sat on it.

4. **Budapest**. What a city! With its palaces, squares and bridges it could be the most beautiful city in Europe, but its faded glory deserves a fresh coat of paint. Take just a few steps off the beaten path recommended by the tourist office and the poverty is all too visible. I have never seen so many angry faces as in Budapest: perhaps they haven't yet realised that faded glory is better than no glory.

HOTEL: design hotel Lanchid 19, is a little worn, but nice, and the location, right on the Danube, is gorgeous. And of course, the big, modern, luxurious Kempinski, which is located in the heart of the city.

5. **Bucharest**. Yes, there are holes in the pavement, particularly if you venture out into the bleak suburbs, and also a lot of stray dogs (although the previous government is said to have exterminated most of them). But it is a grand city, full of imposing museums, churches and palaces. They make the best of things, was my impression of the Romanians. The people are friendly, and funny too. And if you accidentally bump into someone, they say they're sorry. Many of them learned to speak good English at school. A city of contrasts: Romanian women are prudish but they wear very short skirts. You may see a classical string quartet playing in a park, only 100 metres away from streets full of sex clubs. Elegant squares, but also Ceauçescu's monstrous palace. Cigarettes and alcohol are on sale everywhere. I didn't see a single pickpocket (they are all in Western Europe of course).

HOTEL: Rembrandt, which as the name suggests, is run by a Dutchman. Well appointed, nice wooden floors, centrally located.

6. **Bratislava**. There are no ordinary shops, such as a pharmacist, in the city centre. Nothing but restaurants catering to the tourists who trail around behind a guide or trundle over the cobblestones in a little hop-on-hop-off train. The other side of the mighty Danube is another story: the old Soviet-era apartment blocks are slightly less grim these days because whole sides of buildings, sometime 80 by 80 metres, have been painted bright yellow, red or blue.

HOTEL: Kempinski. A five-star hotel that is too luxurious for the likes of me. At breakfast, the over-solicitous wait staff kept asking me how I was doing, but by the third time, it was starting to get on my nerves. The reception desk was excellent and the health club phenomenal, with a 25-metre swimming pool on the tenth floor, and a view of the Danube.

7. **Brussels**. Now that I've spent more time there, I understand why it's called *Petit Paris:* its boulevards, palaces and churches have an air of grandness, but combined with the ambiance of a village, especially in the squares around the Sint Katelijn church, where I had some very good fish at *Bij den boer* .

    HOTEL: Stanhope, a little too business-like for my tastes, and I had to pay the full price, something I hoped to avoid. Directly across the street from the offices of EVP, the Christian Democrats.

8. **Copenhagen**. Even the cemeteries here are friendly and hospitable: Assistens, where Kierkegaard and Hans Christian Anderson are buried is a place where people hang out, including girls in bikinis. But everyone is quiet and polite: they're Danish after all. Copenhagen perennially scores high on the list of the world's 10 most beautiful cities, and its reputation is well-earned, although it also scores high on the list of the world's most expensive places.

    HOTEL: Babette. Good location at the edge of the city centre, close to the water and the overrated symbol of the city, the mermaid. Hip and beautifully decorated, excellent staff, delicious breakfast. Number 2 in my Hotel Top 10.

9. **Dublin**. I think that all Irish are funny: old men in pubs, random girls on trams, but I can't say for sure because they are unintelligible.

HOTEL: Waterloo House. Small and very pleasant, with excellent staff. Youropean Irene is the singing manager of the breakfast room.

10. **Helsinki**: OK, it is cold and dark for six months out of the year, but in the summer, there is no finer city. The city centre, Vironniemi, is a peninsula with a beach that has so far miraculously escaped being ruined by expensive hotels and tacky bars. There is nothing here but peaceful yacht harbours, the docks for the big ferries, and some smaller ones for the wooden ferries that connect thousands of little islands. A tourist tip (with romantic potential): take her or him to Merisatamanranta at the end Vironniemi and take a ferry to Liuskasaari (those crazy Finnish names were a challenge), a little island only 50 metres away. Choose a spot on one of the big flat rocks, warmed by the sun. You'll probably be alone there as this is Helsinki, and therefore quiet. Look out across the sea and watch the big ferries to Estonia and Stockholm disappearing into the distance, and drink that bottle of wine that was so shockingly expensive, even in a supermarket.

HOTEL: Klaus K, a pleasant boutique hotel. Or Seurahuone, a *grande dame* directly opposite the train station.

11. **Lisbon**. One of my favourite cities, for many reasons, including its location on hills next to a mighty river, the Tagus, and the weather. And because of its history, its grandeur as the capital of the huge empire that Portugal once was. But above all because of its authenticity. Lisbon, on the edge of Europe, is less commercialized than other cities, and instead of shopping streets full of the same brands you see everywhere in the world, you can still find an old shoemaker next door to a hip clothing store.

And if it is raining in Lisbon, or the sun is working overtime, go to a museum. Take tram 15 to Belém which is just outside the city centre and was therefore spared the destruction caused by the great earthquake of 1755. Bypass the tourists waiting to get into the Monastery of Jerónimos and the Tower of Belém, and go into the Museu Coleção Berardo. It is big, square and modern (and cool and dry). It is also free, which is perhaps why it is so quiet, so quiet that with a little luck it can be like attending a private showing. It is a modern art museum — or rather a museum for *the best of modern art*: there are one or two works by every major artist. Maybe not very exciting from an art-historical point of view — like *best of* CDs, critics may turn up their noses, but I don't care.

HOTEL: I have tried at least eight in Lisbon, and they were all good. The best are Mercy Hotel, Janelas Verdes and above all LX Boutique, a beautifully restored hotel in what was until recently a bad neighbourhood. One hundred metres away from the Tagus. Number 1 on my Hotel Top 10 list. Check out their site to see why.

12. **Ljubljana**. A nice village, and you can see it all in about an hour. Nebotičnik, the Slovenian word for skyscraper, has a pleasant rooftop terrace.

HOTEL: Antiq Palace. A small city palace where my room was a three-room apartment.

13. **London**. It's big.

HOTEL: none, I stayed with a friend.

14. **Luxembourg**. Others may find this city boring, but I like peace and quiet, and the feeling that the city has been standing still since the fifties, or at least walking at a much slower pace than other capitals. And it has a spectacular alley, a *grand canyon,* 80 metres deep and about 200 metres across, which forms a

natural division between the downtown, or Grund area, and the rest of the city. The streets were almost paved with euros – I found more coins on the street than in any other city.

HOTEL: I stayed with a friend.

15. **Madrid**. Where it only rains one week a year: the week that I was there. But it gave me more time to visit a few beautiful museums (Thyssen-Bornemisza!), and the city's most beautiful theatre, the Estadio Bernabéu, where I saw Christiano Ronaldo play with Juventus. Madrid, the third largest city in the EU (after London and Berlin) is grandiose, the monumental centre of a country (and of what was once a world empire).

HOTEL: none. I stayed with friends.

16. **Nicosia**. My first, and probably last time in Cyprus: why would you come to this European outpost? Well, many British tourists come, as do rich Russian expats. But they probably avoid Nicosia, which is not the prettiest place on the island. The top attraction is the wall that divides the Greek side of Cyprus from the occupied half. They city looks as if it was knocked together over the past three decades without a plan and without love. I'm glad I saw it, and it was nice to be able to wear a T-shirt in November.

HOTEL: none, I stayed with a friend.

17. **Paris**. It's a nice place, too bad the French live there: so goes the cliché, and damned if it isn't true. Nowhere in Europe did so many people bump into me in the street without so much as a mumbled 'sorry', and with their nose stuck in the air.

HOTEL: none, I stayed in a friend's apartment.

HOTEL TOP 10

1. LX Boutique, Lisbon. Beautifully restored in what was until recently a bad neighbourhood. One hundred metres from the Tagus.[16]
2. Babette, Copenhagen. Hip and beautifully decorated, excellent staff, delicious breakfast. [17]
3. Skeppsholmen, Stockholm. Truly idyllic location on a small island a ten-minute cycle from the centre.[18]
4. Europa Royale, Riga. The former town residence of a prominent Latvian family. Wooden staircases and high, decorated ceilings, located next to a quiet park.[19]
5. New Hotel, Athens. In the middle of the city, beautifully designed, gorgeous rooftop terrace, very friendly staff and a good breakfast.[20]
6. Rialto, Warsaw. Gorgeous! An art deco style building in one of the few neighbourhoods to escape destruction.[21]
7. Klaus K, Helsinki. A pleasant boutique hotel in a nice, leafy street.[22]
8. Beethoven, Vienna. Pleasant hotel, very good location, and well-restored. Its charming owner is Youropean Barbara.[23]
9. Antiq Palace, Ljubljana. A city palace where my room was equally palatial: a three-room apartment.[24]
10. Waterloo House, Dublin. Small and pleasant with very good staff. Youropean Irene is the singing manager of the breakfast room there.[25]

18 **Prague**. Everyone knows that it's a beautiful city, provided you stay out of the area around the Charles Bridge, Europe's biggest tourist trap.

   HOTEL: Three Storks. They stole their fifth star, but the price was right (it was January, very low season).

19 **Riga**. A pleasant city with an historic centre that has been designated as a UNESCO World Heritage Site. That is where the tourists congregate in the many bars and restaurants, which seem cheap to them but are beyond the means of most

locals. The sea is close by, a river runs through the city, there are bike paths and parks.

HOTEL: Europe Royale. The former town residence of a prominent Latvian family with wooden staircases and high, decorated ceilings. Number 4 on my Hotel Top 10.

20. **Rome**. The fountains were still intact when I was there a few days before the supporters of my favourite club, Feyenoord, arrived in the city and damaged one of Bernini's famous sculptures during a drunken rampage on the afternoon of their club's match against AS Roma.

HOTEL? No, Airbnb in Trastevere, the hip, bohemian neighbourhood on the other side of Tiber.

21. **Sofia**. Plenty of indications that this is the capital of the poorest country in Europe: holes in the pavement, low prices. Past glory is buried under Soviet concrete or glass cowboy-capitalist office buildings. Around ten years ago, construction workers who were building a new hotel uncovered the remains of an ancient wall. They turned out to be the ruins of a Roman amphitheatre, the second largest in Europe after the Colosseum. At that point you expect archaeologists to take over from the construction workers, and replace the heavy machinery with teaspoons, so that this could become one of Sofia's top attractions. Not in Bulgaria. The hotel was built anyway, on top of the theatre, the walls now just visible on the patio next to the reception desk.

HOTEL: Senses, modern and warm, the nicest hotel in the city.

22. **Stockholm**. The city is perfect, beautiful and well-organised, its inhabitants all tall, good-looking and healthy. They speak English with an English accent. Maybe too perfect: sometimes

it seems as if even the cities minor flaws are well thought-out and planned. And perfection has its cost: the country is very expensive, especially alcohol (if you're drunk in Sweden, you're either rich or you have a low tolerance for alcohol).

HOTEL: Lydmar, too expensive, but beautiful (ask for room 212, which is 80 square metres). And Skeppsholmen, in a truly idyllic location on an island just a ten-minute cycle from the centre. Number 3 in my Hotel Top 10.
In the breakfast room I was seated next to an elderly American woman who as wide as she was tall, and her daughter. 'The room is full of people but it is still quiet. In the US it would be loud,' the mother drawled. She thought about it some more for a minute, then said 'Is it because of the architecture of the room?'

23. **Tallinn**. A beautiful city on a peninsula, and therefore surrounded by the sea on almost all sides, which I love. A compact, prosperous city: things are managed with the usual Northern European efficiency. And although the historic city centre is packed with tourists, it is not quite as twee as most UNESCO world heritage cities are.

    HOTEL: Telegraaf. A chic, attractive hotel in the old city centre. I had someone tape over the little red smoke alarm lights because they were bothering me. The hotel thought it was a strange request, and maybe it was.

24. **Valletta**. Lots and lots of British.

    HOTEL: Hilton. Good, and of course, with a sea view.

25. **Vienna**. In the park people are lying on the grass, a band is playing and some boys are juggling a ball. No barbecues, no ghetto blasters, nobody smoking weed. And this too: the rub-

bish bins on the streets have a special column for extinguishing your cigarette.

HOTEL: Beethoven. Nice hotel, good location and a very competent renovation. The owner is the charming Youropean Barbara.

26. **Vilnius**. I couldn't get into it, not unusual you might say, for an old walled city. But I mean I never really understood it. You get to know a city on different levels, and you have reached the second level if you have located the good restaurants and found out which trams run where. The third level is when you discover it's better not to take the tram at all, but a bike, and you are on such good terms with the waiter in that great restaurant that he fills your glass a little fuller. I couldn't even get to level one: I didn't know which way was north or south, where the station was, or how to cycle to that church I wanted to see. Hopeless. In my defence, I was feeling sick and wobbly for three of the six days I spent there.
Speaking of churches: there are an awful lot of them in Vilnius. A few Russian-Orthodox churches, but all of the others are Catholic. Unlike their protestant neighbours the Latvians, the Lithuanians are papists. There churches attract a particular breed of tourists: religious tourists similar to those who visit Lourdes, Jerusalem and Rome.

HOTEL: Europa Royale, part of the same family of hotels as my hotel in Riga, but this one was clearly a poor relation, and it was a bit rundown.

27. **Warsaw**. If you live in Florence, Lisbon or Stockholm, travelling always involves a bit of sacrifice, since every city is uglier than your own. It's better to come, as I do, from a place like Rotterdam. Like Rotterdam, Warsaw was destroyed by Germany during the Second World War. Late in the war, in 1944,

in retaliation for an uprising. But while the Dutch rushed to rebuild Rotterdam immediately after the war, sometimes with unfortunate results (the Lijnbaan, its main shopping street), the Polish took a different approach. They reconstructed the Stare Miasto, the historic city centre, stone by stone, rebuilding both a castle and a cathedral. Maybe that's why Polish builders are unfazed by your own modest remodelling plans. Poland's top tourist attraction is Krakow, but I prefer Warsaw, even the part outside the historic centre. It's a bit grim and grey, but as we now know, there are different shades of grey.

HOTEL: Rialto. Gorgeous! An art deco building in one of the few neighbourhoods that was not destroyed.

28. **Zagreb**. Their neighbours are not so sure about this, but I think the Croatians are extremely friendly and hospitable. They refuse to let foreigners pay for treatment in their hospitals, and if you ask for directions they will accompany you to your restaurant or a museum. Maybe that is because there are so few tourists: the airport is small, not one of Ryanair or Easyjet's destinations. I hope they stay away for a little while longer, so that Zagreb can remain a well-kept secret: no hop-on-hop-off buses, but an elegant city that is also just a little bit rough around the edges.

HOTEL: Hilton, fifteen minutes by bike from the centre. Good.

GETTING AROUND

I'm Dutch, therefore I bike. That makes me doubly alien in Dublin, and apparently sometimes an undesirable alien, judging from the gestures of the drivers and the honking of the cars and double-decker buses around Stephen's Green and Pearse Street. The odd thing is that, like Berlin, Paris and Barcelona, Dublin has city bikes for hire: every now and then you see a cluster of rickety blue bicycles near a park or museum, but no one ever uses them. I was certainly not foolish enough to get on one, so I looked around for a decent bike rental place.

Neill's Wheels was well hidden, down a dead-end alley behind a youth hostel. In a decrepit rack in front of a grubby shed jam-packed with tools and parts, were four bicycles parked, I chose one with gears. Thirty euro plus a fifty euro deposit. Neill gave me a high-visibility vest, an extra lock and a grimy copy of a map of Dublin. While he adjusted the seat, we chatted a little about football, about his club, Arsenal, agreeing that they should never buy Suarez, because he's crazy. We bonded. Men are simple creatures.

Three days later, when I brought the bike back, Neill was not there, which was slightly inconvenient. His shop was open, and two gas company guys in overalls were lying on their stomachs on the floor next to the trapdoor leading to the cellar. I called him, but he said he's too far away to get back to the shop. What a bother. Or not? 'Just leave the bike and the lock, it's okay.' And the deposit? Neill was thinking. Oh yeah, the deposit. 'Are you in the shop now? Can you see the tool kit? It's closed right?' It was. 'Open the CD player. The key to the toolkit is in there. There are about 15 envelopes with deposits in the toolkit. Take the one with your name on it.' He had 15 other clients!? I followed his instructions, locked up afterwards, thanked Neill and hung up. Later, strolling along under the watery Irish sun, I realised that in most countries I'd been to there were no Neills.

I bicycled in other cities as well, preferably from one appointment to the next, and I noticed that more and more cities are accommodating cyclist and creating cycle paths, where the pace is fast (although foreign cyclists – and even pedestrians! – have a stranger habit of stopping for red lights, something which the Dutch are loathe to do.)

Are those Dublin's ramshackle bikes not to be trusted, in most other places the citybikes are excellent. You can pick one up at many different locations, and return them to an automated bike rack at a different location. Often, the first thirty minutes is free of charge, and the hourly rate increases the longer you keep the bike. Brussels, Budapest, Ljubljana, Paris, Riga, Vienna, Warsaw and Zagreb all have good bike rental systems, many of which are operated by the same company, NextBike, and I used the same app to locate the bike pick up spots in other cities.

Amsterdam, the bicycle capital of Europe, does not have this system. It's hard to say whether it is fear of vandalism that prevents its introduction or lobbying on the part of other bike rental companies who are afraid of the competition.

METRO — UNDERGROUND — U-BAHN

Some cities are too big to be biked, but then there are always taxi's or public transport. Preferably the metro, and real cities have a metro system. In the Netherlands, only Amsterdam and Rotterdam have one. Second-tier Dutch cities, like Utrecht and The Hague, have trams. In Ljubljana, only a few buses ply the streets. The only capital M you'll see in the city belongs to McDonalds (three branches).

18 of the 28 capital cities have metro systems: Amsterdam, Athens, Berlin, Brussels Bucharest, Budapest, Copenhagen, Helsinki, Lisbon, London, Madrid, Paris, Prague, Rome, Sofia, Stockholm, Vienna, Warsaw. Metropolises.

London's system is the oldest in Europe, Budapest's metro is the oldest on the continent, built in 1896. Its Line 1 is spectacular: sometimes the roof of the tunnel is just twenty centimetres under street level, and the platforms and the wooden carriages are so low that I can hardly stand up straight. Line 1 in Paris is also impressive, but for the opposite reason: it is ultra-modern and driverless, and from the first car you stare into the tunnel like a mole and can see the next station approaching.

Riding Sofia's metro probably doesn't cost much to begin with, but in practice it is free because the ticket vending machines do not work. Getting on to the metro is also an unusual experience as the platforms in a number of stations are only half a metre wide, not nearly enough for passengers. They wait in a sort of cave until they can worm their way through openings in the wall and step into a car that has just arrived.

Vienna's metro is old and reliable, like the city. Passengers had left neat copies of the railway's in-house magazine on the seats. In Athens the metro is modern, most of it having been built for the 2004 Olympic Games. There are no ticket checks before or during your journey, but knowing the Greeks, this is unnecessary because they pay anyway. They're like that. The U-Bahn and the S-Bahn in Berlin are part of an extensive, top-end system. There are no booths here either, but every now and then ticket checkers disguised as passengers stand up and carry out a check. I can recognise them now: on the platform they are usually standing in a little group of three people who don't seem to belong together.

In Prague I once lost my ticket: I really had purchased one, but the ticket checker and the colleagues who immediately came to his assistance did not believe me. I had to cough up 800 kroon, or about thirty euro, immediately. An unfashionably low fine in an old-fashioned metro, where the toilets in the stations were clean and there weren't even any attendants. No advertising on the walls and the passengers were almost all white. Metros are a good reflection of the composition of their respective societies: incredibly mixed in Brussels, black, yellow and white, and on the lines travelling through the European neighbourhood, a mixture of ordinary people and expensively-dressed civil servants speaking foreign languages. Brussels has a fine metro system: signs on the platform indicate precisely where the trains are, and the loudspeakers play Prince and U2 during the day, and classical music at night. It is perhaps telling that Schuman Station, which stops in front of the headquarters of the European Commission and the Council, has been undergoing a complete reconstruction for at least two years.

NOTES

1. *Maak werk van je droom*, Business Contact 2013, a book that helps you create your ideal work.
2. Rob Wijnberg, *De Correspondent*, 6 May 2014
3. *de Volkskrant*, 17 May 2014
4. BSD\BGS\Bestuurlijk stuk\Raadsmededeling\061RIS153566_bijlage DH culturele Hoofdstad 2018.doc
5. *The Guardian*, 13 March 2015
6. Cijfers Eurostat, Standard Eurobarometer 83, May 2015
7. NRC *Handelsblad*, 8 August 2015
8. Ewald Engelen, financial geographer associated with the UvA, blog 22 June 2015, http://ewaldengelen.blogspot.nl/2015/06/vijf-jaar-voorgelogen-over-griekenland.html
9. Centre d'action pour la fédération européenne (sous la dir.). L'Europe de demain. Neuchâtel: Editions de la Baconnie re, 1945. 216 p. (L'évolution du monde et des idées), p.76-78
10. Rob Wijnberg, *De Correspondent*, 6 May 2014
11. Veerstichting symposium, Leiden, 1999
12. Alternatieve Troonrede, 15 September 2014, LUX, Nijmegen
13. On the Couch with Europe: The Eurovision Song Contest, the European Broadcasting Union and Belonging on the Old Continent, Cornel Sandvoss, University of Surrey
14. Thierry Baudet, *De aanval op de natiestaat*, Bert Bakker, 2012
15. *de Volkskrant*, 27 December 2014
16. www.lxboutiquehotel.com
17. http://guldsmedenhotels.com/Babette/Babette-Copenhagen-Home.aspx
18. www.hotelskeppsholmen.se/en/
19. http://europa-royale-riga.hotelrigalatvia.com
20. www.yeshotels.gr/category/hotels/new-hotel
21. www.rialto.pl
22. www.klauskhotel.com
23. www.hotel-beethoven.at
24. www.antiqpalace.com
25. http://waterloohouse.ie

MY THANKS TO

Berlin	Martijn and Larissa Boks
Lisbon	Natasha von Mühlen, Marta, Heritage Av Liberdade Hotel, Hotel As Janelas Verdes
Helsinki	Niki Matheson
Dublin	Wibe van de Vijver, Esther Gaarlandt, Waterloo House
Luxembourg	Marc Angel, Raf Roelandt, Cathy Giorgetti
Madrid	Dirk-Jan and Vivian Nieuwenhuis, Aad Hogervorst, Jochem Schoevers, Hans Hoetink
Cyprus	Philip van Dalsen, Christiana Georgiou
Paris	Jurriaan Kien, Anne-Margreet Honing, Marten Mees
Athens	Alexander and Josine Koch, Merel Kleuver, Yiannis Gavrielides and New Hotel
Brussels	Constantijn van Oranje, Mijntje Lukoff, Els Moors, Joe van Waesberghe
Bucharest	Madalina Tanase
Riga	Gerard Bruijnse, Girts Vikmanis
Vilnius	Bernie ter Braak
Copenhagen	Heleen Kist, Marit Scharffenorth, Anders Bo Jensen
Stockholm	Els Berkers, Karin Bruce, Anna Rottier, Jenny Heering
Bratislava	Andrej Kralik, Andrej Brstovsek, Illah van Oijen, Kempinski Hotel
Vienna	Mario Antonio Soldo, Hotel Beethoven
Tallinn	Karoli Hindriks, Hotel Telegraaf
Zagreb	Vedrana Gujic, Boris Savic, Bob van den Bichelaer, Clara Clappendorf, Andrea Komarek, Hilton Hotel
Ljubljana	Laurens Visscher
Warsaw	Beata Zdunczyk, Christine van Exel, Hotel Rialto
Sofia	Martijn Holtkamp, Peter Petrov, Lubomira Kolcheva
Budapest	Ildiko Dudas, Kempinksi Hotel
Valletta	Joseph Zammit-Lucia, Liesbeth Oost, Astrid Vella, Melanie Deguara
London	Barthout van Slingelandt, Monika Kühne, Hank Boot, Vanessa Lamsvelt, Anna MacDonald
Rome	Helvia van Ditzhuijzen, Angela Ariatti
Prague	Carolien Vos, Toscha van Randwijck, Karolina Kottova, Odilia de Ranitz, Lidewij in 't Veld

Amsterdam   Erik Graadt van Roggen, Feije Riemersma, Willem Sodderland, Guido van Dijk, Jeroen Scholten, Roland de Jong, Cecilia Thorfinn, Raul Lansink, Peter Hoogendijk, Machteld Ligtvoet, Sophie Moerman, Poike Stomps, Bruno van den Elshout, Joop de Vries, Udo van Unen

Thanks to the interns from the School voor Journalistiek in Utrecht and Tilburg: Sander, Frank, Marije, Joris, Margit, Roos, Jolien, Eza, Willemijn, Amanda, Riemer, Cas, Rebecca, René

And thanks to the crowd funders who subscribed to the book, bought a question, paid for a flight or contributed financially in some other way to this book.

Thank you Sherida Alvares, Nicholas Aperghis, Jan van Berkum, Hein van Beuningen, Jet van Beuningen, Wendela Bierman-Veenhoven, Willem Bisschop van Tuinen, Annelies Bolhoeve, Rudolf van den Bosch, Madeleine en Hans Broos, Cees Budding, Roger Cox, Bas Derhaag, Arno Dierickx, Jeroen Dijkman, Alarik van Doorn, Martine van Duijvendijk-Bierman, Willem Dutilh, Jolande Eggink, Yolanda Eijgenstein, Anouk van der El, Eduard Elias, Linda Fontijn, Hanke Geertsema, Erik Graadt van Roggen, Jet Hamburger, Dorothee Hamming, Wouter Han, Sabine den Hartog, Joppe Hendriks, Philip Hennemann, Femke Hofstee-van der Meulen, Emilie van Holthe, Unico van Holthe, Constantijn Horák, Roderick van Houwelingen, Frank Hubrecht, Kees de Jong, Roland de Jong, Thijs Kerssemakers, Elise van der Laan, Gert-Pieter Lanser, Dirk Ligtenberg, Herre Kleuver, Maarten van der Kloot Meijburg, Monique Koemans, Alexander Kohnstamm, Coen Koomen, Maaike Koomen, Claartje Kruijff, Claire Mayne, Kiki Mol-van der Lee, Lucas Mol, Xandra Niehe, Josine Opstelten-Koch, Jasper van der Pas, Emilie Patijn, Remco van der Pol, Frederique van Randwijck, Marco Remmelink, Gijs de Reuver, Feije Riemersma, Guusje Roebersen, Nelleke Rookmaaker, Dirk Jan Rutgers, Mariette van de Sande, Marie-Claire Schimmelpenninck van der Oije, Jeroen Scholten, Sofie Simao, Robert Smelt, Lodewijk Sodderland, Willem Sodderland, Frederik van Son, Ewald van der Spek, Jean-Marie van Staveren, Jeroen Surie, Erik-Hein Timmers, Klaas van Veen, Frederik Vernède, Steven van de Vijver, Halbart Völker, Patrick Vriens, Marie Claire de Vries, Jeroen Weidema, Ed Westerweele, Wieger Wielinga, Roderik de Wilde en Sjaak Zonneveld!

Many thanks to Rob de Vormer, for the site.
Merci beaucoup, Monsieur JC de Castelbajac, for the Youropeans-logo.
Thanks a million, Kris Kohlstrand, for translating and correcting all of those interviews and texts for the site!

And thank you Liz, the most beautiful girl in Europe, who now has a refrigerator door full of city magnets.

ABOUT THE AUTHOR

Mark Schalekamp (1968) worked for a bank, as a TV editor, was briefly a lawyer, and was for seven years a social entrepreneur who founded the company Robin Good before choosing a career as a writer in 2007. His first book, *De Rebellenclub*, was a collection of short stories about sports, and his first novel, *De Parvenu*, was published in 2011. Schalekamp's first non-fiction book was published in 2013: *Maak Werk van je Droom:* a self-help book about creating your ideal work. *This is Europe* is a new genre, the result of Youropeans, an experiment in social journalism during which he spent two years travelling through Europe. Schalekamp is a regular contributor, sometimes in the form of an editorial, to NRC, *Volkskrant* and *FD*.

www.ingramcontent.com/pod-product-compliance
Lightning Source LLC
Chambersburg PA
CBHW031308150426
43191CB00005B/129